THE GOLDEN AGE OF STEAM

O. S. Nock

B.Sc., C.Eng., F.I.C.E., F.I.Mech.E.
Past President, Institution of Railway Signal Engineers

THE GOLDEN AGE
OF STEAM

A critical and nostalgic memory of the last twenty years
before Grouping on the railways of Great Britain

ST. MARTIN'S PRESS · NEW YORK

Contents

Illustrations

MAPS

The colour plates are reproduced from paintings by Jack Hill. Plates d, f, and g are based on original photographs by the author.

Acknowledgements

The author and publishers thank the following for permission to use the illustrations as listed:

British Railways: for plates 2a, 3a, 3b, 4a, 4b, 4c, 6b, 8b, 8c, 15a, 16, 19b, 20d, 23b, 23c, 30a, 35a, 40b, 41b, 43b, 44a.

H. W. Burman Esq: for plates 1a, 1c.

Derek Cross Esq: for plate 31.

The Dover Harbour Board: for plates 5a, 5b.

A. G. Dunbar Esq: for plate 32b.

K. H. Leech Esq: for plates 11c, 24a, 24b, 26a, 36b, from the late C. Laundy.

Locomotive Publishing Co. Ltd: for plates 3c, 11a, 14b, 20a, 20c, 21a, 21b, 29b, 40c.

Rev. T. B. Parley: for plate 23a.

Ravenglass and Eskdale Railway: for plates 17a, 17b, 18a, 18b.

Real Photographs Ltd: for plates 2b, 2c, 7a, 7b, 7c, 9b, 10a, 10c, 12a, 13a, 13b, 14a, 15b, 19a, 20b, 24c, 25a, 27a, 27c, 29c, 35b, 35c, 36c, 37c, 38a, 38b, 38c, 40c, 44c, 45a, 45b.

R. D. Stephen Esq: for plates 29a, 30b, 30c, 33a, 33b, 33c, 33d, 34a, 34b, 34c, 41a, 42a, 42c.

Dr Ransome-Wallis: for plates 15c, 22a.

The remaining photographs are from the author's personal collection, and include the work of the late F. E. Mackay, the late E. Mason, the late K. A. C. R. Nunn, the late R. J. Purves, the late W. J. Reynolds, the late W. H. Whitworth, and his own photographs.

Preface

UNTIL THE OUTBREAK of war in 1914 railways were unquestionably the pre-eminent mode of travelling in Great Britain. Within the confines of the cities and larger towns electric trams and a few motor buses were beginning to make inroads upon the railway situation; but for long distance travel, and in the conveyance of minerals and almost all form of goods the railways were in a commanding position. The war years seemed to strengthen their hold, but in the confused period that followed the Armistice of November 1918, discussions about post-war reconstruction were accompanied by many glances over the shoulder, towards what the more discerning sensed were the beginnings of strong disruptive competition.

The twenty years from 1902 to 1922 saw both the zenith and the end of the old railway companies of Great Britain. Their pre-eminence remained to the very end of the pre-grouping era, but it was to vanish like a dream in a very few years afterwards. To enthusiasts of the present age—and their number grows every year—there must often come the question as to what the British railways were really like in what can be called a truly Golden Age. My own clear recollections go back to the years 1908–9, and in this book I have made a nostalgic, and certainly critical, revisitation of the railways as I knew them between my own very early years and the Grouping which came on New Year's Day, 1923.

In fifteen years I travelled by the trains of nearly all the major companies, and some of the minor ones too. As a preparatory schoolboy, I commuted on the Great Western, and on the South Eastern and Chatham; travelling for pre-war family holidays took me also on the South Western, the Brighton, the Great Eastern and the Isle of Wight Central; and then in 1916 came the great family move to the north. I saw the North Western and the Midland in their greatest years; the Furness, the Maryport and Carlisle—not to mention the Ravenglass and Eskdale—were now on our doorstep, and further family movements brought in the Lancashire and Yorkshire, and the North Stafford. I have written extensively of Leeds and what lay to the east of it, and the beginnings of my university career opened up the opportunity of travelling by various alternative routes from Barrow-in-Furness to

Preface

London. In such wise I encountered the last of the trunk lines of England, 'the amazing Great Central'. In one of the first of my long summer vacations I journeyed to Scotland.

The youngest of my own memories of the old railway companies is now more than fifty years old; but the interposition of a professional life concerned almost entirely with the design and manufacture of equipment for railways, and the swiftly changing circumstances to the breathless modern 'image' of the non-steam railways of today have not dimmed those early memories. Indeed, the writing of this book has made them clearer and more vivid than ever before as I have come to appreciate retrospectively the significance of some of the things I saw so many years ago. My memories are as much of people as of things. At the time, of course, most of the big personalities in the British railway world were no more than names of which I read in *The Railway Magazine* and elsewhere; but in later years my professional work has brought me into contact and into the friendship of many men who worked with some of the giants of the pre-grouping era, and so the characters of men like Sir Henry Thornton, C. J. Bowen-Cooke, Churchward and Sir Cecil Paget have fairly come to life.

More recently when I was being interviewed by a television commentator the question was asked as to when my interest in railways began, and how it was initially 'sparked off'. As far as I can recall it dates from my cradle, and I never cease to be grateful to my father and mother for the way they encouraged and fostered my childhood interest in railways. As to more recent times, for nearly forty years Olivia, my wife, has been my companion on countless journeys that have taken us far beyond the tight little railway network with which this book is concerned. As secretary and literary critic, in addition to all her other tasks as wife, mother and grandmother, her counsel and help has been invaluable.

Since the book was written the Museum of the British Railways Board at Clapham, to which reference is made several times in the text, has been closed. Arrangements are being made for the establishment of a new Railway Museum at York.

Silver Cedars   *O. S. Nock*
High Bannerdown   *December* 1972
Batheaston
Bath

CHAPTER ONE

The pinnacle of orthodoxy

THE BROAD GAUGE is dead. Long live the Broad Gauge! I have no doubt that the enterprising Board and chief executive officers who were leading the Great Western Railway into the twentieth century with such vigour would have been shocked to think that my second sentence could have been their slogan. Yet if not in material things, then certainly it was in the enthusiasm and pioneering spirit in which Brunel set out to create 'the finest work in England'. The management of the early 1900s was undisguisedly out to re-establish the Great Western in its one-time, but briefly held paramount position. Furthermore, the characteristics of early broad gauge days prevailed in another marked respect. It was not only in the broad gauge that Brunel built differently from everyone else. There were other features of equipment and working that distinguished the Great Western of pioneer days: there was the 'bridge' rail; the longitudinal-sleepered track; the disc and crossbar signal—not to mention some of Brunel's specialities that proved failures, such as the timber piling under the track, and the ill-starred 'Atmospheric'. And as the rejuvenated Great Western steamed majestically into the twentieth century it standardized, in the twenty years to grouping a surprising number of engineering and operational features that were its own, and remained near-exclusively so in that period.

Yet this opening preamble of mine does not give the impression of orthodoxy—rather the reverse. To the casual onlooker, and particularly to him with an eye for railway detail but without much knowledge or interest in what lay behind it, the Great Western was the most orthodox and conservative of railways. From my early boyhood at Reading I remember it all so vividly; and what I saw then, and had no difficulty in retaining in my memory, has since fitted in closely with the technical and historical features of which I learned later. Until 1910 Reading was the veritable 'grand junction' of all the Great Western express passenger services from London. Until then the entire traffic for Birmingham, Wolverhampton and the north passed through it, and as evidence of the policy of developing long-distance non-stop running one could, at various times of the day, see non-stop express trains between Paddington and Birmingham, Bristol, Cardiff, Exeter, Plymouth and

Worcester. The crack South Wales expresses then passed Newport without stopping, and Worcester had several non-stops. Great prestige value was set upon the making of these long runs, and still more spectacular projects were under consideration, when war came in 1914.

The significance of the trains that came racing through Reading at what then seemed tremendous speeds was to be appreciated later; but what made an immediate appeal to those whom the Great Western publicity department so happily apostrophized as 'boys of all ages' were, of course, the locomotives. The cynics may accuse me of re-viewing the sights of my boyhood through rose-tinted spectacles, but in that retentive memory of mine I cannot recall seeing *any* dirty Great Western locomotives—large or small. The large new 4-6-0s could be counted on the fingers of two hands; but there were swarms of 4-4-0s, tank engines of all shapes and sizes, 0-6-0 goods and, of course, the smaller passenger engines—2-4-0, 4-2-2 and the occasional 2-2-2. The majority of the older engines still had their polished brass domes. One incident remains particularly in mind. It would have been in 1908, and I was 'train spotting' at Southcote Junction with my mother. While we were watching, an up-goods came crawling up the Basingstoke branch; it was headed by a 0-6-0 goods engine and, though at that tender age I was not able to distinguish to which of the various Dean or Armstrong varieties it belonged, I remember clearly how the sun glistened on that polished brass dome. It stood at the home signal for several minutes, for the signals were pulled off for a down train to take the Westbury line. The latter train, when it did come, would have been for the Weymouth line, for it was headed by an outside-framed 4-4-0.

In my earliest 'spotting' days Churchward was in process of greatly simplifying the livery of both locomotives and carriages. I cannot recall having seen an engine with the red underframes and the three-panel painting on the tender, except on my own 'Gauge I' Bassett-Lowke model of the 'Atbara' class 4-4-0 No. 3410 *Sydney*. The elaborately worked scroll lettering, with GWR intertwined on the centre panel of the tenders, was being replaced by the coat of arms of the company encircled by a garter. This device was to get the Company into trouble with the College of Heralds some twenty years later. Apparently no one took any notice of it until Royal sanction was sought before engine No. 6000 was named *King George V*, in 1927; and in the blaze of publicity that surrounded the visit of that engine to America and the numerous public excursions run to Swindon, someone with

1. THE CHANGING SCENE ON THE G.W.R.

(a) Down stopping train near Acocks Green, including two clerestory-roofed slip coaches, hauled by 4-2-2 engine No. 3067 *Duchess of Teck* rebuilt with Belpaire firebox, and dome painted over.

(b) A 'Barnum' 2-4-0, as working on locals round Reading in the early 1900s, rebuilt with domeless parallel boiler: No. 3222.

(c) Down Birmingham express (via Oxford) near Acocks Green, hauled by one of the new 'County' class 4-4-0s, No. 3814 *County of Chester*, with a great mixture bogie and six-wheeled stock.

heraldic, rather than railway interests, raised the question of the validity and, indeed, legality of the device that had been carried by several thousands of Great Western engines. But in those halcyon days before World War I it was one of those emblems that was taken so much for granted as to be thought everlasting!

Although Churchward greatly simplified the locomotive livery by eliminating the red underframes, Great Western engines still remained very gay, with the brass and copper work positively burnished, whether the locomotive in question was one of the latest four-cylinder 4-6-0s, or a saddle-tank 0-6-0 working some remote branch line. The name GREAT WESTERN was splendidly displayed on tender and tank sides, and the full lining out, with all its highly polished embellishment was applied also to the heavy freight tank and tender engines, just as the Aberdare 2-6-0s originally had the red underframes. Churchward also changed the historic chocolate and cream livery of the passenger carriages to a one-colour scheme. I must say that the brown-lake style looked very fine, set off by much gold lining, and scarlet roof-boards. Even so, an enthusiast of no more than my tender age was made aware of the old 'chocolate and cream' not only by pictures, but in the 'hard-ware' of my own 'Gauge I' clerestory carriages that *Sydney* used to hustle round my somewhat limited system.

Passing from purely personal recollections to the results of many years of study and research, the locomotive position on the Great Western in those distant pre-war years was extraordinarily diverse. Churchward's great programme of standardization was only just beginning to gather momentum. By midsummer of 1910, when the short route via Bicester was opened and the principal expresses from London to Birmingham and the North ceased to run via Reading, there were only 30 four-cylinder 4-6-0s in service, and Churchward was still contemplating the construction, concurrently, of both 'Saints' and 'Stars'. The 'Court' series of two-cylinder 4-6-0s was not commenced until late in 1911. The only other engines of the new 'standard' designs regularly in evidence in and around Reading were the 4-4-2 'County' tanks, which were on the faster London suburban trains. The express passenger 'County' class 4-4-0s were not much in evidence. Their principal duties at that time were on the West to North route via the Severn Tunnel, between Bristol and Shrewsbury.

The Great Western had the largest route mileage of any British company, and in those pre-war years the new Churchward standard locomotives were thinly spread over those 3,100 miles, After all, there were less than 200 of them in 1910, out of a total locomotive stock of more than 3,000. The rest made up an extraordinarily variegated lot, that was the

2. LOCOMOTIVE VARIETY IN 1910

(a) Churchward's giant: *The Great Bear*.
(b) One of the 2-4-0 tank engines used on some London surburban services.
(c) One of the '157' class 2-2-2s as rebuilt and working from Oxford until 1914.

delight of railway enthusiasts and the bane of a maintenance engineer's life. The consti-tuents of the 'Flower' class of express passenger 4-4-0s provides no more than a simple example. They all had 6 ft. 8½ in. diameter coupled wheels, and cylinders 18 in. diameter by 26 in. stroke; but that, at one time, was about all the similarity they possessed. All except the final batch, which was actually named after flowers, went through various stages of physical change. The 'Armstrongs' and the 'Badmintons' had begun their careers with domed boilers fully in the highly-developed Dean tradition, and then came the 'Atbaras' with parallel domeless boilers. There were two experimental variations among the 'Bad-mintons', and many of the earlier groups at one time had parallel domeless boilers of the 'Atbara' type at an intermediate stage in their lives. Eventually all these early varieties received the standard tapered boilers fitted to the 'Flowers' proper; but to the end of their long lives one could easily recognize the ancestry of an engine of the 'Flower' class by the shape of the outside framing. All varieties were different.

At the time of which I am now writing however this degree of standardization had barely begun, beyond that is, the stage of fitting parallel domeless boilers to some of the 'Badmintons'. The systemized policy of locomotive naming was getting well into its stride in the years 1908–10. It is true that the 'Atbara' class taking the road just at the turn of the century mostly had names of places, events, and personalities prominent in the development of the British Empire at that period, though some of the names were likely to lose their popular significance fairly soon. *Terrible*, for example, would be more likely associated with such North Western appelations as *Thunderer*, *Titan*, *Vesuvius*, than with a ship of the Royal Navy that rendered distinguished service in the South African war. But the 'Flower' class proper were all named after real flowers, and there is reason to believe that this was the one class for which Churchward himself chose all the names. He was a keen and highly skilled horticulturalist, and some old Swindon men who knew him well always felt that the twenty flowers named on engines 4149 to 4168 were among the favourites that flourished in his own garden: the simple, as well as the exotic—*Primrose* and *Marigold*, alongside *Begonia*, *Camellia* and *Stephanotis*.

At the time, of course, it was natural that one's interest centred upon the passenger engines, and there were enough varieties of these to be sure! The various 2-4-0 classes, derived from designs prepared for the narrow gauge sections of the line when the broad gauge still remained on the West of England main line, provided a fascinating study of their own; and then there were the singles! Many of the big 7 ft. 8 in. 4-2-2s were still working through Reading in my boyhood. Some had their great domes painted over green; but although that took away some of their nineteenth-century splendour, those green domes were 'got up' by the cleaners no less finely, and seemed to give the engines a more modern look. Those with domeless parallel boilers had the safety valves highly burnished, and looked magnificent. Some of the older 2-2-2s had domeless boilers, and they looked compact and businesslike, rather than beautiful. The same applied to the 2-4-0s of the Barnum class that had similar boilers. But statistically very few of the older engines acquired domeless boilers. The numerous stud of saddle and pannier tank engines went about their duties with glittering brass domes, and those on branch line duties in the country made a real contribution to the rural scene.

There was a vast difference in the tempo of affairs on the main lines, and on the branches. Perhaps I ought to have made the distinction between the crack trains and the rest, because there were many trains on the main lines that were anything but speedy. This is where the traditional orthodoxy of the Great Western showed itself. Its activities were attuned to life in the rural communities of the West, and that meant the conveyance of horses, hounds, milk and vegetable products frequently by passenger trains. The four-wheeled, and six-wheeled vans used for such traffic were not suitable for running at very high speeds, and the booked times of many 'intermediate' main line trains were arranged so that schedule time could be kept without exceeding 60 m.p.h. The time allowances at stations were generous, to permit of vehicles being attached or detached as required. The station staffs fully entered into the spirit and responsibilities of this rural traffic, and life was not hurried at such stations.

Behind this gracious façade was the old-world orthodoxy of directors and senior officers, continuing in the happy relationship that had grown up from broad gauge days. Posts like the Chief Engineer, the Superintendent of the Line, and the Locomotive, Carriage and Wagon Superintendent—as the title went in the early 1900s—were virtually autonomous. They reported only to the appropriate committees of the Board, and so long as the financial side of their activities remained satisfactory they were allowed to carry on almost as they liked. But although relations between chief officers and their particular directors were usually cordial in the extreme the arrangement did have the disadvantage that sometimes major decisions were taken by one officer, without any consultation with colleagues. In the leisurely days of the nineteenth century 'major' decisions did not often impinge upon the activities of another department; but things began to get more difficult when the enterprise of the twentieth century began to burst the banks of individual departments.

The then Chief Engineer, James Inglis, was appointed General Manager, in 1903. From his previous post he had naturally been aware of the virtually autonomous position he had enjoyed; but whereas on the majority of other British railways at that time the General Manager was the chief executive officer, a commander-in-chief to whom all other senior officers were responsible, on the Great Western it had never been so. He was a figurehead, but not even a co-ordinator, since the other senior officers acted independently and all attended Board regularly. As General Manager, Inglis readily appreciated the weakness of this system of organization, and he worked out a new one in which the General Manager, and he alone of senior officers, would attend Board, and would take entire responsibility for the whole organization of the railway. There was more to it than a mere change in the organizational tree. He had plans for imposing a stricter and more uniform system of financial control upon what could be described as the 'spending departments'. It was not that the company was in any form of financial difficulty. Since 1902 the dividend on the ordinary stock had never been less than $5\frac{1}{4}$ per cent, and it had been maintained steadily for around ten years. The Board and the Shareholders had every reason to be satisfied. So also were the customers. The Great Western was a favourite with travellers; it was an institution in the countryside and towns that it served.

In putting forward his scheme for reorganization Inglis stirred up a positive hornet's nest; and behind the placid orthodox façade of this most orthodox of railways 'the knives were out', as the modern saying goes. It struck at the very foundations of existing Great Western management. Directors and senior officers had been close personal friends. Alike in their leisure-time pursuits they lived the lives of country gentlemen; it was all very pleasant. Among British railways at that time only the London and North Western was paying a better dividend—so why change? Among the chief officers Churchward was staunchest in opposition, and he was supported by many directors. In vain Inglis argued that it would make for smoother operation, cut costs, and make possible even better dividends. The chairman, Viscount Churchill, saw clearly the tremendous upheaval that would be caused if a serious attempt was made to impose such a 'reform' and to the mortification of James Inglis it was quietly pigeon-holed; it was not brought out again until 1921. And so the nineteenth century edifice of management remained, entirely orthodox. Outwardly all had been serene, save for a mild disturbance in 1910, the significance of which was scarcely apprehended at all, at the time.

So far I have written only of the fight to retain the *status quo*. I must now turn to those back-stage activities that were, in due course, to show that Great Western propensities for 'doing things differently' were as strong in the early 1900s as they were in the day of Brunel. The great programme of mechanical engineering modernization on which Churchward embarked was to some extent sparked off by the high-management policy of making lengthy non-stop runs with the principal express passenger trains. He had to provide rolling stock for these trains. and locomotives to haul them. These two facets of his overall responsibilities were closely interlinked. The handsome clerestory-roofed carriages of the Dean era pulled rather heavily for their dead weight, decidedly more so than contemporary stock on other British railways. Something had to be done about coach resistance. Large and powerful locomotives were needed; but Churchward was well enough aware that unless one is very skilful in design large engines can also be large consumers of coal. It was no use having a big powerful engine if it needed so much coal to fire it that no fireman could sustain the physical effort to complete one of the long non-stop runs desired by the management. Thus the new engines had not only to be much more powerful than previously, but proportionately more economical.

Unlike many of his leading contemporaries in Great Britain at the time Churchward

3. PASSENGER TRAINS: 1910–14

(a) The Cornish Riviera Express passing Old Oak Common: engine No. 4012 *Knight of the Thistle*.

(b) Up two-hour Birmingham Express (via the new route) near Park Royal: engine No. 2903 *Lady of Lyons*.

(c) Branch line train in South Wales, hauled by 0-6-0 saddle tank engine No. 1285.

was very keenly aware of what was happening in the locomotive world overseas. He had also the rare gift of knowing a good thing when he saw it, avoiding being dazzled or mesmerized by strident publicity—which was common enough in the railway engineering world, even in those distant days; and it would probably have come as a profound shock to the 'orthodox', intensely English Great Western, if it had been realized that the new locomotives that began to emerge from Swindon works from 1904–5 onwards were a blend of American and French practice, with very little that was traditionally English about them, except the genius that made so successful an integration. There was first of all the boiler. The tapered barrel was the rule rather than the exception in the U.S.A. in the latter part of the nineteenth century, but its adoption on the Great Western was not immediate. The final designs of the Dean era at Swindon incorporated one of its major advantages without going to the extra expense of the coned barrel. By raising the outer shell of the firebox well above the top of the boiler the steam space immediately above the hottest area was increased, and this facilitated the rapid raising of steam, and minimized foaming at the water level. The outward effect of these raised fireboxes, as shown most markedly in the 'Atbara' class, was not pleasing; and Churchward was criticized for spoiling the appearance of Great Western locomotives. Feeling his way, as the constructional techniques were developed at Swindon works, he ultimately arrived at the fully-coned barrel, entirely in the American style. It was certainly something very different from traditional British practice, but it was outstandingly successful as a steam raiser.

Then there was the question of getting greater efficiency, or in other words getting more work out of the steam raised in the boiler. It was in this quest that Churchward turned to France, where the performances of the du Bousquet—de Glehn four-cylinder compound 'Atlantics' on the Northern Railway were one of the railway sensations of the day. Churchward arranged for one of these locomotives to be purchased from the Société Alsacienne, in Belfort, M. de Glehn's firm, and it was tried on the Great Western. But those de Glehn compounds were complicated machines to handle, and while the French engine-men became extremely expert and got remarkable results, this was achieved by a very rigid allocation of one crew to one engine, even to the extent of sending the driver into the factory when an engine was booked for major overhaul. On the Great Western, even in the spacious days before World War I engines were pooled, and at large depots like Old Oak Common in West London, the driver had the engine for the job, rather than his 'own' engine. Had compounds been adopted as a standard they would have been handled by many different crews, and Churchward felt they were too complicated to give the best results in such common-user duty. And so he went all-out to produce a single expansion locomotive that would be the equal of the compounds in thermal efficiency. This he succeeded in doing with a clever, original, and at that time most unorthodox layout of the traditionally British Stephenson's link motion. One did not need to see the coal sheets to realize that the new Great Western 4-6-os were economical in fuel consumption; a look at their remarkably small tenders—for engines running non-stop to Plymouth—was enough to confirm this.

The carriages were equally original in their conception, and the idea of them may also have come from the U.S.A., in length at any rate. It was a time when the railways running north from London were introducing very large and heavy new carriages; but while Churchward's carriages were certainly long, they were remarkably light and free running. They were 70 ft. long, and the third class included 10 compartments, each seating 8 passengers—80 people in one corridor carriage. The tare weight was no more than thirty-three tons. In contrast to the traditional clerestory-roofed stock the new vehicles had exceptionally wide bodies, and a high elliptical roof. They had a new design of bogie, with bar frames—another American idea—and pulled much more lightly, thereby allowing the locomotive to pull a longer and nominally heavier train for the same consumption of coal. Churchward thus made a two-fold advance in the science of train running, by providing his drivers and firemen with large, powerful and economical locomotives, and building up the trains with coaches that took less pulling.

It is true that in the years before World War I the new coaches, like the new engines, did not come from the works at Swindon very rapidly, and the majority of the express trains in the 1910–12 period included many of the older clerestory carriages. Considerable numbers of them were indeed still in main line express service in the early 1920s; but the formula of replacement had been established, and the like of those 70-ft. coaches was not seen anywhere else on the British railways. Before leaving the question of long non-stop running I must mention the Ocean service that was being assiduously developed in connection with the calling of inward-bound trans-Atlantic liners at Fishguard. Liverpool was then the home port for both the Cunard and the White Star Lines; but by calling at Fishguard a full day was saved on the journey between New York and London. The colour plate facing page 64 shows the scene at Fishguard prior to the departure of the first special from the liner *Mauretania*. On that and one subsequent occasion a stop was made at Cardiff to change engines; but plans were in hand in 1914 to facilitate non-stop running over the entire distance from Fishguard to Paddington. The war unfortunately cut these preparations short, and with the changed sailing arrangements after 1919 the Fishguard scheme never eventuated.

In these days of smokeless zones, and the constant campaigns being waged against atmospheric pollution it is difficult to imagine how bad the winter fogs in England used to be. On several railways the locomotive engineers were trying to devise better means of repeating the indications of the wayside signals than by the noisy and expensive detonators that required large numbers of men stationed at the various signal locations along the line. In retrospect, it is interesting to recall that the initiative towards providing an indication inside the engine cab came from the locomotive, and not the signal engineers. Inventors were busy among the contractors, but the two systems that had the widest application in the 'twenty years to grouping' were those of the North Eastern and the Great Western Railways. The North Eastern gave warning only when the signal concerned was in the caution, or danger position; but the Great Western succeeded in establishing as long ago as 1905 all the principles that are now embodied in the system in standard use over many thousands of miles of British Railways today.

In the development of this system the Great Western was not only different from everyone else, but several *decades* ahead of current thought on the subject of cab signalling. The first point was that the driver was given entirely separate and distinctive audible indications for warning and clear: a blood-curdling little siren for the one, and the ringing of a bell for the other. But the vitally important underlying feature was that the system was 'fail-safe', as the modern terminology goes. Whereas the North Eastern arrangement gave no indication for 'all clear', it was open to the risk that if the danger indication failed to work the driver could be misled, in the absence of any indication, into thinking the line was clear. The Great Western apparatus was, on the other hand, so designed that if current to ring the 'all clear' bell was not picked up, even though the signal itself was clear, the siren would be sounded. In other words the 'failure' was on the safety side.

There was another very important feature incorporated in this Great Western system of audible cab signalling. The driver was required to acknowledge receipt of a warning indication; if he failed to do this an automatic application of the brakes was made and the train brought to a stop. Those who criticized the system argued that a driver could acknowledge and then continue at full speed without heeding the warning he had been given; but the entire philosophy of Great Western Railway operating, whether on locomotives, in signal boxes, yards and everywhere else was based on the sense of responsibility of every individual man. A Great Western man was expected to have a very high sense of responsibility, and it was strongly felt that no mechanical or electrical device should be introduced that would relieve the man of his responsibility, nor give any indication that the management had any doubts of his ability. The audible cab signalling system, with its associated automatic control of the brakes in emergency, was an aid to the driver; not something that did part of his job for him. It was installed on the main line between Reading and Slough, and from the excellent results obtained, was gradually extended to cover the entire main line network.

Although the origin of the system lay in the locomotive department it naturally became a co-operative effort with the signal department, and this leads me to mention the interesting trends in signalling practice that were taking place in the latter part of the 'twenty years to grouping'. The Great Western would ordinarily have been considered the most conservative and orthodox of British railways, particularly in its operating procedures; but unlikely as it might seem they were experimenting with three-position *upper quadrant* signals towards the end of the pre-grouping era. Collectors of vintage railway photographs will be familiar with the one signal of this type on the departure line at Paddington, and when the new 'Ealing and Shepherds Bush Railway' was equipped, in 1920, the same type of signals were used throughout. The fact that this line became more familiar to London commuters as an extension of the Central London tube railway tended to obscure the fact that it was partly owned and completely equipped, so far as the signalling was concerned, by the Great Western Railway.

As things turned out this venture into electrically-operated upper-quadrant signals was no more than a passing phase on the Great Western; in general British practice the day colour-light signal came to supplant the three-position semaphore. But that passing phase was yet another example of how Great Western engineers were thinking far outside the traditional, for the future equipment of the railway. Very little of this was apparent to the outside observer in those years. The glittering engines changed to plain unlined green in the war years—none too well cleaned either; and much of the old-time glamour went out of the Great Western scene. But in Swindon works and elsewhere a wealth of new experience was being built up in manufacturing much precision equipment for the war effort, so that when the time came to resume the development of locomotive practice there were newly-learned workshop techniques to aid in improving the traditional accuracy of construction with which Great Western locomotives had always been made. And in the grouping era, as in the broad gauge days proper, and in the 'twenty years to grouping' the Great Western was at the same time a pioneer, and for much of the time a 'loner'.

CHAPTER TWO

The Dover Road

THE SOUTH EASTERN and Chatham was a railway for which interest and affection grew on closer acquaintance. At Reading, where I first saw its trains it cut a very minor figure beneath the brilliant elegance of the Great Western. It was 'beneath' in a physical sense too, because the line came into Reading from the east to the terminus on ground level, whereas the Great Western strode across the vista seen from the Forbury Gardens on a high embankment. The South Eastern trains were very much the poor relations, and today, in the welter of route rationalization by the nationalized British Railways all traces of the one-time station have been swept away, and replaced by a huge car park. Even so, Reading, of South Eastern and Chatham days was far removed from being merely the terminus of a branch line. Up the embankment of the Great Western there climbed a double-line connection from the South Eastern, and over those tracks passed a few important express passenger trains. The Great Western, despite its isolationism in so many respects, developed a very comprehensive system of through train and carriage workings with its neighbours: carriages, and indeed whole trains passed over its tracks from the London and North Western, Midland, Great Central, London and South Western, and even from the Caledonian.

The South Eastern share in the working of this complex network of services was the through train between Birkenhead and Deal, and it was by this service that I first travelled on the line. In those early years of the twentieth century travelling for family holidays involved more packing, and far more luggage than one would dream of taking on a world tour today. Use of the modern jetliners has certainly taught us how to travel light. I remember as clearly as if it had been yesterday the mountains of trunks, portmanteaux, and other paraphernalia that was gradually assembled before we set out for a month's stay at Folkestone; and in such circumstances a through carriage was veritably a 'must'. So instead of taking one of the ordinary trains from the South Eastern terminus at Reading we sought out the Birkenhead–Deal express, which ran from the Great Western station, and descended by the connecting line. By this we avoided changing at Redhill. The journey

26

thence from Reading always seemed endless, and stations like Wokingham, Farnborough, Ash Junction, Guildford, and Dorking loomed large in the railway map that was beginning to build up in my youthful mind.

Although I have not got copies of the actual timetables of that period it would seem that the train services were not greatly improved from those in the latter part of the nineteenth century which inspired the inimitable E. L. Ahrons to one of his wittiest exaggerations: 'If anyone desired to sample the South Eastern in its palmiest state' he wrote 'I should have recommended him to try the Reading line. Reading to Redhill is $46\frac{1}{4}$ miles, and the fastest train appeared to average about four miles an hour, with occasional spurts to five. I know that this is not far from the mark, because I once tried it myself, and decided to walk if ever I had to go that way again.' In my boyhood the engines used on the Redhill trains, and also on the through expresses to and from the Great Western were mostly James Stirling's domeless-boilered 4-4-os; and although in later years I came to appreciate their distinctive design and superb workmanship they were not such as to provide any serious counter-attraction to the ceaseless glamour parade through Reading on the Great Western. Before my father's place of business was transferred from Reading in 1916, however, a number of these engines were rebuilt with domed boilers, and as the S.E. & C.R. was then up to the hilt in a glamour parade of its own, on its principal main lines, the appearance of these engines certainly did something to brighten up the Reading line—if not the time-keeping!

I must add one further experience of my own, concerning the Reading end of the line before we venture out on 'The Dover Road' proper. In the early spring of 1914 we moved house, to an old farm house in the little village of Hurst, and as a preparatory schoolboy I became a season ticket holder on the S.E. & C.R. between Reading and 'Sindlesham and Hurst Halt!' It was about five miles from Reading, and our train every morning was hauled by one of the newly-rebuilt Stirling 4-4-os, with their polished brass domes and copper-topped chimneys. The only trouble was that they nearly always showed a strong reluctance to running anywhere near schedule time. Morning after morning I had to explain, to sceptical masters, why I was late for school. It was all the more embarrasing for me, because when we had lived on the other side of Reading and I had travelled in by one of the Basingstoke locals, I had been a model of punctuality! Fortunately the family stay at Hurst was not very long; but before my own embarrassment ended the S.E. & C.R. had plunged many points below zero in the family esteem.

It is perhaps a little unfair to have opened this chapter at the westernmost tip of the line, at the terminus of a branch that had its own complications in operating before it reached anywhere near to Reading. The London and South Western had running powers over the last six miles, from Wokingham, and the South Eastern not only passed through Guildford on L. & S.W.R. metals, but used them from Ash Junction, $5\frac{1}{2}$ miles to the west of Guildford, and for a mile to the south at Shalford Junction. This 'by your leave' working was naturally conducive of delays, because when any question of priority was concerned it was no more than natural for the owning company to give preference to their own trains. The only consolation to the slowness of this particular journey was that the line passed through beautiful country. Then the final complication, so far as this cross-country route was concerned, came at Redhill itself, for some of the slow trains that eventually made their way into Reading started from one or another of the London termini of the South Eastern.

Redhill had once been a junction of the first magnitude. Its track layout was simple enough. There was the main north to south line forming part of the London, Brighton and South Coast route to the south coast, and immediately south of Redhill station two South Eastern lines diverged, one to the west—that which led eventually to Reading—and the eastbound one to Folkestone and Dover. But one could not run directly from the Reading line to the eastward continuation. It was necessary to turn in to the station, and reverse direction, with a fresh engine at what had been the rear of the train. When I first knew it Redhill had been relieved of much of the old complication. The South Eastern had its direct line from New Cross to Tonbridge, while the Brighton had built the Quarry Avoiding Line, whereby the principal Brighton expresses by-passed Redhill altogether. Even so, we always seemed to be in the station for ages, while engines were being changed. The only consolation for me was that it gave occasional glimpses of fast Brighton expresses on the distant Quarry Line. But I must hurry away from these areas of leisured travel and tangled up junctions, to see the South Eastern and Chatham at its finest and most spectacular.

Holidays at Folkestone, with excursions therefrom to Dover, Canterbury and Margate, were an absolute fascination for one who already had transport affairs in the blood. The coming and going of cross-Channel steamers, the arrival and departure of the various boat trains led my parents to spend much more time on the harbour piers, than in the more usual parental holiday task supervising the building of sand castles. Since then I have had much pleasure in piecing together the full picture of the remarkable services that I saw in early childhood. For me, and indeed for enthusiasts of all ages the S.E. & C.R. stimulated interest in all its activities by the publication of a splendid series of coloured postcards showing locomotives, carriages, stations, ships and so on. They cost a penny and each week the sum total of my pocket money went on adding another card to my collection. In those days the packet services from Dover and Folkestone were many and various. Ships sailed, as now, to Calais and Boulogne, and to Ostend, but also to Flushing. This latter was a highly competitive service to Holland and Germany, in opposition to the Great Eastern service to the Hook of Holland. But one of the most important traffics through Dover were the Continental and Imperial mails. The Indian mail then went overland from Calais to Brindisi, thus saving much valuable time, while one of the principal Continental mails left Cannon Street at nine in the morning. The S.E. & C.R. had special postal vans on which the lettering was bi-lingual: '*Royal Mail* : *Malle Royale*'.

4. VARIETIES IN S.E. & C.R. 4-4-0S

(a) Built for Great North of Scotland Railway, by Neilson, Reid in 1899, bought by S.E. & C.R.
(b) A Stirling 'F' class, in wartime dark-grey.
(c) A 'Wainwright' in its full glory: 'D' class No. 577.

Golden Age of Steam

My first visits to Folkestone and Dover came not many years after the working union of the two once-deadly rival companies had taken place; and while Folkestone had always been exclusively 'South Eastern' there was plenty of evidence at Dover of the competitive presence of the London Chatham and Dover Railway. Only a few weeks before the writing of this particular chapter, when I took part in a television programme and spoke, on the spot, upon the problems faced by the engineers in construction of 'The Dover Road', I marvelled once again at the daring and skill of William Cubitt and his men in carrying the South Eastern through the Folkestone Warren, and through the great Abbots Cliff and Shakespeare's Cliff tunnels. The Chatham line came into Dover 'by the back way', as it were, and whereas the last eight or nine miles of the South Eastern journey from London were within sight, and at times almost on the shore of the English Channel, the Chatham came through one tunnel after another until the last one brought the train suddenly and excitingly to the very brink of the harbour. Both railways then had extension lines leading on to the Admiralty Pier. In those days Britain was a free-trade country, and there was no question of customs examination on departure and arrival. The trains drew up opposite to their respective steamers, and passengers simply walked from one to the other.

The Admiralty Pier of those days was little more than a massive, immensely long breakwater, wide enough to carry two lines of rails, while on the western side the parapet was a little higher than the tops of the trains. The original arm extended about two train-lengths from the shore, as far as a fine lighthouse. There were berths for three steamers on the harbour, or inner side, and two at which steamers could berth on the *outer* side of the breakwater. One imagines there would be many times when the use of those outer berths would be hazardous, if not impossible owing to the roughness of the sea. A long extension seaward from the lighthouse was built from 1903 onwards, with a number of additional steamer berths on the harbour side. Despite the massive parapet wall on the seaward side of the pier transfer from the train to boat was often most unpleasant in times of winter gales, and there were occasions when the sea broke over the parapet with such force and such volume as to damage and even derail carriages standing on the pier. The co-ordination of the activities of the South Eastern and of the London Chatham and Dover Railways under the working union of 1899, led to a number of important improvements at Dover; but before mentioning these the situation in the old competitive days needs some reference.

Both companies had terminal stations for ordinary traffic almost on the shore, and then single tracked lines led on to the pier. These drew alongside at the pier-head, but there was no connection between the two. The South Eastern line was nearest to the parapet wall, and the Chatham within a few feet of the steamer berths on the harbour side. The rails were set flush in cobblestones like the rails of street tramcars, and everyone walked about at will. One of the earliest moves made after 1899 was to put in a scissors crossing at the pier-head so that trains from either of the tracks on the pier itself could run to either the South Eastern or the Chatham line, and at the outer end the rails were extended round the base of the old lighthouse, on very sharp curves to reach the berths on the outer extension. When I first went to Dover the great project of the marine station was already in hand. A huge area from the Lord Warden Hotel to beyond the old lighthouse was being reclaimed. The berths on the original and most landward part of the breakwater were already out of use, and all the steamer traffic was being operated from the berths beyond the old lighthouse. A public promenade extended throughout the length of the breakwater, and long though the walk was I remember how I could scarcely wait to get to the far end and look down upon the steamers.

The boat trains had their run from London lengthened by about a quarter of a mile during this period, and I remember being thrilled by the arrival of the 2.20 p.m. express from Charing Cross, not only by its splendidly ornate engine but by the speed at which she came along the pier, and most surprisingly of all round those curves past the old lighthouse. At this distance in time I cannot remember to which of the two new classes of 4-4-0 that engine belonged; but the 'E' class, with their Belpaire fireboxes were quite distinctive from the earlier 'D' class. Both were supremely elegant examples of British locomotive design, not only in their gorgeous colouring, and in their profusion of polished brass and copper work, but in the exquisite symmetry of their lines. They were not merely handsome to look at; they were massively constructed, and many of them, of both classes, were still in traffic 50 years after their first introduction. I shall tell later in this chapter how a number of them were modernized in the early 1920s; but many also remained in their original condition throughout their long lives, though not of course in their original livery. One of them has been restored, and is now on exhibition in the Museum of Transport at Clapham.

Technically both the 'D' and 'E' classes were a simple epitome of British locomotive practice of the period, and in detail an interesting blend of the former Chatham and South Eastern styles. The locomotive, carriage and wagon superintendent, Harry S. Wainwright, was a 'carriage' man—nothing of a locomotive designer; but he had as chief draughtsman Robert Surtees of the Chatham, a first-rate locomotive engineer. Because of the limited manufacturing facilities of the Chatham works, at Longhedge, Battersea, no great accuracy of construction was possible, and locomotives were built with generous clearance in the working parts to compensate for inaccuracies in erection. The locomotives of the Chatham did remarkably well on the line, even though they were noisy and rough. South Eastern men who drove them in later years used to call them the 'clatterbangs', because their own engines built to greater precision ran like sewing machines. In the 'D' and 'E' classes the designing skill of Surtees and the precision methods of South Eastern construction were blended to give the happiest of results.

At Dover one saw the former Chatham engines and an occasional domeless-boilered Stirling 4-4-0; but the new 'D' and 'E' classes dominated the Continental boat train working by both routes to London. One of the most important outcomes of the working agreement of 1899 was the multiplicity of routes to London that were made available from both Folkestone and Dover. Although most of the Channel packet services usually kept very good time they were dependent upon the running of trains that had travelled very long distances on the Continent: from the south of France, from Austria and the Balkans, from North and South Germany, and so on. While the London suburban area was not then so heavily worked as it is today, a boat train running half-an-hour out of its normal path could be an embarrassment to the traffic people. At the same time in those pre-war years Charing Cross was the principal passenger terminus for Continental traffic, while the very important overseas mail business was handled at Cannon Street, because of its proximity to the General Post Office at St. Martins-le-Grand. Some trains like the morning boat express started from Charing Cross, and then doubled back into Cannon Street to pick up the postal vans before proceeding to Dover.

When boat trains had to be dispatched in quick succession from Dover it was not unusual for one to take the South Eastern route to London, and one to go via Chatham. Then one would sometimes be lucky enough to see the two engines waiting on their respective tracks at the entrance to the pier. It is from a photograph taken in these circumstances that Jack Hill has produced the beautiful painting reproduced facing page 65. The alternative routes have been of priceless value at times when one or other of the lines has been blocked. The line from Folkestone beneath the 'White Cliffs' may be very picturesque, but it has suffered more than its normal share of accidents from natural causes. The chalk is sound and stable enough in the great headlands; but the Folkestone Warren has been a frequent source of anxiety, chiefly through wave action at the base of the cliffs causing instability. The first of such troubles came in 1877 at the eastern end of the Martello Tunnel, when some 60,000 cubic yards of chalk came down and blocked the line for two months. But a far more serious instance took place just before Christmas 1915, in the middle of World War I. For security reasons no news of it got into the newspapers and technical journals; but in fact the landslip in the Warren was of such magnitude that the line was closed for the rest of the war.

From a line of cleavage 180 yards from the eastern end of the Martello Tunnel the line was badly damaged, and pushed completely out of alignment for nearly two miles almost to the western end of the Abbots Cliff Tunnel. Quite serious consideration was given to closing the line altogether. All the special war traffic to and from Dover was taken by the Chatham route, and the twin bores of the Shakespeare's Cliff Tunnel were used for the storage of ammunition trains. The decision not to attempt to repair the damage during the war was not taken lightly; but the first examinations of the huge area that had become so dislodged suggested that it was not a straightforward landslip, but the result of complex geological factors. A highly scientific survey of the conditions seemed necessary, and personnel for this could not be spared during the war. The Chatham route was available and additional traffic was put through Folkestone. The line was re-opened in 1919. Although it is passing well beyond the period of this book I must recall the oddest of unlucky coincidences that have affected this line through the White Cliffs. World War II had scarcely broken out when there was a heavy fall of chalk between Abbots Cliff and Shakespeare's Cliff Tunnels, on 28 November, 1939, when 25,000 cubic yards of chalk came down, tore up the railway and pushed it out to sea. Fortunately, as in 1915, the vigilance of the men on the spot prevented any damage to railway traffic, and the line was opened again early in 1940, in time to take its share in the ever-memorable evacuation from Dunkirk.

5. DEVELOPMENT AT DOVER

(a) The Admiralty pier extension under construction.
(b) Reclamation work for the new Marine station—photo taken in
    May 1913.

The continental workings at Folkestone involved an operation of the most awkward complexity. Cubitt carried the South Eastern main line high above the town, crossing the valley on the lofty Foord viaduct. To get down to the harbour involved a back-handed connection near to the western end of the Martello Tunnel, a very steep gradient, the crossing of a swing bridge, and then a very sharply curved line through the actual harbour station platforms. In the running of the boat trains the main line engine had to be detached at the junction, the direction of running reversed, and the train taken gently down the bank to the harbour; but getting heavy trains up was even worse, and usually three tank engines were necessary, all going flat out. This procedure prevailed until multiple-unit electric trains took over from steam. It was always exciting to see a boat train start away from the harbour, with two or three engines, exhausts shooting sky-high and their chimneys barking like gunfire. Until well beyond the period of this book the little domeless Stirling tank engines were on the job. But with the laborious climbing of that severe incline, changing direction and engines at the junction, boat trains took longer to do the shorter distance from Folkestone to London than they did from Dover.

The development of Folkestone as a packet station did not go entirely according to plan. For one thing, the South Eastern Railway did not, in the first place, intend to have a secondary port to Dover. Other interests supervened, and the awkward line from high level down to the harbour came as a second thought. But as things developed the South Eastern became anxious enough to have a second port, and a very ambitious scheme was built up which could have left Dover to the London Chatham and Dover Railway and to the Admiralty, and given the South Eastern an entirely independent, first-class packet station of their own. To realize the advantages of this to the full a much better access was needed, and a plan was prepared for a new line to continue the Hythe branch, tunnel under the high cliffs between there and Folkestone Harbour, and terminate on the foreshore immediately to the west of the existing harbour station. Boat trains would be able to make a fast and undelayed approach; all the inconvenience of changing engines and reversal would be eliminated, and the trains could be worked to London in considerably less time than the L.C. & D. could manage from Dover. But Folkestone, as well as being a small, and growing packet station was also a health resort, catering for the 'genteel', and keenly aware of its position in relation to other South Coast resorts such as Eastbourne, Worthing and Bournemouth. It was feared that the establishment of a major railway terminal on the fore-shore, beneath the fashionable Leas promenade would so interfere with the local amenities as to destroy the town's status as a resort, and this local opinion killed the project. And so, all the inconveniences have continued, with little relief, right down to the present time.

Amenities apart, however, both Folkestone and Dover played a massive and vital part in war transport in the years 1914–18, and it was during that time that a profound change came over the appearance of S.E. & C.R. locomotives. In 1913 Wainwright had been succeeded by R. E. L. Maunsell, and with the setting up of an independent department to be responsible for locomotive running, Maunsell was given the title of Chief Mechanical Engineer. In the exigencies of wartime working the extremely elaborate and decorative style of engine painting, which was applied to all locomotives, passenger and goods alike, seemed quite inappropriate, and there was adopted a style of finish that was the very antithesis: a plain dark grey, unrelieved by any lining out, with the complete suppression of all polished metal work, and with the engine number rendered in large white *sans-serif* numerals on the tenders, or on the side-tanks of the suburban and shunting tank engines. It was as though the S.E. & C.R. had abandoned its gay peacetime uniform for a wartime battledress. Certain other British railways simplified their engine-liveries during the war, but none so drastically and completely as the South Eastern and Chatham.

I must confess however that when I saw the engines again, first briefly, in 1919, and then more frequently from the summer of 1921 onwards, I was impressed by the simple dignity of that austere turn-out. For one thing the engines were mostly very clean; but I realized also that all the finery one can bestow does not in itself make a handsome engine, and that those Wainwright and Stirling 4-4-0s had a balanced symmetry of line, and a dignity that would still have made them handsome engines in the most work-a-day of garbs. But by the time I came to London to begin my engineering studies, in 1921, there were some new-comers amongst them, the workings of which I found most interesting to study. Locomotive engineers of both the Chatham and of the South Eastern railways had worked under severe restrictions of axle loading; and the working union of the two old companies had not brought much relief, except that the old speed limit of 60 m.p.h. everywhere on the South Eastern was raised. Faced with the increasing loads of the boat trains the locomotive department had worked out proposals for new engines of the 4-6-0 type; but first one design, and then another had been vetoed by the civil engineer, and the best that could be done was to provide some modified 4-4-0s with superheaters. Acceptance, even of these, was grudging, and they were not allowed to run over any part of the former London Chatham and Dover line.

After the war the traffic department decided to concentrate all the Continental business at Victoria, and by so doing put the locomotive department in a difficulty, in that the most powerful engines could not be used, due to the weight restrictions over the 'Chatham' part of the route. Maunsell and his staff thereupon embarked on a very notable project, namely to rebuild some of the 'E' class 4-4-0s with superheaters, but without increasing the weight on any of the axles. Every means of reducing surplus weight was examined. The broad wheel-splashers were narrowed; the heavy cast-iron drag box beneath the footplate was replaced by a lightweight steel assembly of equivalent strength, and these and other detail modifications saved enough weight to compensate for the addition of the superheater. But even more important than the saving in weight was the thorough modernization of the front-end and valve gear. Large diameter piston valves were substituted for the original slide valves, and the Stephenson link motion had its setting revised on the lines of that most successfully fitted and standardized on the Great Western Railway. The re-built engines proved immensely fast and powerful, quite beyond their modest size, and they held the fort on the boat trains for five critical years, until well after the grouping, when the civil engineer of the newly-constituted Southern Railway was ready to allow 4-6-0s of the 'King Arthur'

6. NOTABLE S.E. & C.R. TRAINS

(a) Through express from Dover to the G.W.R. line via Redhill and Reading, leaving Sandling Junction, hauled by Stirling 'B' class 4-4-0.

(b) One of very few photographs showing the new 'L' class 4-4-0s of 1914 (built by Borsig of Berlin) in pre-war livery. Engine No. 773 hauling up Continental mail train near Folkestone Junction.

class on the principal boat train routes.

In the last summer before the grouping, that of 1922, I spent many hours at the lineside of the S.E. & C.R., watching the train workings, and taking photographs in the beautiful Kentish countryside. And as the smartly groomed, dark grey engines came pounding up the banks, towards the tunnels burrowing beneath the crest of the North Downs I found myself reflecting upon the striking metamorphosis that had befallen the railway since the days of the colourful glamour-parade of pre-war years at Folkestone, and since those school mornings when I waited impatiently on the little platform of 'Sindlesham and Hurst Halt' for the belated train, wondering for how long those masters would believe it was the train, and not counter-attractions in Reading itself that was making me so consistently late! But there was another interest on the post-war S.E. & C.R., as well as the rebuilt 4-4-os, and the old favourites of pre-war years in their modern dress. During the war Maunsell had produced two new designs—represented it is true by no more than a single prototype of each—but which were destined to be the cornerstones of a scheme of complete modernization on the railway. One, No. 810, was a 2-6-0 tender engine, and the other No. 790, a 2-6-4 tank. Though dating from 1917 their story really belongs to the post-grouping era; but, waiting with my camera by the lineside at Elmstead Woods, Chislehurst, or Orpington, there was always the hope that one of these two might come along one day. But so long as my camera was concerned they were most elusive.

The bane of my schoolboy life, the Reading service, did not entirely escape me even in my post-war admiration of the smartness of the main line working out of London. For I also spent long hours beside the Brighton line south of Croydon, and sure enough the old Stirling 4-4-os, rebuilt with domeless boilers and likewise austere in the all-pervading dark grey came chuffing slowly along on the old line to the south, cut so deeply into the North Downs before it dived into Merstham Tunnel. I had no occasion to travel by those trains, but they did not seem to be hurrying even then, any more than they did when I spent so long waiting for them at Sindlesham and Hurst Halt!

CHAPTER THREE

A railway in transition

TO SOME WHO try to view the past in true historical perspective the period between the end of the Boer War, and the fateful August of 1914 often has the look of a golden age for the railways of Britain. It was no less a highly critical era, and while some of the old companies continued more or less in their set ways, the managements of others, cognisant of the new trends that had barely come to the surface in 1914, were setting in motion certain important lines of development that were fairly to revolutionize their entire practice before many years were out. Towards the end of this period no English railway was more completely in transition than the London and South Western. Many writers have lingered nostalgically over its old-world charms; upon the nineteenth-century atmosphere of both its branch and its main lines in Wessex, the New Forest and East Devon. Those who delighted in what might be termed the 'folk lore' of railways could certainly have found ample material covered by the initials 'L.S.W.R.'; but step inside the headquarter offices at Waterloo, into the new locomotive works at Eastleigh, or on to the quaysides at Southampton Docks, and one was caught up in a positive whirlwind of activity.

One did not need to go into the offices at Waterloo. The old station was, stage by stage, being torn down; the track layout in the approaches altered beyond recognition. Property on both sides of the line was being acquired, demolitions were in progress, and the bewildering complexity of a huge reconstruction scheme evident on all hands. Not all that the South Western had in prospect in the London area was yet even beginning to be apparent. The decision was about to be taken to electrify much of the suburban area. Already the South Western was in the forefront of modern signalling development in England, and the fabulous Dugald Drummond was to live just long enough to see the consummation of his greatest work—the planning and construction of the new locomotive and carriage works at Eastleigh. The abrupt change in locomotive design practice had yet to come; while Drummond lived the older traditions prevailed, though not flourishing so bravely as of old. Apart from this however, every department of the railway was on the move, under the inspired leadership of Herbert Ashcombe Walker, who came from the London and North Western to become General Manager in January 1912.

The reconstruction of Waterloo Station was a colossal undertaking. At the turn of the century it had 18 passenger lines, grouped into what were generally known as the north, old, and south stations. But it had been enlarged piecemeal over the years and was the most higgledy-piggledy jumble anyone could possibly imagine. Many of the lines lay between two platform faces; there was an engine shed sandwiched in between the old and the south station, and right in the middle of the whole ensemble there was a through single line that led out of the back wall, crossed the Waterloo Road and made a junction with the South Eastern Railway. From the western end the station was approached by six running lines. But quite apart from the purely railway complications things could be bewildering in the extreme for passengers who did not know their way about. The platforms were not numbered consecutively. It was only on the signalling diagrams that any form of order prevailed, and that was not of much use to a harassed passenger with only five minutes to catch his train, and horrified to discover that platform No. 2 was by no means where he might expect to find it. But it was one thing for an enterprising and far-sighted management to decide on the complete reconstruction of such an outdated and cumbersome layout; it was far otherwise to carry it out. Even at the turn of the century Waterloo was one of the busiest stations in the world, and the reconstruction had been done while the traffic continued to flow.

The South Western carried the heaviest passenger traffic of any British railway. It proudly advertised that it ran 'In the path of the sun, for health and pleasure', and at holiday times the traffic in and out of Waterloo was tremendous. The record of working on a certain Saturday in the summer of 1892 gives the following remarkable figures:

Regular passenger trains arriving	255
Special passenger trains arriving	37
Regular passenger trains departing	250
Special passenger trains departing	31
Empty stock trains entering Waterloo	72
Empty stock trains leaving for sidings	84
Light engines arriving from shed	80
Light engines leaving for shed	70

The total number of train and engine movements in the 24 hours was thus 879, and as most of this would be taking place in the 18 hours between 4 a.m. and 10 p.m. there would be a movement to be signalled and regulated nearly every minute of the day!

The new layout was planned by J. W. Jacomb-Hood. Until his untimely death in the spring of 1914 he was what we should now entitle the chief civil engineer. But his official title was 'Resident Engineer'. This was a picturesque survival from the earliest days of the London and Southampton Railway, of which the great pioneer Joseph Locke was engineer. After the railway was opened for traffic in 1840 Locke was retained as engineer, though in little more than a consultative capacity. The man on the spot, who had to deal with the day-to-day activities and eventually to take responsibility for the numerous extensions was the 'resident engineer'; and this latter title survived long after Locke's death, and the disappearance of the post he had held. Jacomb-Hood had a very talented assistant in Alfred Weeks Szlumper, the London Divisional Engineer, on whom much of the day-to-day

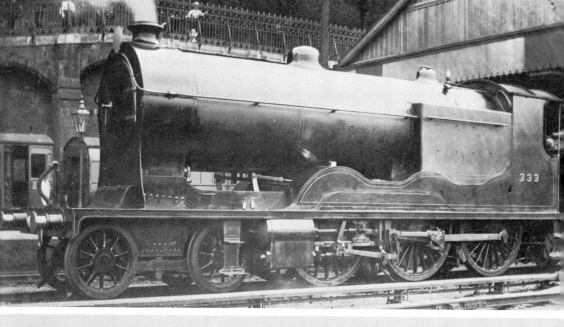

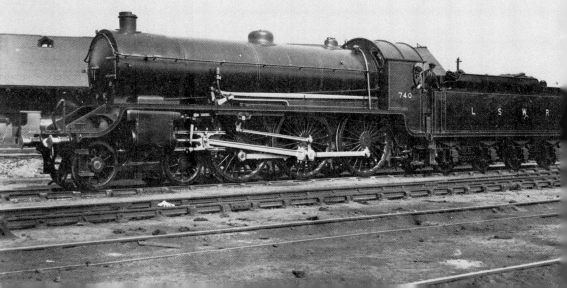

responsibility for the reconstruction of Waterloo devolved. The general plan of the work was to start with the old South station; demolish it, and gradually work across the whole area towards the north. Stage by stage a group of two or three platforms would be closed to traffic, and the trains accommodated elsewhere in the station. As the reconstruction enlarged the platform and track capacity so the business of re-routing became easier; four or five new platforms would take the place of the original three, and so on. From the passenger point of view the lofty glazed roof, and the wide concourse at the head of the platforms were much appreciated features.

While the actual work of construction was in progress the track layout leading into temporary platforms and sidings had frequently to be altered, with appropriate changes in the signalling. On the L.S.W.R. the 'resident engineer' took the ultimate responsibility for signalling, and it was fortunate that Szlumper had an interest in this work far greater than that of merely delegating it to a specialist assistant. Szlumper read a fascinating paper to the Institution of Civil Engineers on the Waterloo signalling, as it was modernized in 1892, and during all the complicated 'stage-work' that accompanied the successive phases of the station reconstruction the signal engineer had his full co-operation in a very intricate task. Arthur Johnson was signal engineer, a very able man who had gained wide experience of the latest electrical techniques during an extensive tour of the U.S.A. His introduction of 'power' signalling on the L.S.W.R. did not, however, include anything at Waterloo itself; there he was constrained towards modifying and extending the very fine mechanical plant of 1892.

What Szlumper himself called 'The Waterloo Signal Station' was one of the wonders of the British railway world. This is no place to enlarge upon details of the many ingenious mechanical contrivances that were built into the huge interlocking machine in the signal box on the bridge spanning all the approach tracks. It was the tremendous array of semaphore arms carried high above the roof of that signal box that so caught the eye. When the plant was put into commission in 1892 there were no fewer than *sixty-one* semaphores at that one location, with another eighteen, on the Westminster Road signal bridge, a little further out from the terminus, with another *eighty-four* on separate cantilever bracket posts at the entrance to the platforms. But it was, above all else, that amazing 'skyline' of signals above the box that made so arresting a spectacle. For lovers of the old railways a sight like that was almost the equal of some gleaming vintage steam locomotive and its train; and I must admit I had some mixed feelings in the 1930s when my professional work involved the design of many utilitarian structures that were to replace the old 'A' box at Waterloo, and its numerous semaphores.

7. OUTSIDE CYLINDERS ON THE L.S.W.R.

(a) An Adams 6 ft. 7 in. 4-4-0 of 1893.
(b) Dugald Drummond's enormous 4-cylinder 4-6-0 of 1905.
(c) R. W. Urie's 'N.15' class, 2-cylinder, of 1918, forerunners of the
    S.R. *King Arthur* class.

In taking the London and South Western Railway well to the fore in the adoption of 'power' signalling Johnson installed the low-pressure pneumatic system. It was sometimes called the 'all air' system, and used compressed air at a pressure of no more than 15 lb. per sq. in. Jacomb-Hood considered it was cheaper than the electro-pneumatic system, and on his recommendation it was standardized. A total of 25 signal boxes was so equipped, including large main line installations at Clapham Junction, Basingstoke, and Salisbury. It was complicated in its lavish use of piping, because it required three pipes for each signal— one for lowering it, one for restoring it to danger, and a third for the return indication to show that the signal *had* gone back to danger. Although it was not adopted as standard by any other British railway the 'low pressure pneumatic' gave long years of trouble-free service on the London and South Western; in fact the plant at Basingstoke, and the automatic signals between there and Woking were not replaced until a few years ago, having been in commission for around sixty years.

Those automatic signals between Woking and Basingstoke were one of the great sights of the L.S.W.R.—very much the 'railway in transition'. They covered a stretch of 20 miles of quadruple-tracked main line, and each automatic signal location consisted of a bridge spanning all four tracks, with a signal post for each on the bridge. Each post carried a home and distant arm, and all were pneumatically operated according to the occupancy of the track circuits ahead. They were actually 'three aspect' signals. They normally stood with both semaphore arms in the clear position. When a train passed, both arms went to danger. Then when the train had passed the next automatic signal bridge ahead the upper or 'home arm' was lowered, and when the preceding train had passed the second bridge ahead the lower or distant arm cleared. Johnson was sometimes criticized for using two separate arms to give his three indications, when by use of upper quadrant arms all three could have been given by one arm; horizontal for stop; inclined upward, one section clear; vertical for two sections clear—as the Great Western did at Paddington and on the Ealing and Shepherds Bush line. The latter arrangement was of course becoming quite common practice in the U.S.A. But however much the L.S.W.R. was 'with it' in other modernizing techniques Johnson stood resolutely out against three-position semaphores. He always said it was like trying to tell the time from a 'one-armed clock'!

Installations of the low pressure pneumatic signalling system were made on the westward continuation of the main line from Basingstoke, but not on the original main line—the parent stem of the entire system—down to Southampton. It was there that I first travelled on the London and South Western, journeying from Reading for holidays at Southsea, the Isle of Wight, and Bournemouth. There the transition, that was gaining such momentum elsewhere had scarcely begun to touch the railway in pre-war years. From the 'Hants' fork of the 'Berks and Hants' line of the Great Western we changed into the distinctive two-tone non-corridor carriages of the L.S.W.R., salmon coloured above the waistline and with blackish-brown bodies. Many trains were worked by the Adams outside-cylindered 4-4-0 locomotives, which looked so grandly impressive as they came sweeping in to a station stop. Eastleigh was our changing point for Portsmouth and Southsea, but I have a recollection that on one expedition we had to change at Southampton. The original line, as engineered by Joseph Locke and opened in 1840 came straight down beside the river Itchen to a terminus near to the old town centre. When I first travelled that way it was known as Southampton Town, and the line to Bournemouth and Weymouth turned sharply to the right at Northam Junction less than a mile from the terminus. The present main station was then Southampton West, and some trains used to enter the town station, and then proceed west over the triangle junction that led to the new line. Today the old 'town' station has disappeared, and my most vivid recollection of this part of the line is of riding the engine of an Ocean Liner Special, starting from beneath the very bows of the great Cunard White Star liner *Queen Elizabeth*, and then running non-stop to Waterloo.

This, however, is a recollection of much more recent times, though it was certainly a development for which the seeds were already being sown in the years before World War I. The eminence of the port of Southampton stems directly from the enterprise of the London and South Western Railway. In the early years of the present century, apart from the packet services to the Channel Islands, Havre, and the Breton ports the overseas traffic from Southampton did not extend much beyond the South African and South American mails. For the British steamship lines Liverpool was the premier port for transatlantic traffic, while through the enterprise of the Great Western Railway ships from America based in various European countries were calling at Plymouth on their eastbound journeys. But while the Cunard 'flyers' *Mauretania* and *Lusitania*, holding the Blue Riband for the Atlantic crossing were firmly attached to Liverpool, the L.S.W.R. was doing everything it could to attract the rival White Star line steamers to Southampton. The Trafalgar graving dock, then the largest in the world, was opened in 1907. It was 875 ft. long, 90 ft. wide at sill, and 125 ft. wide at cope level. It was scarcely finished before an announcement, by the White Star Line, caused some consternation at Waterloo.

In competing for the immensely valuable ocean traffic between England and the U.S.A. the White Star made no attempt to match the Cunard in speed. Instead they decided to build two luxury liners, of what became known as the 'palace hotel' category, that would provide every known convenience and luxury in travel, but at a lesser speed than the express mail steamers of the Cunard. These two giants were the *Olympic* and the *Titanic*; but it was their size that nonplussed the L.S.W.R. They would be too big for the largest graving dock in the world! After much consideration a decision was taken to enlarge the Trafalgar dock to an inside length of 897 ft., and to a width at entrance of 100 ft. The disaster to the *Titanic* on her maiden voyage stunned the whole world; but in due course the *Olympic* came to Southampton. In those previous years however, before the 'palace hotel' liners were calling regularly there was a weekly service to New York by White Star from Southampton, by lesser ships, and these liners used to call at Queenstown. The L.S.W.R. hit upon the idea of issuing tourist tickets to Ireland via Southampton, and landing at Queenstown by tender. The White Star Liners on the New York run were then the *Adriatic*, *Majestic*, *Oceanic* and the *Teutonic*, and the fares from Waterloo to Queenstown were 91s. first class, and 67s. second class. Presumably passengers made their own way back.

So far as speed was concerned the principal competitor of Cunard on the North Atlantic run was the North German Lloyd Line; and plans for enlargement of the Trafalgar Dock had scarcely been started before the German Line announced the laying down of an even larger ship. This was the supremely beautiful *Imperator*, but she had not long been in service before war broke out in 1914, and the likelihood of her needing the facilities of a graving dock at Southampton vanished—for a time. But after the war the whole pattern of steamship services on the North Atlantic changed. For a time the premier British lines were carrying practically all the traffic. For the convenience of tourists going direct to the Continent both Cunard and the White Star made their first European calls at Cherbourg, and Southampton, instead of Liverpool, became the terminal point. The facilities built up in pre-war years by the London and South Western Railway were of almost priceless value. The transition set in motion had indeed paid off, and the development was continued throughout the lifetime of the Southern Railway. I need only add that the *Imperator* was handed over to Cunard, as war reparations, and was renamed *Berengaria*.

So far I have touched no more than incidentally upon the locomotives of the L.S.W.R., which in those pre-war years were synonymous with the name of Dugald Drummond. Never the most placid of characters he came to the South Western as a frustrated and embittered man. His early career, first on the North British, and then on the Caledonian had been one of unbroken success, and in its later stages of rich financial reward. But he was tempted by a prospect of vastly greater fields of activity to relinquish his post on the Caledonian in favour of a glittering project in Australia. This fell through, and he set up a locomotive manufactory of his own in Glasgow. This again was unsuccessful, and when the post of locomotive superintendent in the L.S.W.R. fell vacant he was glad enough to take it, at a salary far less than that he had enjoyed on the Caledonian. Though he came to London as a disappointed and no doubt a disillusioned man, no personal sentiments were allowed to enter into his management of the department. Furthermore the esteem in which he was held by his former staff and workmen on the Caledonian was amply shown by the number of Scotsmen who came south to work for him on the L.S.W.R. His tenure of office on the line was an outstanding success, except in one particular; that unfortunately is one that was prominently in the eye of railway enthusiasts, and in consequence tends to give a wrong impression of the latter and final phase of his career.

Drummond was ever to be remembered in railway history for the family of medium powered 4-4-0 express passenger locomotives, from the 'Waverley' class of 1876 on the North British, the '90' class on the Caledonian, which won such fame in the 'Race to the North' in 1895, to his brother's 'Small Ben' class on the Highland Railway. Incomparably

8. THE DRUMMOND 4-4-0 DEVELOPMENT

(a) The original 'T9' 4-4-0 batch, without cross water tubes.
(b) An 'L.12' 4-4-0, No. 434 decorated for a Royal special.
(c) Drummond's last design, the 'D.15' 4-4-0 of 1912, with inside Walschaerts valve gear.

the finest of all was his 'T9' on the London and South Western. In my own opinion this was one of the best, and most long-lived small-power locomotives of all time. But then, while maintaining a strong and efficient management of the locomotive department, and securing first-rate workmanship in the locomotive shops, his work as an engine designer strayed into the unorthodox, and there was a striking parallel in this respect to the career of F. W. Webb, at Crewe, on the London and North Western. Both men were the most utter autocrats, and their most senior assistants would scarcely have dared to comment, still less to criticize their proposals in locomotive design. Dugald Drummond drifted from the simple, straightforward 4-4-0 locomotive that had already brought him such renown, to a series of large four-cylinder 4-6-0s. They were tremendous things to look upon, grandly impressive in their elegant outward proportions yet, except for the last series, strangely sluggish and ineffective in traffic.

It is true that there were only 26 of them altogether; but their very size, and the flourish with which they took the road naturally brought them very much into the public gaze, and their shortcomings were highlighted to a greater extent than might otherwise have been the case. What made the first two groups sluggish in passenger service can only be conjectured; but to preserve a remarkably neat and closed-in outside appearance the steam passages, and inside valve gear had many bends and convolutions. It was also noticeable that drivers seemed disinclined to let them run fast downhill. The older 4-4-0s were doing some of the fastest running in the country at that time, frequently reaching speeds in excess of 85 m.p.h.; but the bigger engines rarely got much over seventy. The London and South Western Railway did not, however, enjoy one of the best tracks in the country. The alignment was splendid, but the roadbed was such as to set up severe rolling and vibration with large engines. The last batch of four-cylinder 4-6-0s, known by the men as the 'Paddleboats', from their huge paddlebox-like splashers, were much the best. They could run freely, but being rather awkward to fire sometimes ran short of steam. Drummond was a constant striver for high thermal efficiency, and resisted the current trend to apply a high degree of superheating to the steam. By this latter practice a certain amount of valuable heat was thrown away in the exhaust. Churchward had the same inclinations, on the Great Western, and used no more than a moderate degree of superheat. Drummond designed his own 'steam dryer', which was fitted to all his later engines.

In 1912 he had reached the age of 72, and was still as vigorous and forthright as ever; but in November of that year, while on the footplate he received a very severe scald in the leg. The injury was so serious that the limb had to be amputated, and at his age the shock was too great. He died the next day. He was succeeded by Robert W. Urie, Works Manager at Eastleigh who, like Drummond himself, had a distinguished career on the Caledonian before coming south to the L.S.W.R. In personality Urie was the very opposite of Drummond—no less incisive, no less master of the department, but a mellow, charming character, who got his results by leadership rather than dictatorship. All the same Urie, like so many men who had come from Scotland to work on the L.S.W.R., would have been the first to acknowledge the debt of gratitude he owed to Drummond, even though he

46

9. NINE ELMS SHED IN 1920

(a) Engines from top towards camera are 'T9' No. 301; another 'T9' unidentified; an 'M7' 0-4-4 tank; 'S.15' mixed traffic 4-6-0 No. 502; a small-wheeled 4-4-0 under repair; Adams 0-4-4 tank No. 197 and an 'M.7' 0-4-4 tank.

(b) Isle of Wight Railway, 2-4-0 *Ventnor*.

proceeded at once to reverse some of his predecessor's most cherished practices in loco-motive design. In one respect he anticipated, by nearly forty years, the 'engine' layout that was standardized by the nationalized British Railways from 1951 onwards.

Urie's first new locomotive was a large 4-6-0, and in this he used two cylinders only, outside, with the Walschaerts valve gear, also outside, Everything was outside and readily accessible. There was no need to get the engine over a pit in order to do routine maintenance work. This became his standard engine layout, and it was applied on several varieties of 4-6-0 and on some large tank engines of the 4-6-2 and 4-8-0 types used in connection with traffic in and around the large marshalling yard built at Feltham shortly after the war. Urie also discarded the steam-dryer, and substituted a conventional type of superheater designed at Eastleigh. This change greatly increased the reliability of the 'Paddleboat' series of Drummond 4-6-0s, and also that of the larger 4-4-0s of the 'L.12' and 'D.15' classes. I remember with what interest I read in *The Railway Magazine* of the building of the 'N.15' class of 4-6-0 express passenger engine, in 1918; I was in the North at the time, but when I came to London in the autumn of 1921 one of my first expeditions was to the L.S.W.R. lineside to see these engines at work. Then I had my first personal experience of the transi-tion that was so profoundly affecting that railway. I went to Surbiton, and duly saw the 11 a.m. West of England express sweep through, headed by an 'N.15'. But much else was changed from the railway I had known in pre-war years.

One of the most striking innovations was the new rolling stock embodied in the five-coach 'Tea-car' sets newly introduced on some of the Bournemouth expresses. Restaurant cars had never been plentiful on the L.S.W.R., and what cars there were shared the narrow-bodied, flat-sided profile of all the rest of the main line passenger stock. But these new carriages were something quite different. Both in width and height they were built out practically to the limit of the loading gauge, with a smooth, almost bulbous exterior profile. There were only a few of them in service when I first came to London, but again the South Western proved a pioneer, and those tea-car sets became a prototype for the new standard coaches of the Southern Railway, built in large numbers in the grouping era. In quite a superficial respect also the coaches were getting a 'new look' after the war. The old two-tone livery of 'salmon and sepia' was being replaced by olive green of the same shade as that of the locomotives.

The sense of transition was completed on the London and South Western Railway by the swift comings and going of the new electric trains. In these, as in so many other things the railway was an anticipator. The system of traction chosen in 1914, was a new one so far as British railways were concerned, and in the use of the 'third rail' for pick-up and returning current through the two running rails it pioneered the system that has now been extended throughout the entire main line network in Kent and Sussex, and been extended to Portsmouth, Southampton and Bournemouth. How it came to be preferred to that of the neighbouring London, Brighton and South Coast Railway, when a choice had to be made for the future standards of the Southern Railway is a story that belongs to the grouping era. It is enough here to record that the system of the L.S.W.R. was standardized.

CHAPTER FOUR

'Sweedy'

ONE SATURDAY MORNING in 1948, at the height of the summer traffic, I was in the Platform signal box on York station, watching the traffic working and listening to the almost ceaseless telephone and aural instructions by which the Assistant Stationmaster was co-ordinating the control of train running in the entire York area. There was no colour light signalling at that time, and he was in constant communication with no fewer than 9 signal boxes, in addition to 'Platform', and those 9 boxes had a total of 907 levers between them. It was just after 10 o'clock, with the busiest time for southbound trains approaching, and he spoke to the senior signalman at Clifton Junction; 'I'll have Sweedy next'. Here, in the year of grace 1948, was a survival of an old railway nickname that dated back to upwards of a hundred years. In day-to-day railway talk at Doncaster or York no one used to refer to the Great Eastern; it was always 'Sweedy'. But I must say I was intrigued beyond measure to hear the old nickname still in use 25 years after the Great Eastern had ceased to exist. That cryptic 'phone call in 1948 referred to the 10.12 a.m. express from York to Lowestoft, the engine and coaches for which were waiting ready in one of the sidings at Clifton Junction.

'Sweedy': what memories the name arouses! It would not be heard in the teeming eastern suburbs of London, where the Great Eastern derived so much of its passenger revenue, nor yet on the lordly 'Hook of Holland' boat express; but one had not to travel far into East Anglia, north through the Fens and into Lincolnshire to realize the extreme many-sidedness of Great Eastern operation. It was where it connected with other railways to the north of March and Peterborough that its old nickname could be heard. It arose from the predominantly agricultural country that it served; but even though the Great Eastern had a substantial traffic in grain, turnips, sugar beet—and swedes!—these far from represented the sum total of its freight traffic in the northern sector of the area it served. Like many another traveller, my own first introduction to it, in pre-1914 days, was by a holiday express from London to the East Anglian coast; but it will be as well to take a look at the system as a whole before referring in any detail to a particular traffic.

East of a line drawn from London to the Wash it had East Anglia almost, but not quite to itself. There were two 'intrusions'. The northern one in the shape of the Midland and Great Northern Joint Line did not trouble the Great Eastern unduly. Two westerly prongs of this little system converged at King's Lynn, and then made a hilly and difficult course over the Norfolk 'breckland' to Yarmouth. The Great Eastern lived in more or less peaceful coexistence with this line, and even after the grouping of 1923 it still remained a joint concern, henceforth of the L.M.S. and L.N.E.R. The other 'intrusion' into its own territory was the London, Tilbury and Southend, the sphere of activity of which was succinctly covered in its title—not always the case among the pre-grouping railways of Britain. Great Eastern relations with the 'Tilbury' were rudely shattered in 1912 in a matter that had profound effects on the future of both railway systems. But first of all let us seek out 'Sweedy' in his northern associations, and how his nickname became a household railway word as far north as York.

I need not delve back into nineteenth-century railway history beyond saying that outright ownership of the line north ended just north of March, and from there onwards, through Spalding, Sleaford, Lincoln and Gainsborough there ran the celebrated Joint Line, owned by the Great Eastern and the Great Northern. At Black Carr Junction, $2\frac{3}{4}$ miles to the south of Doncaster the Joint Line made a junction with the Great Northern main line from King's Cross, but the Great Eastern exercised running power for a further 32 miles to the north of Doncaster, to reach York. In the competitive spirit that animated the British railway companies of pre-grouping days the Great Eastern advertized 'The Cathedrals Route' to the north, and ran a restaurant car express between Liverpool Street and York. Actually there was only one more cathedral than on the direct route, passing Ely and Lincoln instead of Peterborough; and despite the level country traversed it was infinitely slower. More than that, apart from the brief intermissions of ecclesiastic splendour the line throughout from Cambridge to York, in the flat monotony of the countryside, was one of the dullest scenically that it was possible to make in Great Britain. But much of it was grand country for swedes!

The Joint Line was, however, far more important as a coal carrier. At Doncaster it was in connection with some of the richest colliery districts in England, and over it went a constant stream of heavy trains bound for many parts of East Anglia and also the eastern districts of London. Not all of the Great Eastern traffic in coal came from the Doncaster district. Trains from the East Midland collieries came eastwards from Peterborough, and March was the 'grand junction' of the Great Eastern heavy freight business. Five main lines converged at this point. Going round the compass clockwise they came from Peterborough, Spalding (the Joint line), Wisbech and King's Lynn, and finally Ely—the main line to London via Cambridge. The importance of March grew in the years following the grouping, and it became the scene of the first-ever completely mechanized marshalling yards in Great Britain. Despite its nickname however, in 1913 vegetables formed no more than 3 per cent of the total tonnage of the freight traffic of the Great Eastern, which then amounted to some $13\frac{1}{4}$ million, annually. Some of the individual totals contributing to this are interesting to recall.

50

Coal, coke and patent fuels	5,078,840 tons
Other minerals	2,436,226
Grain	1,088,275
Stone	507,785
Vegetables	361,706
Bricks	287,570

Great Eastern engines worked into Doncaster on both passenger and freight trains, while the passenger engines continued north to York, and in their magnificent blue livery contributed to the kaleidoscopic effects to be witnessed at that station in pre-grouping days. At Doncaster the Great Eastern had its own allocation of space in the big locomotive depot on 'the Carr', as the one time marshy district to the south of the town was known. At one time it had been a game decoy, much loved by the sporting gentry of the neighbourhood. Contrary to what might have been expected the Great Eastern enginemen based at Doncaster never seemed to suffer from any feelings of inferiority complex towards their counterparts on the Great Northern, despite the proximity of the famous 'Plant Works' and the G.N.R. locomotive headquarters. Outpost Doncaster may have been so far as the Great Eastern was concerned; but the enginemen had a superiority rather than an inferiority complex! For many years I had on my staff at Westinghouse an engineer whose father had been a driver at Doncaster. When I first learned of this I naturally assumed he was on the Great Northern; but my friend was horrified at the mere suggestion, and told me, bursting with pride, of how his father had risen to be the senior *Great Eastern* driver, working the crack 'lodging turns' down the Joint Line.

In the foregoing paragraph I referred briefly to the Great Eastern engine livery. It certainly was magnificent. I saw it first in the smoky precincts of Liverpool Street Station in London. The royal blue, which was the basic colour, was apt to darken slightly with age; but the scheme of lining out, accompanied by the profusion of polished metal-work of various kinds, made a truly splendid *ensemble*. It is preserved, for posterity to see, on two locomotives in the British Transport collection in the museum at Clapham. The 'blue' had a slightly purplish hue, quite different from the original dark 'Prussian blue' of the Caledonian; it was set off, and the purple effect intensified by much red lining. The preserved engines are a mixed-traffic 2-4-0 and a suburban passenger 0-6-0 tank, neither of which carried the livery in excelsis. To behold it at its grandest one had to visit Liverpool Street just before the departure of the Norfolk Coast Express and gaze upon a 'Claud Hamilton' class 4-4-0, or better still, one of the new superheated 4-6-0s of the '1500' class, which came out just at the end of 1911. On these the splendid blue with its prominent red lining was supplemented by much polished brass- and copper-work, with the coupling rods red, and their ends highly polished steel.

The new 4-6-0s had not come upon the scene when I first travelled on the Great Eastern Railway. Then the great majority of locomotives had severely plain stove-pipe chimneys, like the two that are preserved in the museum at Clapham. This, and the mounting of the dome very close behind the chimney gave them a style of their own, quite apart from their gay livery. But, to revert to the 4-6-0s, their introduction revealed to outside observers a pecularity in the main line engine working that might not have been appreciated while the 'Claud Hamilton' class 4-4-0s were in general use on the principal express trains. Very few of the crack workings were operated by London crews. The large depot at Stratford was 4 miles out of the terminus and light engine running would have increased congestion on what was always a very busy section of line. Consequently the turns were arranged so that engines came up from the country, and waited for their return trains in the engine yard at Liverpool Street. Five of the new 4-6-0s were built in 1911–12 and, after some preliminary running from Stratford, they were allocated to Parkeston Quay shed, Harwich, for the Continental boat train workings. The crack expresses on the Cromer run, including the celebrated 'Norfolk Coast Express', were allocated to Ipswich and Norwich sheds, and these remained 4-4-0 hauled during the summer of 1912. It might appear strange that an express running non-stop in each direction between London and North Walsham should be worked by locomotives from Ipswich and Norwich, when both places were passed without stopping; but these 'star' duties involved lodging turns for the men.

The 'diagram' by which Ipswich men worked the down Norfolk Coast Express was typical. They began with the 10 a.m. Ipswich to London, arriving just before 11.30 a.m. Then they took the 'non-stop' to North Walsham, and continued to Cromer, before returning to Norwich, where they booked off for the night. Next day they took a 'slow' from Norwich to Cromer; then the 1 p.m. up Norfolk Coast Express running, as in the down direction, non-stop from North Walsham to Liverpool Street, and then finally home to Ipswich in the evening. The Norwich men, working on alternate days, began by taking the morning slow to Cromer; then the up Norfolk Coast Express, and then down from Liverpool Street to Ipswich where they booked off for the night. Then next morning they took the 10 a.m. up to London; down to Cromer with the Norfolk Coast Express, and then home with the evening 'slow'. In those days it was considered that only the very *élite* of engine crews were allocated to lodging turns, yet nowadays they are avoided wherever possible! The second batch of 4-6-0s, completed in the early months of 1913, were divided between Ipswich and Norwich sheds specially for the Cromer trains. But their introduction was marked by a tragedy. Engine No. 1506, the first of the new batch was on the up Norfolk Coast Express on 12th July when, through an operating mistake, a light engine strayed on to the line in front of it at Colchester. In the ensuing collision the big engine, strangely enough, got very much the worst of it; her driver was killed and the brand new engine damaged beyond repair.

10. GREAT EASTERN LOCOMOTIVES

(a) One of the Holden 'T.19' 2-4-0s as rebuilt with large Belpaire boiler and leading bogie, No. 748.

(b) Engine No. 1—a 2-4-2 suburban tank, of class nicknamed the *Gobblers*.

(c) Standard 0-6-0 goods engine No. 1217.

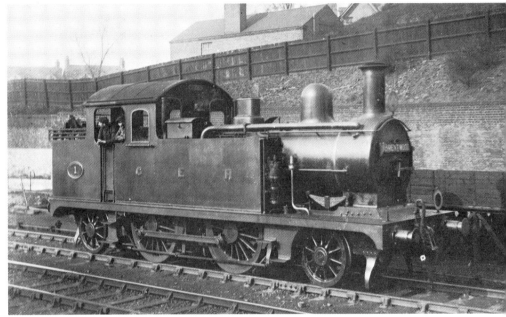

These Great Eastern 4-6-os were splendid engines in traffic, though in outward appearance they gave the impression of being larger than they actually were. Since the introduction of the 'Claud Hamilton' class of 4-4-o all new Great Eastern locomotives had been equipped with very large cabs giving ample protection from the weather, and they gave a very massive, 'important' look to the engines themselves. Inside, however, they had very large tool boxes built over the coupled wheel splashers, and this made a relatively narrow channel leading to the firebox. On the 4-6-os the distance between the shovelling plate of the tender and the firehole door meant taking one or two steps with each charge of coal, instead of being able to pick up and swing in a single movement. The Great Eastern men were used enough to this, and were proud and fond of both 'Claud Hamiltons' and the 4-6-os; but although it is stepping somewhat outside the period of this book I must mention a later phase in the life of the 4-6-os. When, in L.N.E.R. days, many larger engines were put into the former Great Eastern domain, and a number of the 4-6-os became redundant, they were drafted to Scotland to work on the former Great North of Scotland Railway. Their relatively light axle loading made them admirably suited to a line where fairly severe weight restriction prevailed, and where nothing but small 4-4-os had previously been permitted to run. Although their new duties in Scotland bore no comparison, for sustained hard work, to what they had done on the Great Eastern in earlier days, the men found the firing of them a trifle laborious, particularly in the little 'walk' they had to take with each shovelful of coal. They promptly nicknamed them the 'Hikers'. So far as coal consumption on the G.E. was concerned, on the Hook of Holland boat express, in making the run of 69 miles from Liverpool Street to Parkeston Quay in 82 minutes the firing rate was roughly $1\frac{1}{2}$ tons an hour. Seeing that the official limit for a single fireman in British Railways days was fixed at 3,000 lb. per hour, that is $1\frac{1}{3}$ tons, the Great Eastern top-link men were certainly expected to work. That they did it with a whole heart was typical of the intense pride all employees took in the wellbeing of their railway.

Trains like the Norfolk Coast Express, the Hook of Holland boat, and the Cathedrals Route express to York, prestige symbols though they were, did not represent the dividend earning potential of the Great Eastern. The passenger traffic statistics for the year 1913 throw a vivid light upon the general situation. Although the number of passengers conveyed does show an enormous preponderance of third class, and workman's rate journeys a high

II. 'SWEEDY' IN ACTION

(a) Typical of branch lines in East Anglia—a Holden mixed-traffic 2-4-o on a light stopping train. One of these engines has been preserved in the Railway Museum at Clapham.

(b) Semi-fast train on the main line: the 2.22 p.m. London to Ipswich, composed mostly of four-wheeled coaches (!) passing Brentwood hauled by Claud Hamilton class 4-4-o No. 1806.
THE TAKEOVER THAT WASN'T

(c) L.T. &. S.R. One of the largest standard express 4-4-2s, No. 82 *Crowstone*, at Plaistow, in 1911.

proportion of these would be relatively short. Nevertheless the totals are impressive.

NUMBER OF PASSENGERS IN 1913	
1st class	1,849,548
2nd class	2,103,005
3rd class	65,570,111
Workmen	27,949,982

Up to the outbreak of World War I the London suburban services, although very intense, were in an intermediate phase. The great majority of the trains were composed of four-wheeled carriages seating six aside, in both second and third class. The thirds had bare boards for seats, with rests only up to the 'small' of one's back. They were a direct descendant of the old travelling 'box', in which one sat or stood anywhere convenient. Attempts were being made to provide more modern coaches for the commuters, and several 'converted' trains were in service, consisting of 27 ft.-bodies of former 4-wheeled coaches mounted in pairs on 54 ft. underframes and carried on two 4-wheeled bogies. But the standard Great Eastern London suburban train of the immediate pre-war period consisted of seventeen 4-wheeled coaches, and usually hauled by one of the standard 0-6-0 tank engines, of the type represented by No. 87, now preserved in the museum at Clapham. The peak-hour suburban trains on the Colchester main line loaded so heavily that some of these were made up to no less than twenty 4-wheeled coaches.

Engine No. 87, as now preserved, had the typical stove-pipe chimney; but in years just before the war an increasing number of these engines had copper caps fitted, like the main line express passenger classes. There were, when at maximum strength 230 of these 0-6-0 tank engines, differing in certain details but all generically of the same design. There was another large group of tank engines, of the 2-4-2 type; these were used mainly on the country branch lines, of which there were many. With larger coupled wheels, a longer wheel-base, and less adhesion weight they were naturally not so handy for the intense service around London, which required a 'nippy' little engine with a capacity for rapid acceleration. The 2-4-2 engines also had a reputation for having a healthy appetite for coal, and acquired the nickname of 'gobblers'! In the London area they were used on the Southend trains, which being an 'outer' service, with fewer stops, gave the engines a better chance to develop the speed that their larger coupled wheels made possible. The loads of the busiest Southend 'all-stations' trains were usually 15 four-wheelers, and a mention of these trains leads me on to that great 'bone of contention', the London, Tilbury and Southend Railway.

This smart and very well managed little railway operated in the heart of the busiest area of Great Eastern activity, an area where the nickname 'Sweedy' could well have been unknown. There was precious little in the way of turnip and beet conveyance originating in the Hackney Marshes, up the Lee Valley, and out to Romford and Chelmsford. In earlier days the Great Eastern had kept a benevolent eye on the 'Tilbury'; they permitted their locomotive engineer, William Adams, to design 4-4-2 tank engines for their little neighbour, and there is no doubt that the Great Eastern Board looked forward to a 'take-over', at some future time. But the 'Tilbury' prospered, and their strong and independently-minded Managing Director, Arthur Lewis Stride, voiced the unanimous feelings of the Board and shareholders in resisting all offers that were made. It was a peaceful coexistence. The 'Tilbury' had running powers into the Great Eastern terminus at Fenchurch Street, and paid appropriately for this convenience. Their Southend traffic was more of an 'express passenger' character than that of the Great Eastern, and whereas the latter company came into the centre of Southend from the north the 'Tilbury' served a whole chain of growing residential towns along the Thames estuary.

One would not have thought that a change of general managers on the Midland Railway would have had profound repercussions in south-west Essex. But the new man on the Midland was the redoubtable Guy Granet, and he had not long been in office before the British railway world realized that they had an immensely strong personality in their midst—and one who could be very unorthodox too. What went on behind the scene can only be conjectured, but by the year 1912 Stride of the Tilbury had been persuaded to sell out—not to the Great Eastern, but to the Midland! The surprise and shock to all Tilbury employees can scarcely be exaggerated; but the news fairly stunned the Great Eastern Board, It took them completely by surprise. Lord Claud Hamilton, the chairman, was furious. But whatever sentiments may have been expressed within the walls of the Liverpool Street offices it was realized that the only way to play the new situation outwardly was by co-operation. Granet had been long enough in the saddle for other British railway managements to realize that awkwardness, or outright opposition could easily lead to disaster. When the Midland Railway promoted their Parliamentary Bill to ratify the merger that had been negotiated between Granet and Stride, the Great Eastern opposed it, more or less on principle; but to quote *The Railway Magazine* of June 1912: 'Owing to the amicable understanding arrived at with the promoters, the Great Eastern company withdrew its opposition to the Bill, and entered into an agreement to extend Fenchurch Street station, to widen its own lines running therefrom, and to equip the same for electrical working by Midland trains'. The outbreak of war in 1914 postponed almost indefinitely the fulfilment of this project.

Amicable understanding or not, Lord Claud Hamilton had been so shocked that the Midland–Tilbury take-over could have been concluded, under their very noses, without the Great Eastern management getting a whisper of what was going on, that he had lost all confidence in his general manager. It so happened that on 15 July, 1912 the company celebrated the Golden Jubilee of its incorporation, with a commemoration dinner at the Great Eastern Hotel, Liverpool Street. Some of the most distinguished personalities in the railway world of London were there, including Sir Gilbert Claughton, chairman of the L.N.W.R., and the general managers of the Great Northern, Great Western, London and South Western, and of the London Underground lines. It was noticeable however that there was no one there representing the Midland Railway, despite the supposedly 'amicable understanding'! But the surprise of the whole function came when the Lord Mayor of

London rose to propose the toast of the evening—'The Great Eastern Railway Company'. Instead of the felicitous speech that was expected, and deserved, he said, in as many words, that he thought the whole concern was in a decline; it had always been in low water, and that the sooner it remodelled itself on French lines the better! One can imagine that Lord Claud Hamilton with a prepared response to what was expected to be a gracious speech had to do some pretty quick thinking to reply 'off the cuff' as it were, to such an indictment. He took up immediately the suggestion of 'going French', which he retorted 'would produce a revolution, and we should be hounded from the positions we now occupy'.

All the same, the summer of 1912 was generally an uneasy one for the Great Eastern, when to add to the business worries, and the undercurrent of dissatisfaction with the top management the holiday traffic was terribly dislocated, and immense damage done to the line and its equipment by the almost tropical storms that swept East Anglia in late August, and caused some of the most widespread flooding in the Norwich district that has ever been known there. Flooding apart, the Tilbury episode had convinced Lord Claud Hamilton that he needed an infinitely stronger man than W. H. Hyde in the position of general manager to deal with the matters of co-ordination with the new owners of the Tilbury line. Now it so happened that Lord Claud himself, and certain other Great Eastern shareholders had considerable railway interests in North America; indeed, such was the unofficial backing given by some of them to a new project in British Columbia that it was named the Pacific Great Eastern Railway. Anyway, Lord Claud came to the conclusion that a transatlantic 'go-getter' might be the most adequate match for the dynamic Guy Granet, of the Midland, and choice eventually fell upon Henry Worth Thornton, General Superintendent of the Long Island Railroad. He was then no more than forty-one years of age. Trained as a civil engineer he had 'made good' in a variety of railway posts including the Pennsylvania; but it was significant that very early in his career he had moved from the engineering to the management side of railways, and had shown exceptional ability as a senior executive officer, albeit so far on a relatively small American railway.

His appointment as general manager of the Great Eastern caused surprise in England, and not a little offence when Lord Claud Hamilton suggested that the choice was due to the dearth of suitably qualified railway officers in this country. It is true that there were not many Guy Granets, or Herbert Ashcombe Walkers about, and in the Board Room at Liverpool Street it was, by now, fully realized that the hitherto placid, amiable 'Sweedy' had got a tough fight on its hands. But Thornton himself quickly proved not only to be one of the ablest of general managers, but also one of the most likeable. While he certainly lived up to the expectations of being a human dynamo he made his changes in organization and traffic working methods without upsetting people—in strong contrast to his counterpart on the Midland! There must have been many details of the Great Eastern scene that he found curious, and perhaps a little archaic, such as the track layout at Cambridge; but he planned wisely, and within a restricted budget. The onset of war halted his plans for development on the Great Eastern, but gave opportunity for his own stature and power of influence to be greatly enhanced. That in turn made even greater the confidence the Great Eastern Board had in him. For example, at the end of 1916 the chief engineer, Horace Wilmer retired; Thornton immediately took personal charge of the department himself, which his early training in the U.S.A. fully qualified him to do.

But so far as the running of the railway was concerned his most important move was the appointment of F. V. Russell, as superintendent of operation in 1915. This was a new post, normally reporting to the chief traffic manager, but with very wide powers for the re-organization of train working procedures. In selecting Russell for this job Thornton had to a large extent followed his own career in the U.S.A.; for Russell had been trained as a mechanical engineer, and after completion of his apprenticeship in the locomotive depart-ment at Stratford and some outside experience on inspection he entered the drawing office, and had advanced quickly to be chief of the new design section, to take major responsibility for the 'Claud Hamilton' class 4-4-0, first introduced in 1900. He was thus by training and by major experience very familiar with the potentialities of the locomotive stock of the company, and this proved greatly to the advantage of all concerned when he planned the great scheme of train service modification in East London put into operation after the war.

Many railwaymen of the period, if instructed by the management to increase an already intense service, would have thought first in terms of electrification, of lavish schemes of improved signalling with expensive alterations to the track layout, and possibly a complete renewal of the rolling-stock. But in the Great Eastern case no money was available for large capital investment. Russell had to get his results with existing steam locomotives, mechanical signalling aided by Sykes 'Lock and Block' apparatus, and the traditional 4-wheeled coaches, with their spartan interiors. Every single facet of the working was organized to the last detail. As there would be many more trains it was considered that the standard formation could be reduced from 17 to 16 four-wheelers. This would permit a more rapid acceleration from stops, and give an extra 27 ft. in the platforms at Liverpool Street. This was very important, because the light engine movements for each train were timed to a split-second. At the outer end of each platform there was a short shunting neck, long enough to accom-modate two tank engines. As an incoming train arrived an engine for the next outward working would be ready, and the points would be changed and that engine on the move almost before the train had drawn up to the buffer stops.

From his long railway experience Russell knew that much time could be lost at suburban stations by passengers looking for carriages of the right class. While there was a heavy pre-ponderance of third class passengers, all these 16-coach suburban trains included first- and second-class carriages as well, and passengers who had paid more would hardly be inclined to pack in anywhere in the interest of getting the train smartly away from a station. There was no chance of moving once you were in! So the passengers had to be organized as well as the enginemen, signalmen, and porters. The carriage doors of the second and first class compartments were painted in bright distinctive colours; and as they did not alter in position on the trains, or from train to train, the regular first- and second-class passengers at intermediate stations got to know where to stand, and could entrain in the same split-second standards of timing that were expected from everyone else concerned with the service. Because of the brightly coloured doors they became known as the 'Jazz Trains', and the nickname survived well into the 1950s, when the one-time Great Eastern suburban lines were electrified.

The 'Jazz' service was introduced in 1920, but use of the coloured doors had been discontinued when I first travelled on the Great Eastern again after the war. Apart from the train working, which I always found amazingly 'slick', there was one big change from pre-war days: the beautiful blue engines had gone, never to return. As a war economy all engines were painted a plain 'battleship grey', and so they remained until the G.E.R. became part of the London and North Eastern Railway with the grouping of January 1923.

CHAPTER FIVE

The North Western in peace and war

IT IS A little difficult sometimes to explain exactly how the old individual railway companies of Great Britain exercised their several attractions upon enthusiasts of all ages. In this respect there is no case more inexplicable—on the surface at any rate—than that of the London and North Western. Literally, kaleidoscopically, it was the least colourful of all the old railways. Its engines were black; its carriage bodies were so dark a brown that they could be roughly described as 'black and white', and its principal stations bore the grime of a hoary and hard worked antiquity, rather than of any sociological elegance. It is true one had the Doric Arch at Euston, and Philip Hardwick's incomparable Great Hall; but those gems of architecture were encompassed by such a bewildering jumble of 'train sheds', undistinguished office buildings and miscellaneous hutments as to be lost upon the great majority of the travelling public. As for the rest, Lime Street in Liverpool, Manchester (London Road), and the great joint stations at Birmingham, Carlisle and Preston were starkly utilitarian.

Yet for all this the North Western undoubtedly had, up to the end of 1922, the largest number of devotees among those who loved railways for their own sake. That in its business status, its traffic, and in the punctuality of its train services it was pre-eminent is apart from my immediate theme. Just now I am looking at it through the eyes of an enthusiast—not as a potential customer. In the former guise I can only refer to my own experience. In the foregoing chapters of this book I have written much about railways I knew in my early boyhood—four of the most colourful and individualistic it would be possible to imagine. They were colourful in their gay liveries, and spotless turnout, colourful in the exciting places to which they took us for holidays; and to a boy who loved the sea and ships Dover, Felixstowe, Southsea, Weymouth and Bournemouth were then very exciting indeed! But then, fostering interest at a very early age, my father used to bring home copies of *The Railway Magazine*, and I read of the Great Northern, the Midland, and the Scottish lines. Then came *The Wonder Book of Railways*, with its magnificent coloured reproductions of some of the famous 'F. Moore' paintings, and my allegiance to the railways that served

Reading began to totter; and believe it or not, before I had ever set eyes upon a Crewe engine I was rapidly becoming a most ardent North Western fan. I cannot explain why! There was something in cold print, and half-tone illustrations that gripped my imagination. A boy not yet ten years old was not to know it then, but I was actually looking on the surface of one of the greatest and most efficient railway organizations of the age.

Then, as now, the line out of Euston was the busiest of any in Great Britain, and at that time it is doubtful if there was another 150 miles of railway anywhere in the world that bore such an intensity of traffic as that running between London and Crewe. The coaches were not so luxurious as those of some other lines, but because their punctuality could be relied upon the trains were heavily patronized, and the locomotives had to be worked hard to keep the smart schedules then operated. In the decade before the outbreak of World War I the general standard of speed between London and the principal cities of the Midlands and Lancashire was an overall average of about 55 m.p.h.; and there were plenty of trains running up to this standard. To a mere onlooker the great fascination of North Western train operating was that in this period the express passenger engines were all, without exception, named. There had been no whimsical changes in livery to suit the 'ego' of individual engineers; the painting style had remained unchanged since 1873, and all express engines, ancient and modern alike, bore their names in simple sunken black letters on narrow brass plates that were polished and *burnished* till they shone like gold. Furthermore, the livery may have been 'black'; but at this distance in time it is difficult to convey the impression of the amazing, lustrous, *deep* shine that the cleaners used to work up on those engines. In sunlight it used to reflect the blue of the sky, and was sometimes termed 'blackberry black'.

None of those North Western engines running until the year 1913 were very large, and although they performed prodigies of hard work there were times when the patronage of the trains was such as to overpower the capacity of a single engine, and so a second was attached in front. The double heading of important express trains was one of the most picturesque North Western characteristics, because the assistant engines were nearly always vintage specimens of late Victorian days, which had been the pride of the line in their own era. In the period just before World War I the pilots, as they were usually known, were little 2-4-0s of Webb's 'Precedent' or 'Whitworth' classes, affectionately called 'Jumbos'. They could run like stags, and it was a great sight to see one of them coupled ahead of one of the newer engines and racing down the country at the head of a long train. But the time was not so distant from when the still smaller 'Lady of the Lake' class 7 ft. 6 in. single-wheelers were being used as main line pilots. They had gone before I began to take notice of railway matters—but only just. The last of them was withdrawn in 1906.

It was not until 1916 that I first travelled on the London and North Western Railway; but in more recent times extensive studies of engineering practice and traffic operation have enabled me to build up a fairly complete picture of the line as it was worked in the days when I knew it only through the pages of *The Railway Magazine*. As an engineer myself it is naturally to engineering matters that I turn first, and inevitably to that amazing

12. NORTH WESTERN, WEBB TYPES.

(a) One of the 6 ft. 3 in. 'Whitworth' class 2-4-0s (*6 ft. Jumbo*), No. 2158, *Sister Dora*—a regular Camden pilot of 1920.

(b) *Alfred the Great* class 4-cylinder compound 4-4-0 No. 1947 *Zillah*, as modified by Whale with separate outside Joy valve gear.

establishment, Crewe. While to the present generation of enthusiasts the name of Crewe will be associated first, second and always with locomotives, it was, in the first decades of the present century, one of the most remarkable all-round railway engineering plants to be found anywhere in the world. The vast extent of its activities stemmed from the attitude of the great chairman of the L.N.W.R. in Mid-Victorian times, Sir Richard Moon. Tough, puritanical administrator that he was, constantly seeking means of reducing the operating costs of the railway, he encouraged his engineers to do everything possible within their own works; to avoid using proprietary manufactured articles, to eliminate agents, and 'middle-men', and build locomotives and all else from the basic raw materials. In John Ramsbottom, and then F. W. Webb he had engineers of outstanding competence. In 1864 the first-ever plant for manufacture of steel by the Bessemer process was set up at Crewe, and from then onwards the North Western rolled all its own rails, as well as providing all the steel needed for locomotive, carriage and wagon construction. At a later date Crewe began the manufacture of all the signalling equipment required on the line, and production methods throughout the works, of whatever product was involved, were second to none in the engineering industry all over the world. But even Crewe did not deal with carriage and wagon construction. This was carried on at Wolverton and Earlestown respectively.

But it is above all as a locomotive works that Crewe was world-famous at the turn of the century, both in its immense output, and in the very distinctive quality of the engine designs produced. Compared to the large 'Atlantics' and 4-6-os that were being introduced on other British railways the North Western 4-4-os of the 'Precursor' class, which were the mainstay of the express traffic on the Southern Division until 1910, were slender machines of undistinguished appearance, save for that lustrous 'blackberry black' and the fascinating variety of their names. But an immense capacity for hard work had been built into them. They had a boiler that could produce steam very freely, and although they used a lot of coal they were easy, and not unduly fatiguing to fire. Then the cylinders and valves were well designed, so that the large volume of steam could be used to the best advantage. So, while many of their larger contemporaries on other railways were hauling trains of 200 to 300 tons, the 'Precursors' took 350 to 400 tons on the fast 55-m.p.h. trains between Euston, Crewe, Liverpool and Manchester.

That they made plenty of noise about it goes without saying; but the roar of *Achilles* or *Thunderer*, climbing the long incline out to Tring, equally matched by others of the class bearing less appropriate names like *Daphne*, *Fairie Queene* or *Senator*, was the kind of appeal to the emotions that endeared the North Western to its lineside supporters. And when the load became too heavy even for *Ajax*, *Tubal*, or *Vesuvius* and one of the little 2-4-os, *Caractacus*, *Merrie Carlisle*, *Gladstone*, or *Luck of Edenhall* was coupled on ahead the peculiar delights of the railway enthusiasts knew no bounds. Yes, *Luck of Edenhall!*—an extraordinary name for a locomotive, but perhaps not so strange when one recalls the catholicity of choice that prevailed throughout the 75 years when Crewe was the principal locomotive centre of the London and North Western Railway. For all its business efficiency, for all the splendid dividends it paid to its shareholders, for all its manufacturing prowess

(a) Great Western Railway. Engines 3402 'Halifax' and 4108 'Gardenia' leave Fishguard with the first 'Mauretania' Special on 30 August, 1909.

JACK·HILL

JACK HILL

not only at Crewe, but also at Wolverton and Earlestown the North Western had an intensely human side to it. There was nothing systematic in its engine naming. When a locomotive was scrapped its name was handed down to one of a modern type then under construction, and some of the names were in almost continuous use for upwards of a hundred years.

But one of the most delightful features of Crewe locomotive naming was the extent to which contemporary events and personalities were honoured. Then, a name of no immediate significance would be taken off and put into cold storage as it were, and a special new one put on. The only difficulty, as time went on, was to trace the origin of some names the topical interest of which became dimmed with the passing of the years. Who, for example, was *Sir Salar Jung*, a title carried by one of the 'Jumbos'—a class that included such diversities as *Patience*, *Penrith Beacon*, *Wizard*, *President Lincoln*, *Mabel* and *The Auditor*! But the locomotive requirements of the L.N.W.R. in the early 1900s demanded more than could be provided by a systematic replacement of older units, and consequently more names had to be found. The 60 engines of the 'Experiment' class of 4-6-0s built in 1908–10 included 25 names of shires of England and Wales, ranging from *Middlesex* to *Northumberland*, from *Bedfordshire* to *Carnarvonshire*. Here was system of a kind; but another 10 of these engines all had proper names beginning with 'B'. It looked as though someone had taken a dictionary and extracted *Babylon*, *Byzantium*, *Bactria*, *Bellisarius*, *Bellona*, *Berenice*, *Bacchus*, *Berengaria*, *Britomart* and *Boniface*!

Reference to the years 1908–10 leads me on to a very important change in the management of the locomotive department on the L.N.W.R. The 'Precursors', and the 'Experiments' that followed them, were essentially a drawing office job. George Whale the Chief Mechanical Engineer was an out-and-out 'running' man. He knew what was wanted to work the traffic, laid down certain broad requirements, and left the drawing office to get on with it. They produced two first-rate designs entirely in the traditional mode of Crewe. The 'Experiments', which were, of course, not experiments at all, but merely taking the name of the first of the class, were not such an immediate success as the 'Precursors'. The firebox was something new to North Western footplate men, and they took some little time to master the technique of firing them; but the engines themselves were extremely free runners, and they had not been long in traffic before one of them was clocked at 93 m.p.h. At the end of 1908 George Whale retired, and he was succeeded by Charles John Bowen-Cooke, who until then had been Running Superintendent of the Southern Division of the L.N.W.R., with his headquarters at Rugby.

Although Bowen-Cooke, like his predecessor, had held high responsibilities for 'running' he was, at once, a man of much wider interests and technical achievement. His father was a clergyman, and as with many young men of his generation part of his schooling was spent abroad. One recalls the witticism of the columnist who used to write in 'Engineering' under the pen-name of *Capricorn*: 'Sons were often sent to Crewe because fathers felt it was the last hope for boys whose school results were too depressing for any of the traditional professions. If not the Church, then Crewe would have to do'! It so happened that part of

(b) Dover 1903. Two Wainwright 'D' class 4-4-0s waiting to couple on to the London bound Continental expresses.

young Bowen-Cooke's education was spent in Germany, and at the age of 16 he was done with school and entering Crewe as a premium pupil. Although his entire working life of 46 years was spent in the service of the London and North Western Railway there is no doubt that his sojourn in Germany, at a relatively early age, gave him an outlook far beyond that of his own railway, and indeed of the British Isles. He succeeded Whale at a time when the one-time insularity of the British railway outlook was beginning to break down. His famous contemporary on the Great Western, G. J. Churchward, had already incorporated features of French and American design in his latest locomotives, and in view of his boyhood acquaintance with the country it was perhaps not unnatural that Bowen-Cooke took more than a passing interest in current German practice.

At that time the majority of the states comprised in the German Empire had their own railways. There was no central co-ordination of engineering practice; but some of the individual railways, and equally the leading manufacturers, had to use a modern colloquialism 'gone all scientific'. Although the standards of punctuality of service was far behind what would then have been tolerated on the North Western there were certain points in locomotive design that interested Bowen-Cooke. One thing was the German application of superheating. Several British railways were running superheater engines by the beginning of 1909, most of them using forms of the apparatus designed by Dr. Schmidt, of Berlin. Some of them were taking advantage of superheated steam to lower boiler pressures, maintaining roughly the same tractive power of their non-superheated engines, but reducing the costs of boiler maintenance through the lower steam pressure. Others used the minimum degree of superheat using it merely to dry the steam, and eliminate condensation. At Crewe however, Bowen-Cooke took the 'Precursor' class 4-4-0, with its magnificent boiler and firebox, put on a Schmidt superheater of high capacity and kept the boiler pressure the same. The result was a phenomenal raiser of highly superheated steam.

This was not all. The 'Precursor' had the conventional form of slide valves, but the superheated version had piston valves—not only so but with a relatively much larger opening to steam and exhaust. The combination of highly superheated steam, with its natural fluidity, and the redesigned cylinders and valves made the new engine outstanding in its performance. It was completed at Crewe early in 1910, the year in which King George V

13. (a) A remarkable combination at Crewe: Euston–Manchester express hauled by 'Claughton' class 4-6-0 No. 1159 *Ralph Brocklebank* piloted by a North Staffordshire Railway 4-4-0 No. 170.
(b) J. H. Adams's 0-6-2 mixed traffic tank, North Staffordshire Railway.
(c) A historic occasion of double significance on the L.N.W.R. The afternoon Scotch 'Corridor' express hauled as usual by the War Memorial engine No. 1914 *Patriot* is piloted by the 8 ft. 6 in. single *Cornwall*. This latter engine was used to haul the C.M.E.'s private saloon, and it had brought C. J. Bowen-Cooke from Crewe to London, when he was en route to Cornwall for a holiday, on which he died. This double-heading of the 'Corridor' was the immediate aftermath of Bowen-Cooke's last journey on the L.N.W.R.

ascended the throne of the United Kingdom, and with the usual North Western facility in choosing topical names for its locomotives the new superheated 4-4-0 was named *George the Fifth*. It would perhaps be invidious to suggest, that, particularly in respect of its size and weight, it was the most outstanding locomotive yet to run the rails in Great Britain. Nevertheless superheaters cost money, and Crewe had ever been mindful of first-costs in locomotive construction. So Bowen-Cooke built a second engine with the improved cylinders and piston valves, but using saturated steam, as on the 'Precursors'. This was the *Queen Mary*, and for several months she was run in competition with the *George the Fifth*, while details of running costs and general performance were collected.

The superheated engine proved incomparably superior in every way, and it was adopted in the standard express engine of the line. The performance of these relatively small engines, weighing without their tenders no more than 64 tons, takes some believing today. On the 55 m.p.h. express trains, which meant going uphill at 50 m.p.h. and down at 70, the 'Precursors' had not much in hand when the loads exceeded 350 tons; but the 'George the Fifth' class not only took 400 tons easily, but could readily make up time to the tune of about ten minutes between Euston and Crewe, when delays occurred. In the later days of steam on the nationalized British Railways much scientific testing of modern designs was carried out, and one of the bases of comparison was the rate of evaporation sustained in the boiler. Various classes of 4-6-0, designed in comparatively recent times, produced evaporation rates of between 22,000 and 26,000 lb. of steam per hour; yet it is a sobering thought to recall that the little *George the Fifth* 4-4-0, of 1910 vintage, used regularly to steam up to 20,000 lb., and on occasions to a maximum of 22,000!

To use a human simile however, they were taxing their own strength—in other words they were developing more power than their frames could normally withstand. The frame design was the same as that of the 'Precursors', but the superheater engines on occasions sustained an output of power some 30 per cent higher than the 'Precursor' maximum; and while engines in first class condition could stand this tremendous output from so small a machine, North Western engines were worked for very long mileages between successive visits to Crewe for overhaul, and while in service they covered lengthy daily mileages, often necessitating the employment of two crews, one to relieve the other 'at half-time', as it were. In consequence, the 'George the Fifth' class, brilliant runners as they were, tended to suffer, with increasing age, from cracked frames and rough riding. In the years 1911–16 the work of the 90 engines of the class was little short of phenomenal.

There can be little doubt that the power output of these engines exceeded all the expectations of Crewe. The trains were not speeded up, and the loads were not greatly increased; but on the L.N.W.R. drivers and firemen would seem to have made it a point of honour to make up lost time, from signal checks, speed restrictions and such like, and it was then that the 'George the Fifth' class engines were really extended, and sometimes overtaxed their strength. But almost from the moment that he became Chief Mechanical Engineer C. J. Bowen-Cooke was thinking in terms of much larger engines—to provide a reserve of power, and to enable the heavy, fast trains to be run with greater economy, and without the engines having to be worked so nearly at their limit. But of course the restriction in size and weight of any rolling-stock is whatever the track will bear, and in axle loading Crewe locomotives were already getting near to what the civil engineer would accept. In 1910, however, there was another factor to be considered, and towards this Bowen-Cooke's knowledge of German locomotive practice could have had considerable influence.

With the introduction of progressively larger and heavier locomotives, and the increase in size and weight of the working parts, the question of balancing was becoming of great importance. The rotation of heavy members, and the back and forth oscillation of the pistons produces an unbalancing effect, and would, if not compensated for, result in a rough-riding, if not actually dangerous engine. The traditional way of balancing in the past had been to put heavy weights in the wheels, the rotational effect of which was to counteract the unbalancing action of the pistons, cranks and so on. This certainly lessened, almost to the point of elimination, the rough and dangerous riding; but those weights in the wheels produced what is termed a 'hammer-blow' effect on the track. It increased with speed, and made the effect of a locomotive running at high speed far worse than its dead weight per axle might suggest. Bowen-Cooke was well aware of this, and one of his 'George the Fifth' class 4-4-0s had a 'dynamic augment'—to use the technical term—that at 75 m.p.h. put the maximum combined load per axle, from the dead weight of 19·1 tons up to no less than $33\frac{1}{4}$ tons.

Bowen-Cooke had studied with much interest the 4-cylinder compound 4-6-0s then running on the Bavarian State Railways. All four cylinders drove on to the leading coupled axle, and with this arrangement all the rotating and reciprocating parts balanced themselves. There was no need for any additional weights to be put into the wheels, and the 'hammer-blow' was completely eliminated. By use of this principle it was thought that an engine having a much heavier dead weight per axle than the 'George the Fifth' could be built for the L.N.W.R. A large new four-cylinder 4-6-0 was designed in the drawing office at Crewe, and its weight diagram submitted to the civil engineer. Unfortunately, however, the significance of the finer points of engine balancing was not then appreciated; dead weight was the only thing that counted with those responsible for track and bridges, and the proposed new locomotive was rejected, as being too heavy. Bowen-Cooke had to set the Crewe drawing office on to a revised design, with a smaller boiler, so that the dead weight per axle should not greatly exceed that of the 'George the Fifth' class.

Although it was a great pity that this 'super' locomotive did not materialize, Crewe made a remarkably fine job of the 'compromise', of which the first example took the road early in 1913. This was engine No. *2222, Sir Gilbert Claughton*, named after the Chairman of the company. Knowing a little of what had gone on behind the scenes it could be seen that the boiler looked a little short for so large an engine; but when its technical details are compared with those of the famous Great Western 'Star' class—a 4-6-0 of roughly the same size—it could be seen that there was nothing lacking. And when the 'Claughton' engines went into traffic it was soon evident that they had quite astonishing capacities for load haulage and high speed. Two test runs carried out in November 1913, with the engine *Ralph Brocklebank*,

69

one from Euston to Crewe, and the second from Crewe to Carlisle, produced by a considerable margin the highest outputs of power that had then been recorded with any British locomotive up to that time. These were no isolated bursts of power, but efforts that were sustained with little or no intermission for around two hours at a time. The maximum cylinder horsepower recorded was 1,669, at 69 m.p.h.

When war came, in August 1914, a second batch of 10 'Claughton' class engines was under construction at Crewe, and their great haulage capacity was soon put to invaluable use in working the greatly increased train loads. Trains hitherto run separately were combined to make engines available for troops and other special trains; but at first the speed of expresses was unchanged. There was a remarkable instance of this in the Northern Division of the L.N.W.R. To make the loads more readily manageable the morning Anglo-Scottish express from Euston, which conveyed portions for both Edinburgh and Glasgow was, in peace time divided at Crewe; the two sections, one for Edinburgh and one for Glasgow each attached through portions from Birmingham, and the weight of the Glasgow train varied from 200 to about 290 tons. It was booked to cover the 141 miles to Carlisle in 159 minutes—an average speed of 53 m.p.h.—including the ascent over Shap, where the line rises to an altitude of 915 ft. in just over thirty miles. But in 1915 the two sections were run as one train from Crewe to Carlisle, to the same 53 m.p.h. timing. Although there was some cutting down in the number of carriages run the load was never less than 400 tons, and usually around 450.

Never was the capacity of the 'Claughton' class engines, and the skill of their drivers and firemen shown better than in the running of this very heavy train over the mountains. The official load limits for these engines over the more level parts of the line, from Euston right through to Carnforth, in North Lancashire, was 420 tons tare, which could be increased to 450 tons with a full complement of passengers and much luggage. Drivers would have been entitled to take assistance over the mountains; but time and again the engines were in such 'cracking' form that they took loads of 420, 430 or even 440 tons up the fearsome $4\frac{1}{2}$ miles of 1 in 75 of the Shap Incline single handed. I have in front of me detailed notes of two journeys, one with the engine *E. Tootal Broadhurst*, and a load of 420 tons, and the other with the pioneer engine of this class *Sir Gilbert Claughton*, with an even heavier train of 440 tons, on which the average speeds from Crewe, to Carlisle were 54 and $54\frac{1}{2}$ m.p.h. But I have more to say about the particular problems of working trains over Shap in a later chapter of this book.

It was in 1916, when my father's place of business was moved from Reading to Barrow-in-Furness, that I first travelled on the London and North Western Railway. The war was in a critical and anxious stage. Crewe works, although engaged in large scale production of war material was still turning out many new engines, for the additional traffic was enormous; and true to tradition many of them bore names connected with the war. There were battlefields like *Gallipoli* and *Suvla Bay*; memorials to grievous losses like the Cunarder *Lusitania*, and names of great war leaders, both of the British Empire and our allies; *Admiral Jellicoe*, *Lord Kitchener*, *King of the Belgians*, *Raymond Poincare*. There were, no less, intensely

14. NORTH WESTERNS IN THE GOLDEN AGE

(a) Excursion train on the North Wales line near Rhyl, hauled by
    7 ft. 6 in. 2-2-2 engine No. 1435 *Fortuna*.
(b) Liverpool and Manchester express entering Crewe, hauled by
    'Prince of Wales' class 4-6-0 No. 1134 *Victor Hugo*.

human touches, such as *Edith Cavell*, and *Captain Fryatt*. But as the war went on, and the materials became scarce, the naming of new express locomotives ceased for a while, to save the brass that would have been needed for their nameplates; and 27 engines of the 'Claughton' class, built to sustain the wartime traffic in 1917 were the first North Western passenger locomotives built in the 72-year history of Crewe works that were not named.

It is perhaps understandable that this chapter about the London and North Western Railway has been mainly concerned with locomotives, because it is after all locomotives that form the first link in the chain towards dividend earning. But a special word must be put in about the carriages. Those on long-distance express trains were broadly speaking of three types. There were the older bogie corridor coaches with relatively narrow bodies, near-flat roofs, and having a length of 45 ft. Then there was the 57-ft. stock, some with high elliptical roofs and some with a semi-elliptical profile. These were the most modern coaches on the majority of the long-distance express trains. But then there were the 12-wheelers—I can never think of these coaches, whether the dining cars that ran on the principal expresses, nor of the special compartment stock used on the afternoon Anglo-Scottish expresses between London and the Scottish cities, without getting a feeling of acute nostalgia; for they were without question the best riding and most comfortable British carriages I have ever travelled in. But all the North Western carriages rode well. It was not until my express travelling began to extend beyond the line between Euston and Barrow that I learned of coaches that did ride roughly at times!

The smooth riding of North Western express trains was not solely due to the design of the coaches. The company claimed, with some justification, to have the finest permanent way in the world, and one can appreciate the reluctance of the civil engineer to accept heavier locomotives, even though his reluctance in the case of the Bowen-Cooke 4-6-0s was to a large extent based on ignorance of what the smaller and nominally lighter engines were regularly doing to the track. But another factor that contributed to the pleasure of travelling on the North Western was the care and skill with which drivers operated the vacuum brake. This arose, in the first place, from the older men having had to cope with that ingenious, but impracticable contraption the Clark and Webb Chain Brake. To operate that successfully on a long train without the kind of snatches that led to broken couplings needed a high degree of expertise, and made the main line express drivers very 'brake-conscious'. When the company adopted the automatic vacuum brake the drivers found that they could get an exceptionally smooth deceleration, and jerk-free braking became as much a point of honour with them as making up lost time when trains had been delayed. One noticed sometimes the change, so far as braking was concerned, in through L.N.W.R. carriages when they passed on to other companies' lines. I had plenty of experience of this in my journeys between London and Barrow for at Carnforth we passed on to the metals of the Furness Railway. I am not for one moment suggesting that the Furness drivers were 'slap-dash', or inexpert in their handling of the brake. It is only that there were *occasionally* moments when one remembered that we were no longer on the North Western. And having reached Carnforth, as it were, it is time to look at the Furness Railway in some detail.

CHAPTER SIX

The Furness Railway: a thriving local enterprise

MY OWN PLEASURE that the family home was to be transferred to the North West of England, in 1916, was at first slightly tempered by the realization that we should not after all be living on the London and North Western Railway, but on a local line on which I had done next to no prior reading. My perusal of *The Railway Magazine* in those days was inclined to be spasmodic, and I had missed a couple of very comprehensive articles on the Furness Railway that had appeared in 1913. My only recollection, prior to that momentous removal in 1916 was of an old photograph showing one of the Sharp Stewart 4-4-0s standing on the very sharp curve of the Furness platforms in Carnforth station. To a boy whose mind was naturally running on the largest and latest of engines it is curious that the memory of that old Furness engine persisted. But it certainly did.

But once we arrived in the district interest grew by leaps and bounds. For one thing, our new home was not ready for occupation and for several weeks we lived at the Furness Abbey Hotel, immediately beside the railway, and with beautiful gardens that gave excellent views of the passing trains. I had yet to see the tremendous industrial activity that was centred upon Barrow in those war years; only a few miles away, in that oddly named 'Vale of Deadly Nightshade', Furness Abbey with its picturesque station and pleasant hotel might have been in the heart of the Lake District. It was still, even in wartime a centre for those who sought a brief relaxation from urgent affairs, and even as a schoolboy I began to sense the remarkable atmosphere that this little local railway had created in the tourist business. I have always been an inveterate 'collector' and my early acquisitions of coloured postcards published by the Locomotive Publishing Company has already been mentioned in this book. There were none of these to be seen on the bookstalls of Furness Railway stations, or at the reception desk of the Furness Abbey Hotel; but there were new and exciting things. Many of the British railways of pre-grouping days published their own ranges of picture postcards, depicting locomotives, carriages, stations, and scenes on the line. The majority of these were in monochrome, some in photogravure, and it was only a few, like the South Eastern and Chatham that blossomed out in full colour.

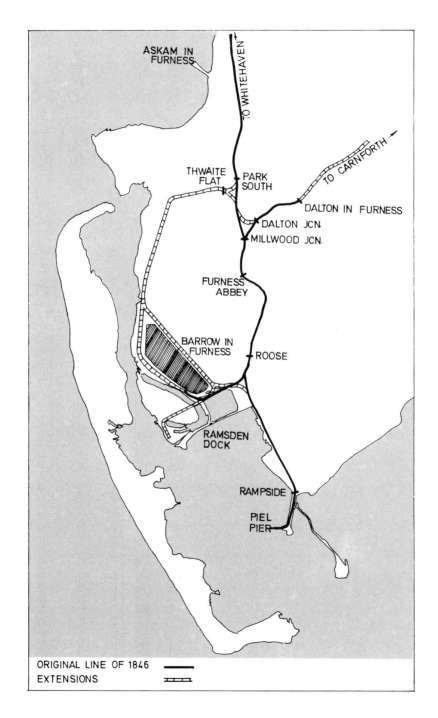

MAP I: FURNESS RAILWAY, AROUND BARROW

74

The Furness Railway, as I quickly learned to my delight, did nothing by halves, especially when it came to publicity. Certainly they had a series of fine glossy-printed photographic cards, showing locomotives, carriages, and the very picturesque little steamers that plied on Windermere and Coniston lakes. But they went one better, and in a way that provides an interesting association with my present publishers, who were then producing the celebrated series of 'Colour Books'. In 1905 a volume on *The English Lakes* appeared, with no fewer than 75 reproductions in colour from paintings by the distinguished Lake District artist, A. Heaton Cooper. This was an opportunity too good to be missed by the enterprising management of the Furness Railway. Arrangements were concluded between the publishers and Rapheal Tuck & Sons, for the issue of a series of coloured postcards, on which the illustrations from *The English Lakes* were exquisitely reproduced. The Furness Railway coat of arms appeared on the back, and on the front the only imprint other than the title was the name of the nearest station to the scene depicted. I still have a number of these beautiful cards, which I must have bought more than fifty years ago, and the colour rendering and quality of reproduction yield nothing to those in a de-luxe edition of the book itself.

Furness Railway publicity was already weaving its spell on a boy barely entering his teens, even before he had set eyes on one of the lakes. In 1916 an attempt was still being made to sustain something of the normal business of railways, and many of the combined tours through Lakeland were still in operation, by rail, coach and steam yacht. At one time there were 20 of these tours run daily, and they were incredibly cheap. The 'Four Lakes Circular Tour', which included Windermere, Rydal, Grasmere, and Coniston, cost a modest 5s. 9d., while if one made a straight trip from Furness Abbey to Grasmere and back, including sailing the 11-mile length of Windermere both ways, the fare was 2s. 9d.!! My father was then in process of taking over a new business, while my mother had to get our new home going and cope with all the unfamiliar problems of housekeeping in a district so different from that we had left behind. So that excursions from Barrow were not frequent in that first summer. But I had a bicycle; the roads were not busy, if the surfaces were atrocious, and so I started exploring. And so from this rather personal introduction to the Furness Railway I can pass quickly on to an account of this most interesting line as it was in its independent days.

The geographical situation of Barrow might suggest that it would inevitably be a terminus for trains coming from without the Furness district, and that any communication farther north would be made by reversal of direction. So in fact it originally was, except that the terminus at the tip of the Furness isthmus was not at Barrow at all—for the very simple reason that in 1846, when the Furness Railway started operations, Barrow scarcely existed. Lying off the coast at the southern extremity of the isthmus is a tiny island named Roa. The nomenclature is a little confusing, because on Roa Island is the small township of Piel, and yet Piel Castle, an ancient monument, is on the neighbouring Piel Island! Names apart, however, there was a considerable demand for the hematite iron ores of the Furness district, and owing to the difficulty of communication with the nearest parts of Lancashire, thoughts turned to transport by sea. The estuaries of the Lakeland rivers are shallow and sandy, but deep water existed at Piel, and with a railway in view a certain John Abel Smith put forward a plan: 'To connect Roa Island with the neighbouring Island of Great Britain'! So it came about that the first section of the Furness Railway ran from Kirkby-in-Furness on the Duddon Estuary, through Askam and past Furness Abbey to the newly-constructed Piel Pier, on the Roa Island. There was a short branch to Dalton-in-Furness, another district then also rich in iron ore.

From this beginning a complicated layout developed in the Barrow area, as shown on the map on page 74. With the tremendously rapid growth of Barrow itself the line was extended northward so as to provide facilities for through running from the Carnforth direction to the north, while additional connections were put in to permit of the direct running of freight trains avoiding Barrow altogether. The one-time pair of triangle junctions to the north of Furness Abbey lay only a few miles from my home and I remember being much puzzled by the abrupt changes of direction of some of the lines. By the year 1916 both junctions had ceased to be triangles; two spurs had been removed, including a piece of the original main line of 1846. The signal box at Mill Wood Junction remained, however, and a most curiously ornate building it was—roughly circular in plan, very tall, and looking like one of those characteristic watch towers on the Rhine. Through freight trains from the north used to stop at Park South Crossing to take rear-end banking assistance up the very heavy gradient of the line round the spur to Dalton Junction, and up the continuation of the bank to Lindal Moor. The area was intersected with convenient public footpaths and I spent many hours watching the freights blasting their way round the curve to Dalton Junction. It was more than eight miles round the complete circuit of the Barrow loop, but only one mile between the junctions at the beginning and end of the avoiding line.

By the time we went to live in Barrow another piece of the original main line had been removed, namely the direct connection from the north to the Piel branch. The steamers to Belfast and the Isle of Man originally sailed from Piel Pier, but after the opening of the Ramsden Dock in 1879, the boat train services were transferred to the new Dock station, on the Walney Channel. Before World War I both the London and North Western and the Midland Railways made much of their connections with the Belfast steamer sailing from Ramsden Dock at 8.30 p.m. The Midland service was indeed labelled as the 'Royal Mail Route', and from London the journey time from St. Pancras, by the 1.30 p.m. 'Scotch Express' was only half an hour longer than by the rival train from Euston. On the Midland however, a line always very conscious of the need for restricting engine loads, the through carriage service was only from Hellifield to Ramsden Dock. There was a very rapid and convenient connection from the Scotch Express, and the 'boat train' was thence given preferential treatment, with a non-stop run to Carnforth.

The 7.20 p.m. from Carnforth on the Furness line was quite a remarkable train. It conveyed the through London and North Western carriages from Euston to Whitehaven; there was the Midland through carriage from Hellifield to Ramsden Dock, and a coach that was slipped at Grange-over-Sands. Its only regular stop between Carnforth and Barrow Central was at Ulverston; but it stopped by request at Dalton and Furness Abbey to set down passengers from beyond Carnforth, and an unusual provision, in the event of its not otherwise stopping, was a stop by request at Furness Abbey to take up passengers for Belfast. With a sharply curved route that precluded anything in the nature of sustained fast running it needed some smart locomotive work to cover the $28\frac{1}{2}$ miles from Carnforth to Barrow in 47 minutes when both conditional stops were made. The stop at Furness Abbey, used by tourists with much luggage, was often of several minutes duration. The down mail, which left Carnforth at 4.25 a.m. was a train on which passengers were carried almost on sufferance; I well remember the first time I used it, and made the request for a stop at Furness Abbey, to be met with a pre-emptory 'No Sir!' from the ticket inspector at Carnforth. That was shortly after the Furness Railway had been absorbed into the L.M.S. system. The timing was sharper than in pre-war years, allowing only 24 minutes for the 19 miles from Carnforth to Ulverston. The evening express connecting with the Belfast steamer was the fastest in pre-war days, being allowed 26 minutes.

Although it is stretching the story a little beyond purely Furness days I must say that the 24-minute timing of the Mail often had the locomotives in difficulties. There was a disposition at first to draft unwanted Midland engines on to the Furness line, and vintage non-superheater 4-4-0s were not up to the job. From the noise they made it was evident that the drivers were doing their best. But the situation changed completely once the new management sent a small batch of North Western 'Precursor' type 4-4-0s to Barrow. Although they too were non-superheated, and getting elderly, they made short work of the Mail, and I recall several occasions when the last stages of an all night journey from London were enlivened by our going rocketing round the curves by Grange-over-Sands and Kent's Bank at 55 to 60 m.p.h. with one of those much-loved veterans on the job. There must have been something in the system of locomotive allocation that affected it, because I have never travelled on the Mail behind a true Furness engine, although there were plenty of them about, doing excellent work, in the mid-1920s when I began using the train occasionally.

The locomotives of the Furness Railway require special mention and praise, because although it was no more than a small railway, and the total locomotive stock at the time of grouping was only 136, they were admirably suited to the special and varying local conditions. All except the oldest among them had been designed by W. F. Pettigrew, a most distinguished engineer, who had gained a wide experience of locomotive practice before coming to Barrow in 1897. His early training had been on the Great Eastern Railway, and from his pupilage under William Adams he served three successive Locomotive Superintendents, Massey Bromley, T. W. Worsdell, and James Holden, eventually rising to the post of Assistant Works Manager at Stratford. In 1886 he had rejoined William Adams becoming Works Manager at Nine Elms, London and South Western Railway; but in 1897, when he left the larger English railways to join the Furness, he was undertaking far more than the management of just over one hundred small locomotives. His responsibilities included the steam yachts on Windermere and Coniston lakes; the sea-going steamers on the Barrow–Fleetwood service; all the machinery at the railway-owned docks at Barrow,

together with all the associated tugs, barges and dredgers, not to mention all the railway carriages and wagons owned by the company.

But Pettigrew was above all a locomotive man, and during the 10 years he was with Adams on the L.S.W.R. he largely organized the very comprehensive series of trials on one of the Adams outside-cylinder express passenger 4-4-0s. He subsequently won the George Stephenson medal and Telford premium of the Institution of Civil Engineers for the paper he contributed to that Institution, describing the trials. They were, without question, the most scientific that had been conducted on any British locomotive up to that time. On the Furness Railway he naturally had no opportunity to build locomotives capable of the speeds regularly attained by the Adams 4-4-0s on the L.S.W.R., but in a few years he carried out a very thorough modernization of the locomotive stock, introducing massive reliable engines well suited to the local conditions. I suppose it was no more than natural that an engineer who had been so closely connected with scientific testing should wish to carry out tests on his own new engines, and in this connection I have a tale to tell.

As we settled down to life in Barrow my parents came to know many of the senior officers of the Furness Railway, and among these was Edward Sharples, who became locomotive, carriage and wagon assistant to the Engineer after the retirement of Mr. Pettigrew, in 1918. I had the pleasure of meeting him several times when I had begun my engineering training, and knowing something of Pettigrew's literary work and Sharples' participation in it, to the extent of making many of the drawings for the classic *Manual of Locomotive Engineering*, I asked him once if they had ever carried out any 'indicator' trials on Furness Railway locomotives. He sat back in his chair and laughed loudly, and then went on to tell me of an experience they had with one of Pettigrew's 6 ft. 6 in. 4-4-0s of 1900, engines that could well be described as an inside-cylinder version of the Adams 4-4-0 on the L.S.W.R. Certainly the Furness engines were among the neatest and most handsome medium-powered 4-4-0s ever built. Well, the customary shelter for the testing staff was erected around the front of the engine; the steam 'indicators' were fitted to the cylinders and, with Sharples in charge out in the shelter, away they started. The straightest piece of line for a spell of fast running was down the Cumberland coast from Seascale towards Millom, and with a fairly heavy load they gathered speed. 'Near Silecroft', Sharples went on, 'We were tearing along at a terrific speed—for this part of the world—about 62 m.p.h. We were taking diagrams, and I went to use the primitive "inter-com" to speak to the footplate. But all I could hear was the driver swearing blue-murder because he couldn't

15. FURNESS: ANCIENT AND MODERN

(a) The celebrated 'Bury' type 0-4-0 No. 3 nicknamed *Coppernob*—preserved, and now in the Railway Museum at Clapham.
(b) One of the powerful 0-6-2 tanks, used for local trains and banking duties at Dalton.
(c) One of the Sharples 4-6-4 tanks, No. 118 on a Whitehaven to Carnforth express near Grange-over-Sands.

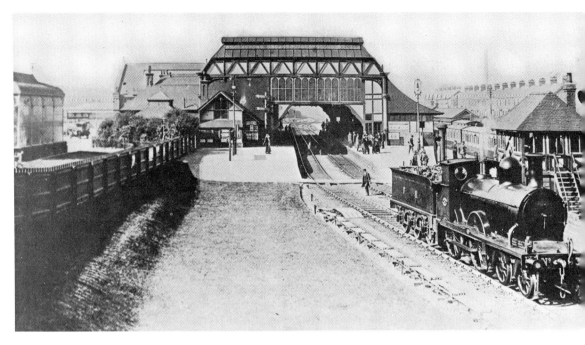

16. BARROW CENTRAL STATION

A panoramic view showing, on extreme left, the glass case containing the 'Coppernob'; the 'covered' main up and down platforms, and the outside platforms to right. The locomotive in the foreground is a Sharp, Stewart 4-4-0 of 1893. The all-over roof was destroyed in the 'blitz' of 1941.

make the engine go faster.' He laughed again, and then added 'We didn't publish any results of those trials!'

Quite apart from any technical details the distinguishing characteristic of nearly all Furness locomotives was their magnificent livery—a rich iron-ore red, smartly lined out in black and white, and with the initials FR on the tenders, or side tanks in the case of the tank engines. The passenger 4-4-0s carried the very beautiful coat of arms of the company on the leading splasher. The intense industrialism of Barrow and of many smaller towns on the coast of the Irish Sea found no place in this device. The centrepiece was the Madonna and Child, which is part of the arms of the Abbot of Furness, while the motto *Cavendo Tutus*—advance with caution—is that of the Cavendish family, whose head, the Duke of Devonshire, always took a very active interest in Furness Railway affairs. The locomotive stock standardized under Pettigrew could be very simply summarized as 4-4-0 for passenger, 0-6-0 for goods and mineral, 0-6-2 for mixed duties and rear-end banking. There were also some powerful 0-6-0 tanks for shunting in the Barrow docks, and 6 very handsome 4-4-2 tanks for working on the Lakeland branch lines. They all had a strong family likeness, and

(c) Midland Railway—The Last Days. A Morecambe-Leeds Express near Bentham in 1921.

JACK HILL

a complete simplicity of outline. During the war a few of the large 0-6-0 mineral engines were finished in 'battleship grey', but this style did not last long.

Apart from occasional casual references I have so far not mentioned the line itself, other than the area of its early origins around Barrow; and having pounded a way up the steep gradients from Furness Abbey, through Dalton, one came to Lindal Moor, through a tunnel hewn out of the solid rock, and having no lining of masonry, no ornamental façade at its western end: just an awesome rough-cut hole in the rock face! Lindal Moor has nevertheless an association of far greater significance than a tunnel 'in the raw' as it were. Like many small railways the Furness was occasionally the unjustified butt of the local humorists, and in 1892 these gentlemen were presented with a Heaven-sent piece of 'copy' when an engine disappeared down a hole! In fact it was an occurrence of deep significance, quite apart from the unfortunate loss of an important engine. Much of the district served by the Furness Railway is fairly honeycombed below ground by small individual iron ore workings. These were at the height of their activity in the later part of the nineteenth century, but towards the 'nineties many of them were getting worked out. At Lindal Moor the mining continued to be extensive, and much of it was beneath the railway. What happened on 22 October, 1892, was simple enough. One of the standard 0-6-0 goods engines was shunting, when just ahead of it a large cavity appeared. The driver and fireman did what they could, and just managed to jump clear before the engine took a 'header' into the hole. By the time the breakdown gang arrived from Barrow the engine had disappeared from view; only the tender was saved.

Travelling farther east the line descends steeply from Lindal Moor to Ulverston, and there one comes to one of those wide, fascinating estuaries in which the Lakeland rivers debouch into the Irish Sea. But before coming to the long, fearfully exposed viaduct by which the main line crosses the River Leven, where a train was once literally blown off the rails by the force of the wind, we must notice the first and most prosperous of the branch lines that the Furness Railway threw out towards the major tourist areas of the Lake District. Although there was scarcely a village in the vicinity a major steamboat pier, railway station, and a refreshment pavilion was established at the foot of Windermere. The station was named 'Lakeside', and luncheon and tea rooms on the most elaborate scale were provided, and during the summer months a string orchestra played during lunch and afternoon tea. Lakeside was the base of operations of the Furness Railway fleet of steam yachts on Windermere. The older yachts, which were built in the style of gondolas, had non-condensing steam engines, and had a 'puffing' exhaust like a locomotive. The Lakeside branch trains from Ulverston were usually worked by one of the handsome 4-4-2 tank engines.

In pre-war days the junction with the main line was a triangle, which thus permitted direct running from the east, and was much used by excursion trains from the London and North Western and Midland Railways. When I first travelled to Lakeside, in 1916, however, the eastern spur of the triangle had been removed to provide track for urgently needed railways behind the battle-front in France. The connection was restored soon after the end of the war. The second branch to the north led off the main line at Arnside, and followed

(d) North Eastern Railway, 1919. Engines at Bridlington. 81

the east bank of the Kent to trail in to the London and North Western main line at Hincaster Junction. Over this line the Furness Railway operated a shuttle service between Grange-over-Sands and Kendal, of five trains a day. In so doing running powers were exercised over the L.N.W.R. line from Hincaster Junction to Oxenholme, and thence over the 2 miles of the Windermere branch into Kendal. One imagines that the Furness would like to have run right into the terminus of the North Western branch, to Windermere Town; but the owners had their own service there, and merely provided connections to the Furness trains at Kendal. Incidentally the one Furness engine, and train was kept pretty busy in running that shuttle service. The first train left Grange at 8.20 a.m. The $14\frac{1}{4}$-mile run to Kendal took 35 minutes, with four intermediate stops, but the service had to be interwoven with the Anglo-Scottish main line traffic of the North Western between Hincaster and Oxenholme, as well as providing the smart main line connections at Grange for which the Furness Railway was notable. The connections onwards to Windermere Town were not good, and they were used in only one of the circular tours.

The branch line from Arnside to the junction with the L.N.W.R. at Hincaster was of great importance in the working of freight traffic. During the war there was a great demand for blast-furnace coke, and through 'block loads' were operated from the Durham coke ovens via Barnard Castle, over Stainmore summit to Tebay, on the L.N.W.R. main line. To enable the haulage to be transferred direct from North Eastern to Furness locomotives running powers were exercised between Hincaster Junction and Tebay, and the big Pettigrew 0-6-0s worked through. Fortunately for the Furness side of the business the loaded trains ran in the westbound direction, and it was only the empties that had to be hauled up the formidable Grayrigg bank of the L.N.W.R. Another interesting use of the branch from Arnside to Hincaster Junction was the running, during summer months, of a through North Eastern train from Newcastle to Barrow, hauled by a North Eastern engine throughout. It was advertised: 'The Shortest and Quickest Route between the North Eastern Railway and the Isle of Man is through Lakeland, via the Furness Railway and Barrow'. Like many an advertisement, it rather strained at the truth, because the route south-west of Tebay skirted, rather than passed *through* the Lake District, though to be sure there is a fine, if distant view of the Langdale Pikes when descending the Grayrigg bank on the L.N.W.R.

Before I had any opportunity of investigating the past history of train services over the Furness line a picture in *The Railway Magazine* had greatly puzzled me. The year was 1917, and the quality of paper available for that journal was getting worse and worse. But somehow or other the publishers managed to include a plate in full colour in nearly every issue. The April number contained a notice that 'A very fine colour plate is in preparation for the May *Railway Magazine*', which when it appeared was simply titled 'North Eastern Railway train on Furness Railway near Arnside'. There was not a line elsewhere in the magazine to explain what to the great majority of readers must have been a quite inexplicable occurrence. Of course the summer through service from Newcastle had ceased on the outbreak of war, three years earlier. There was not a note of acknowledgement of who the photographer was—not even the signature 'F. Moore', though the painting was undoubtedly one of that school. It is a fascinating record of a long forgotten train service.

Going north from Barrow the old main line is re-attained by a circuitous route within sight of the sea, and then it presses on through iron workings at Askam and to Kirkby, the first terminus. All the time the Duddon estuary is close at hand, usually one vast expanse of red sand with the larger iron-working town of Millom on the far side and the most southerly of the Lakeland mountains Black Combe, towering up behind. The railway is making another wide detour here. From Askam to Millom across the sands is only 3 miles; but by the Furness Railway round the head of the estuary it is just 10. At this head point is the little junction of Foxfield, from which the Coniston branch leads into the heart of the mountain region. This is the most picturesque of all the Furness by-ways, for it is carried high above the lake, and gives some charming views. Unfortunately however there was no direct connection between the trains and the lake steamers. The pier at the head of the lake is a good mile from the railway station, and when once we attempted to take a sail on the lake the steamers seemed to be running with a complete disregard for the advertized time-table. We waited in vain for the steamer at the lake head pier, and eventually when we were ensconced in our return train, and had actually started for Foxfield we saw the S.Y. *Gondola* placidly steaming up the lake far below! I should imagine that the Coniston steamers connected more reliably with the road vehicles on the circular tours than they did with the trains.

The most northerly section of the Furness main line ran close to the Cumberland coast for most of the way, only turning inland briefly to pass on the landward side of the bold headland of St. Bees. It was single-tracked from Sellafield northward, because the density of traffic, relieved of the heavy mineral tonnage from the iron working districts of Egremont and Cleator Moor, was much diminished. And so the Furness Railway came to its northern end at Whitehaven, passing from the 'suburban' station of Corkickle through an exceedingly narrow-bore single-line tunnel to Bransty, to make an end-on junction with the London and North Western Railway. It was a wild, lonely track from Sellafield, where the line to Cleator Moor turned inland. The cliff scenery was desolate rather than attractive, and when we once ventured thus far, on a day's outing from Barrow, we took one look at it and then caught the first train back to the pleasant little seaside town of Seascale, 2 miles to the south of Sellafield. Of adventures based on Seascale however I have much to tell in the next chapter.

Returning to engineering matters, there was an important change in organization following the retirement of W. F. Pettigrew in 1918. Until then the civil and mechanical engineering departments had been quite separate, and their chiefs each reported directly to the general manager. But in 1918 the civil engineer, D. L. Rutherford, was appointed Engineer-in-Chief, and added the mechanical engineering departments to his former responsibilities. Sharples became assistant engineer for all mechanical matters, but outside the actual Furness district the new set-up was not widely known, particularly in railway journalistic circles. In consequence of this there has always been some confusion as to the true authorship of some very fine new locomotives introduced in 1920. One evening at my father's house Sharples put the true situation in a nutshell. He said: 'Rutherford said he wanted a 4-6-4 tank, so we had to get on with it.' The basic design was worked out in detail by Sharples and the drawing office staff at Barrow, and the contract for building five of these engines was awarded to Kitsons, of Leeds. They were huge and impressive looking machines, and did their work with ease and efficiency. They were unusual in being the only British engines of the 4-6-4 tank type to have inside cylinders. Despite their great length the chassis and bogie design was such that they rode the curves easily, and became great favourites with the enginemen by their smooth and comfortable riding.

One cannot leave this highly individual little railway without reference to a very important feature of its semaphore signalling. In pre-grouping days while the arms of distant signals had V-shaped ends and the white band was often in the shape of a chevron there was nothing to distinguish such signals at night. Like the home signals they showed a red light in the danger position, and reliance was placed on the driver's intimate knowledge of the road for him to appreciate whether it was a distant or a home signal that he was sighting in that single red light in the darkness. One or two of the railways running south of London used an illuminated chevron sign to the right of some distant signal lamps; but the Furness introduced a highly distinctive form of distant signal lighting at night. They used a flashing red, with the light controlled by the same type of acetylene gas apparatus used in a 'winking' navigational buoy. The result was remarkably effective. There was no mistaking one of those flashing reds for anything else. Their use was discontinued after grouping, because the problem of distant signal lighting had been solved on a national basis by the very simple expedient of using 'orange' as the warning light for a distant signal, instead of red.

CHAPTER SEVEN

Ravenglass and Eskdale

SOME YEARS BEFORE World War I we had an old volume of the *Wide World Magazine* in the house, and in that book was an article entitled 'A Railway in Chancery'. It began 'Hidden away in the wilds of Cumberland is the quaintest railway imaginable . . .' and it went on to describe a journey thus: 'It lurches, and groans, and rolls along in a manner that makes you wonder why you did not invest your spare coppers in insurance tickets. You also speculate whether the bottom will fall out of the carriage, the train pull up the rails, or the whole affair topple over into the river. . . .'

It is no part of my story to attempt to describe the old 3 ft. gauge line, which became subject to an Order in Chancery when it was no more than two years old! It staggered to a close in April, 1913. But memories of that old article in the *Wide World Magazine* came flooding back when *The Railway Magazine* for December 1915 arrived, and with it a lively account of the re-opening of the line, on the 15-inch gauge, powered by a truly magnificent scale model 'Atlantic' locomotive, built by Bassett-Lowke. But while the thought of that little railway gripped my imagination it was consigned to the storehouse of far-off, un-attainable things. At that time Ravenglass might have been in the Sahara for all the chances I then imagined I had of ever going there. And even after we moved to Barrow in the following year the 'penny', that we were then within a day trip's reach of Eskdale, did not finally drop until we made an expedition to Seascale, and two stations before that particular journey's end we stopped at a station whose letters spelled out the name 'Ravenglass'. All we could then see from the Furness Railway train were some sheds in an advanced degree of dilapidation, a few miscellaneous items of 15-inch gauge rolling stock standing in grass-entwined sidings, and a plume of steam rising above some other sheds.

To a boy of 11 dereliction meant nothing. Somewhere out of sight must be that splendid 'Atlantic' engine that I had read about in *The Railway Magazine*, but it was not until the following year that I persuaded my parents to venture on a trip up the line. There were many other things to do beside sightseeing in that first summer at Barrow. When' we reached Ravenglass, and crossed over to the Eskdale Railway station it was to find a surprise, and something of a disappointment; for instead of the expected model 'Atlantic' was a tall 'contractor's' type utilitarian 0-6-0 tank engine which I recognized as of the breed used on the Eaton Hall Railway, in Cheshire, and owned by the Duke of Westminster. It had no cab, a large polished brass dome, and a very tall chimney, and was named *Ella*. Standing nearby was another one of a similar type, but eight-coupled, named *Muriel*. But of the model 'Atlantic' there was not a sign. There were plenty of picture postcards on sale at the station, and from these I discovered that the Eskdale Railway owned not only an 'Atlantic' but a 'Pacific'! Never mind; perhaps we should see one or other of them on our journey up the line. The train consisted only of open four-wheeled carriages, seating 8, in two 'compartments', and having been warned by friends in Barrow of the dire effects of smoke and smuts from the engine we secured seats towards the rear of the long train. We had not yet absorbed the technique of securing virtual immunity from locomotive emissions, by travelling in the very front compartment, where most of the exhaust went clean over our heads!

So we trundled up the line behind *Ella*. The track was very rough. The old rails of the derelict 3 ft. gauge 'Railway in Chancery' had just been moved inwards to provide the 15-inch gauge, and although there was plenty of strength left in them to support the lighter rolling-stock the little four-wheelers jogged and jolted along. But it was part of the fun. Had I appreciated it at the time I might have wondered how the scale-model wheels and motion of the Bassett-Lowke 'Atlantic' and 'Pacific' could have taken to that rough track. Actually, as I shall relate in a minute, they had both been casualties from a very different reason. There was no sign of either of them on that first trip of ours up the line, in the early summer of 1917. The service did not extend beyond Beckfoot in that year. The original terminus of the line was at Boot, and in the last half-mile there was the worst gradient on the line—a full quarter-mile at 1 in 37.

But scale models or not we all enjoyed the trip so much that we went again. As before *Ella* hauled the train that connected with the morning Furness Railway train from Barrow, but this time only as far as Irton Road, 4 miles from Ravenglass. There to my great interest engines were changed, and the model 'Atlantic' came on. From our seats near the rear of the train I could not get a very clear view of the little engine; but there was something odd about her tender. But the change in the style of travel was astonishing. It is true that the gradient is favourable on leaving Irton Road, but we dashed away in most exhilarating style—in the most extraordinary contrast to the jog trot of *Ella*. On leaving Eskdale Green however, on a gradient of 1 in 62, the 'Atlantic' all but stalled, and a number of male passengers got out and pushed. So we came to Beckfoot, and there was a chance for a close look at the little engine. I was shocked. She was stripped of her running plates and driving wheel splashers, and looked very dirty and unkempt; but it was the tender that really puzzled me. The body, instead of being carried on two four-wheeled bogies, as I had seen in photographs, was roughly fixed on a four-wheeled flat truck, that looked as if it had been an open goods wagon from which the sides were removed. I put all this down to the possibility that the day-to-day practical use in such rough mountain country was more than

17. RAVENGLASS AND ESKDALE, IN CHANCERY

(a) Boot station, with 0-6-0 tank engine *Devon* in 1905.
(b) Whit–Monday excursion in 1906, with every item of rolling stock
    the railway then possessed, hauled by the engine *Devon*, shortly
    after leaving Ravenglass.

the finesse of scale models could stand. It was not until many years later that I learned of the true reason for the odd appearance of the 'Atlantic', and the complete absence of the 'Pacific'.

The latter engine had originally been built by Bassett-Lowke's to the order of Capt. J. E. P. Howey for use on his 15-inch gauge railway at Staughton Manor. But the war upset all his plans. Shortly after the engine was completed he left for military service, and very early in the war he became a prisoner in enemy hands. The engine named *John Anthony* was tested on the Eaton Hall Railway, and eventually, renamed *Colossus*, she came into the possession of the Eskdale Railway in 1916. After the war Capt. Howey realized his ambition of having a 15-inch gauge railway for he was the moving spirit in the construction of the Romney, Hythe and Dymchurch Railway. But to return to the Eskdale Railway, where was *Colossus* in 1917? Looking back to the scene as we saw it in that year I am amazed at the 'rough and ready' atmosphere that prevailed. In an age when, even in wartime, locomotives of the main line railways were always smartly turned out, the grimy, uncared-for look of the 'Atlantic' was deplorable. When first delivered at Ravenglass she had been gorgeously finished in Great Eastern blue, with much polished brass- and copper-work, and one would have thought that with all the fascination of a new narrow-gauge railway she would have been kept so. But of course the new management was dependent upon local labour to run the railway, and some of these characters did not seem to have much railway tradition behind them. The driver of the 'Atlantic' was a little hunch-backed man, always incredibly dirty, with a rapid, and vituperous flow of language. *Ella* was driven by a stolid pink-faced youth to whom time did not seem to matter.

Who else was involved I do not know, but apparently through some gross carelessness the 'Atlantic' and the 'Pacific' collided on shed, with such violence that the 'Atlantic' tender was somewhat mangled, and the 'Pacific' was out of traffic for the whole summer! By resorting to the makeshift I saw the 'Atlantic' was got back into service in 1917, though stripped of much of her original finery; but she looked a specimen from the last days of steam in British Railways, rather than the pride and joy of a new enterprise. From all accounts the two scale-model engines had done a good deal of running during the summer season of 1916, when the only other power available was an 0-4-0 'contractors' tank engine, *Katie*, from the Duke of Westminster's railway. But this little engine was hardly up to the sharp gradients of the Eskdale line, and it was very fortunate that the company was able to purchase *Ella* and *Muriel* in time for the start of the summer service of 1917; otherwise, without either 'scale model' they would not have been able to run a service at all. The line was extremely popular in those war years, and when we travelled the trains were always crowded.

In 1918 we spent some weeks in the school holidays at Seascale, and with a push-bicycle it was not long before I had ridden the 4 miles to the crossing of the Eskdale Railway at Muncaster to see what was happening. I was rewarded by my first sight of *Colossus*, seemingly in good shape and with the proper bogie tender. When we made our first trip up the line that year the morning train was run in two portions, with the nameless 'Atlantic'—

88

still as 'scruffy' as ever and with makeshift tender—taking the first part, and *Colossus* the heavier second portion. The line was then open throughout to Boot; we got out at Beckfoot, on a blackberry-gathering expedition, but we waited to see the departure of the train. To assist up the 1 in 37, the 'Atlantic' had returned from Boot, and coupled on to double-head the heavier train. There were some unorthodox workings at times. The last train down the valley that evening was very heavy, and it was taken throughout by both engines, the 'Atlantic' at the head end, and the 'Pacific' pushing in rear; and both engines running tender first! At one time there was some talk of providing turntables, to avoid tender-first running, but these were not installed until much later.

I must recall another adventure on the Eskdale Railway in that same summer of 1918. One evening my father and I decided to travel from Seascale and catch the last train up the valley, and we found quite a different clientele on that run. The passengers, other than ourselves, were all dalesfolk, returning from work in neighbouring places like Egrement, and even from Whitehaven; there were housewives returning heavily loaded from shopping expeditions, and one could appreciate the real value of the little railway in the ordinary life of the dales. Altogether the train was quite heavy, and *Colossus* was obviously not doing too well; she slipped repeatedly on Muncaster Mill Race bank, and one could sense that the driver was relieved when quite half the passengers got out at Irton Road. When we got eventually to Boot we found we were the only passengers returning to Ravenglass that evening, to catch the connecting Furness Railway train to Seascale. We also gathered, while waiting for the re-start from Boot, that *Colossus* was in trouble. She had an overheated axle-box on the tender. The driver was a man of apparent authority, who might have been the manager of the line, and he explained to my father that there was nothing for it but to proceed dead slow to Irton Road, where he *thought* there was a flat truck that we could use as a tender. We thought of our connection back to Seascale, but there was nothing to be done to hurry up the proceedings.

What I do remember was the intense feeling of loneliness up in those quiet dales as the twilight came on, with just my father and me sitting in the front compartment, with a long train of empty carriages jogging along behind us, and the anxious driver coaxing that disabled tender along—again, of course, tender first. How they actually improvised things at Irton Road I cannot say. There was only the driver and the guard to do it, and in the light of lamps it took a long time. What we did know was that there was not a hope of catching the Furness train from Ravenglass. The road to Seascale crossed the railway at Muncaster, so we asked them to put us down there. Once repairs were effected *Colossus* was taken down the gradual descent from Irton Road like the wind, and the trip ended for us with a 4-mile walk to our lodgings in Seascale. With the ending of the war my parents were glad enough to take holidays farther afield and it was several years before I saw the Eskdale Railway again.

In the meantime some important managerial and engineering developments had taken place. At Irton Hall, not far from the line, and a little to the west of Irton Road station, lived Sir Aubrey Brocklebank, then a great shipping magnate. But although his business interests were world-wide he took a keen interest in all activities around his home estate, and particularly in the Eskdale Railway. It was indeed far more than the interest of an amateur enthusiast. He was already much concerned with railways, being not only a director of the Great Western, but chairman of the Locomotive Committee Board. It was he that the great G. J. Churchward once chaffed with the words: 'You're the only b . . . director I've ever met who knew anything about valve gears!' Furthermore, in somewhat earlier years his association with the Great Western, and his brother Ralph's directorship of the North Western, and their comparisons of engine-building costs is generally considered to have sparked off the ill-starred locomotive exchange of 1910, when a Great Western non-superheated 'Star' 4-6-0 was matched against a North Western 'Experiment'.

Thus Sir Aubrey Brocklebank's interest in Eskdale Railway matters was at once expert and highly authoritative. After the war, when the motive power situation could have become critical he personally paid for a new express passenger 'Pacific' engine, put into service in 1919. This was a similar design to that of *Colossus*, but with a few detail changes. The boiler was pitched slightly higher, and she had a six-wheeled tender. But she was generally of 'scale-model' proportions and was subject to the same disadvantages as the earlier engines, in suffering from rough handling on a rough road. Appropriately the new engine was named *Sir Aubrey Brocklebank*, and for some years, with careful and constant maintenance she was the pride of the line. She was notable in not being built by Bassett-Lowke, but by Hunt & Company of Bournemouth. She was the first and only steam locomotive that company had built, but they made an excellent job of her. Like the earlier scale models she was painted blue, and in 1922 I had an excellent trip up the line behind her on the heavy morning train. She was sharing the work with *Colossus* at that time.

Of course the grouping of the British main line railways at the end of 1922 did not affect the Eskdale Railway, and at the risk of slightly overlapping the period of this book two further motive power developments must be mentioned. The origin of the first is historic. This was the Ford Model 'T' tractor, a curiously utilitarian affair, the original suggestion for which came from a lady. During World War I two daughters of C. J. Bowen-Cooke, Chief Mechanical Engineer of the London and North Western Railway, were serving in France as Ambulance drivers, and one of them, in conversation one day with a British officer, was appalled at the hazards regularly experienced in getting men and stores to and from the trenches in pitch darkness, often over ground pitted with shell holes and other debris of war. Movement by day was out of the question. Miss Cooke, when on leave, suggested to her father the idea of having small Ford-engined lorries which could be converted to run on light narrow gauge tracks, that could be laid on the surface of the ground. Bowen-Cooke immediately took up his daughter's idea. The Crewe drawing office was set to work on it, and so emerged the 'Crewe Tractor'. After a certain amount of early 'sales resistance' the War Office accepted it, and a total of 132 was built at Crewe. They were used not only in France, but in Egypt, Mesopotamia, and in Macedonia. One of these came into the motive power stock of the Eskdale Railway at the end of 1922. It proved very useful for light duties, staff trains and such like, for which there was no need to go to the time and

18. RAVENGLASS AND ESKDALE, 15-IN. GAUGE

(a) The Heywood 0-6-0 tank engine *Ella*.
(b) The Bassett-Lowke 4-4-2 *Sans Pareil* poses for a photograph, with
    Muncaster station in the background.

trouble of preparing a steam locomotive.

Until 1922 locomotives had not been specially designed for Eskdale Railway conditions. The Bassett-Lowke 'Atlantic' and 'Pacific' were intended to run on a well-built scale model permanent way, whereas they had to thrash along on the narrowed-down track of the 'Railway in Chancery', at first at any rate. By the time Sir Aubrey Brocklebank took the reins things had been much improved, but it was still rough going at times, and this second 'Pacific' was designed very much in the Bassett-Lowke mould. In those post-war years, thanks to the enterprise of Sir Aubrey himself the railway had a growing traffic in stone, from quarries at Murthwaite, on the side of Muncaster Fell, not far from his home. The old contractor-type engines *Ella* and *Muriel* were coping, not too well, with this heavy work, and it was suggested that a more powerful engine was desirable. From the outset the well-known model locomotive designer, Henry Greenly, had been associated with the rejuvenation of the Eskdale Railway. He in fact was the designer of the Bassett-Lowke 'Atlantic' and 'Pacific', and in 1922 he worked out the design of a powerful freight locomotive specially for Eskdale Railway service. This was a truly massive 2-8-2, named *River Esk*, and the contract for her construction was placed with Davey Paxman & Co. Ltd. of Colchester.

For some reason, which I have seen attributed to the builders, the engine, which was otherwise a thoroughly simple and straightforward job, was fitted with Lentz poppet valve gears, using scaled down components of the standard gear which was then being introduced on to main line locomotives. I think its use, rather than originating with Davey Paxman, can be attributed to the influence of the late Edward Cecil Poultney, who had always great interests in Furness and West Cumberland railways, and who was associated, business-wise, with the development and application of poppet valve gears generally. *River Esk* proved a very powerful engine, and was used both in passenger and freight service. But, as with many a main line engine, the poppet valve gear proved troublesome, and *River Esk* has been an infinitely better and more dependable engine since rebuilding with the Walschaerts valve gear in 1927. When I visited the line in 1970 she was still doing excellent work.

CHAPTER EIGHT
'Midland' in the North Country

IN THESE DAYS of standardization on the British nationalized railway system, or indeed when thinking a little further back to the increasing uniformity of style manifested by the 'Big Four' in the Grouping Era, it is astonishing to reflect upon the differences that existed among the old railway companies of the pre-grouping age. In this book I have taken the reader so far along the line of my own introductions to the various railways: from the Great Western to the South Eastern, the South Western and the Great Eastern, and then northwards, by the North Western itself to the Furness. But the mere act of entering a Midland carriage at Carnforth faced one with something far different from anything previously encountered—quite apart from its beautiful external colour scheme. But why Carnforth of all places, to meet the Midland? Well, we were travelling from Barrow to Skipton, on the way to visit an uncle at Harrogate, and to avoid the crowded purlieus of Leeds in wartime we did the last stage of the journey over the moors direct by car.

To return now to the Midland carriages, by the year 1916 two years of war had dimmed the glitter on many an English railway, but not yet that of the Midland. The first impression on climbing into that carriage from the low platform at Carnforth was one of extreme space and airyness. Thomas Clayton certainly gave his passengers plenty of light. While other carriage designers were rather parsimonious with their window space, and all the railways on which I had so far travelled were uniform in this respect, Clayton provided large rectangular-cornered windows that extended to the full width of the compartment seats and added large rectangular top lights as well. The result was an extraordinary 'light' and cheerful carriage. The effect was enhanced by the gay colour of the upholstery—a kind of green and orange 'autumn tints' effect. To my mind the 'thirds' were far more attractive than the 'firsts', which were upholstered in plain dark blue. The trains running into Carnforth were then non-corridor; but that was nothing out of the ordinary at that time. The only corridor trains that I had ever travelled in up to that time were on the Great Western, between Reading and Weymouth, and of course on the London and North Western main line.

I have mentioned the 'low' platforms at Carnforth. This was not the only peculiarity of the one used by the Midland trains. The North Western main line runs due north and south through the station and even in those days trains used to streak through without stopping at anything up to 80 m.p.h.; but in the short distance of the platform length the Furness line turned an almost complete right angle to the west, and Midland trains were accommodated at a bay platform on the outer periphery of the Furness 'arc'. Thus trains going east from Carnforth left the station in a direction roughly west-north-west! The ensuing track, to attain their ultimate direction, and to cross the North Western at right angles has been described as a logarithmic spiral in reverse, starting on a very sharp radius, and gradually opening out, as a more easterly direction was attained. On reaching the first station out on this interesting cross-country line one could be surprised in those days to see that the station buildings and lineside equipment was still wholly in the Furness Railway style. This first stage of the journey, as far as Wennington, where the main Midland cross-country line from Lancaster and Heysham Harbour was joined, was jointly owned by the Furness and the Midland; and while the Furness maintained the track, stations and fixed structures the Midland worked all the traffic, providing the necessary rolling-stock and locomotives. There may have been an occasional special worked by the Furness Railway, but other than that it was all Midland from Carnforth eastwards.

One's abiding first impression on meeting the Midland Railway for the first time was undoubtedly of the carriages; but then, just look at the fascinating variety of locomotives that worked over this one cross-country line! From notes I made in the five years I was regularly travelling over it there were two varieties of 2-4-0; no fewer than four different classes of 4-4-0; several different ranges of 0-6-0 goods engine, with the occasional 0-4-4 tank thrown in. And when that cross-country line reached Hellifield there were, from time to time, three more varieties of 4-4-0 and the main line goods engines to add—not to mention the Lancashire and Yorkshire engines coming in from the south. But to be more explicit about the locomotives on the line to Carnforth and to Heysham, the graceful little 2-4-0s worked many of the passenger trains, often with astonishingly heavy loads. Most of them were of the Johnson type with outside frames only to the leading wheels; but occasionally we got a Kirtley, with outside frames throughout, and outside coupling rods in the fashion already familiar to me from Great Western engines.

Those little engines had to work hard over that route, because from Wennington eastwards it was a continuous climb for 9 miles on gradients never easier than 1 in 180 and mostly between 1 in 100 and 1 in 120. It was rare to see one of those trains double-headed, however many of the principal main line express trains of the Midland had two engines. The 2-4-0s were all in power-class 1, and so were the smallest of the 4-4-0s. There were quite a number of those beautiful Johnson engines in their un-rebuilt condition working over that line, I believe some of them were based at Hellifield, and were used as pilots on the Scotch expresses. The purists may tilt at my use of the word 'Scotch' instead of Scots or Scottish; but on the Midland Railway every through express train crossing the Border, day or night alike, was labelled 'Scotch Express' in the public timetables. This practice continued on the Midland Division of the L.M.S. for some time after grouping, until, indeed, the special names 'Thames–Clyde Express' and 'Thames–Forth Express' were introduced for the morning services to and from St. Pancras.

There was quite a variety of engines contained within power-class 2. A number of the Johnson 4-4-0s had been rebuilt with larger boilers while retaining their original wheels, frames and motion. These had the Deeley round-top type of firebox, but one could distinguish those with 6 ft. 6 in. coupled wheels from those with 7 ft. more readily after rebuilding than previously, by the distinctive shape of the new splashers. In their beautifully graceful 'Johnson' form the general appearance was the same, except that a keen observer could gauge that the wheels were larger. These first rebuilds were not superheated, and there was a further variety with Belpaire fireboxes, that were also non-superheated. Included also in Class '2' however were some considerably more powerful rebuilds. Strictly speaking these latter should not be called rebuilds at all. They were what could be jocularly described as an 'accountants' rebuild! They were virtually new engines, that were replacements of the originals with just enough of original parts incorporated in them to satisfy the accountants that they were not entirely new. These engines all had 7 ft. diameter coupled wheels, and superheated boilers, and were excellent small-power units.

Reference to the variety of locomotives included in the one power class leads me on to the managerial policy of the Midland Railway that was inaugurated in 1907, and which had been gradually extended to cover all activities on the line by the time I began to travel regularly eastwards from Carnforth. In my book *Steam Railways in Retrospect* I have a chapter entitled 'The Midland Revolution, 1907–22' in which I describe the changes in methods of operation particularly so far as freight train working was concerned. One of its most important and far reaching aspects was to take the matter of decision-making at lower supervisory levels out of the hands of the man on the site, and to provide him instead with a set of regulations on which he had to work. It was a new conception of railway management. Hitherto British railway operation had been based very largely upon the sense of responsibility of individual men, who from their experience were relied upon to make appropriate decisions in meeting the day-to-day problems of railway working. Its application to the loading of locomotives illustrates the general principle admirably.

To make things as simple as possible for establishing the necessary rules the entire passenger locomotive stud was divided into four power classes, and its working out in practice can be seen in the No. 2 class, of which every one of the four varieties worked over the line that leads to Heysham Harbour and to Carnforth. Loads were fixed for various duties according to the speed required by the timetable and the severity of the gradients on the route. Over certain sections, for example, the load for a Class '2' engine was 180 tons. It was then accepted that any passenger engine with a small '2' on its cab side could work such a train to time. No consideration need be given by the man allocating engines to jobs as to what the mechanical condition of the engine was, or whether it happened to be a 6 ft. 6 in. 'round-topped' non-superheater rebuild that was just about due to go to main works for general overhaul, or whether it was one of the virtually new 7 ft. superheaters, in

19. STATELY MIDLAND EXPRESSES

(a) Down 'Scotch Express' leaving Elstree Tunnel hauled by 7 ft. 9 in. 4-2-2 No. 672 and Deeley compound No. 1042.

(b) Up 'Scotch Express' near Armathwaite hauled by Class '4' non-compound 4-4-0 No. 992.

spanking condition. If the engine was serviceable for traffic it was expected to do the job. As a result of this working principle loads had to be fixed on the low side, so that the worst engine on the shed could run the train to time.

Of course, individual shed masters who were not too clerically minded, saw to it that the best engines of a power class were allocated to the most important jobs; but the load limits were strictly enforced, and by the regulations a driver who had one ton over his stipulated load was entitled to a pilot engine. If he was overloaded, decided to 'have a go', and lost time in the process, he could receive a severe reprimand. Looked at from the viewpoint of locomotive achievement, and the delight of those thrilling occasions when an enterprising driver gets some exceptional work out of his engine, the Midland system had the effect of damping out such individual effort; but of course for those who merely enjoyed watching the trains it very often provided the spectacle of two engines instead of one on a train, and a considerable variety of engines on the same train from day to day. I can hardly think that the load-control regulations had been applied to trains over the cross-country line to Wennington and the west when I first travelled over it, when I recall the loads that used to be taken by the little Class '1' 2-4-0 engines.

The section eastwards from Wennington where the line was climbing into the Craven country, was second only to the far-famed Settle and Carlisle line for majestic scenery. I fear however that on many of my earlier journeys I was not in a frame of mind to appreciate it. Returning to school after the holidays a 'deep depression' had usually centred over the small group that came from Barrow by the time the train had left Wennington; while conversely, at the end of term we were all too much in high spirits to notice the passing scene. Appreciation came in later years, when the train was climbing laboriously up the grade from Bentham, and a magnificent prospect of Ingleborough opened out to the north-east. Out on the moors, at the foot of Ingleborough itself was the quaintly named Clapham Junction. It certainly *was* a junction, and there is a village named Clapham some distance away; but its remoteness, and the sparseness of its train service even in those years could not fail to raise a smile from any well-read railway enthusiast, and among the few London boys at school it was, of course, a supreme joke. It was, even then, one of those railway locations the function of which had changed completely with the years.

The line running westwards from Skipton, usually known as the 'Little' North Western, was planned in the first place to provide a direct connection from the West Riding towns to Scotland, and after having crossed the high ground west of Ribblesdale it was pushed on northwards, round the western flanks of Ingleborough and up the Vale of Lune with a view to continuing to make a trailing connection with the London and North Western main line at Low Gill. But the North Western had other ideas. They had no desire to have a protégé of the Midland linking in with their main Anglo-Scottish line, and in the breathless haste of early railway projecting they secured authorization for a branch line of their own, southwards from Low Gill; and so the 'big' North Western met the 'Little' North Western in an end-on junction at Ingleton. So, when I knew the district, the Midland worked a shuttle service between Clapham Junction and Ingleton, but if you wanted to go farther north it was necessary to wait for the next North Western train. And I must add that the connections between the two were not very convenient!

The 'little' North Western was built like many another line that traversed hilly country, and in the first ten miles out of Skipton, where it was negotiating the high ridge between the valleys of the Aire and the Ribble it followed an almost continuously curving track, not so much to lessen the gradients as to minimize the necessity for heavy earthworks. In consequence it has always been subject to a number of moderate speed restrictions. Riding on the footplate from Skipton through to Wennington one notes the same general characteristics throughout. But one passes on this route that place of the most profound significance, Settle Junction, and sees climbing at once, but on an almost straight alignment the route of the Midland Scotch Expresses, to Carlisle and far beyond. The story of how this superb piece of railway came to be built, to be opened for traffic in 1876, and the actual manner of its building is one of the greatest romances, dramas and epics in British railway history. It would fill a whole book, let alone part of one chapter. Here I can only tell how I first saw it, in 1916, how I lived beside it for the next five years, and how some years afterwards I came to ride over it many times on the footplate, and to know it in all weathers and seasons.

The Midland's Railway's first proposal to build the line was no more than a threat: a move in the game of nineteenth-century railway politics, to try and out-bluff the London and North Western. But when the Midland afterwards tried to climb down from the project, its allies, both in England and Scotland would have none of it. Together they brought such pressure to bear on the Midland—realizing the immense traffic advantage of having a route into England entirely independent of the North Western—that a formal decision to build the line was taken. To the honour of the Midland, once that decision was made there were no half measures about the way the line was engineered. On the 'Settle and

20. THE CHANGING 'LOOK' OF MIDLAND ENGINES

(a) One of the Johnson 'Belpaire' 4-4-os of 1903 with original style of painting and double bogie tender.
(b) A Kirtley '800' class 2-4-0.
(c) The grace of a Johnson 7-footer of 1896.
(d) A superheater '999', for the Settle and Carlisle Line.

a

b

c

d

Carlisle', as it was known from the outset, there was no circumventing of obstacles that lay in the direct path. If there was a deep valley ahead the line was taken straight across by an immense and stately viaduct; if there were rocky eminences there was no thought but to blast clean through. As for the tunnels, some of them were among the worst ever to be constructed in England. The result was one of the finest pieces of railway in the country: 76 miles of line through tremendous mountain country, but without a speed restriction worth talking about anywhere.

I have ridden on locomotives over many scenically famous stretches of line in many parts of the world. I have ridden through the Blue Mountains, in New South Wales; up the Montagu Pass, in South Africa; through the spiral tunnels on the ascent to the St. Gotthard Tunnel in Switzerland, and not least through the Kicking Horse Pass on the Canadian Pacific. Yet somehow I do not feel that any of these vividly spectacular stretches of railway gives the same thrill to anyone riding on the engine as does the Settle and Carlisle. For on a Midland Scotch Express there was always the supreme sensation of SPEED. It is a hard enough grind going up the banks in all cases—tremendous on the Canadian Pacific, where sometimes three giant ten-coupled locomotives were needed to lift a heavy Transcontinental express up the grade at 20 m.p.h. But descending it was no more than a crawl; the curves preclude anything in the way of speed. The only sentiments that occur to one are whether the brake shoes are going to get so hot as to set the carriages on fire! The scenery is sublime; the curves and the alignment of the railway are alike breathtaking, even at dead slow speed, but the thrill is towards the pioneer engineering work that made such routes possible.

Then come with me on the footplate of a southbound Midland Scotch Express; a heavy train, over 400 tons; two engines, a 7 ft. Class '2' superheater leading, and a Class '4' 3-cylinder compound next to the train. Kirkby Stephen is passed, climbing hard on 1 in 100. Throttles wide open; reversing screws well forward; a pandemonium of exhaust noise in the rock cuttings, intensified as we blast through Birkett Tunnel. Out on the wildest moorland slopes, speed about 35 m.p.h., and Aisgill summit now in sight, still about 4 miles ahead, at the Westmorland–Yorkshire watershed, 1,150 ft. above sea level. 'Small beer' one might say in comparison to the Great Divide in the Canadian Rockies; but wait. Both these Midland engines are kept hammering away until the last minute round the curve and over the viaduct beneath Wild Boar Fell; and then with the summit reached and the whole long train on the level at the top, steam is shut off and the train brought quickly to rest. There is now no further need for the pilot engine, and the sooner she is returned to Carlisle the better. The Midland, through their 'small engine' policy may have used much double-heading, but no company reduced to such a fine art the business of detaching the pilot engines.

Almost before we were at rest the fireman of the leading engine had jumped down and was ready to uncouple. Then that engine ran smartly ahead of the points. The signalman did not waste a second. Those points were reversed and the pilot was backing into the siding in little more time that it took the driver to reverse the engine; and as we had stopped a little short of the starting signal our driver had actually started the compound before the signal cleared to draw forward. The signal was, however, pulled off in a trice, and we were right away. And the whole operation, from our coming to rest with two engines, and on getting away again lasted just *sixty-five seconds*! From Kirkby Stephen climbing the last 7 miles of the bank, stopping at Aisgill to put off the pilot engine and getting under way again, it took only 17 minutes to pass Hawes Junction, another 3 miles beyond Aisgill; and by that time we were doing $58\frac{1}{2}$ m.p.h. That 65 seconds to detach the pilot at Aisgill was no special stunt; it was the normal procedure, which I clocked on several other occasions with different classes of engine and on different trains.

From Hawes Junction, running southwards, we were entering upon the most spectacular and exciting part of the line. It is carried, almost level, at a high altitude of around 1,100 ft. on great hillsides, looking down sheer into valleys where tiny villages of closely packed stone cottages cluster beside infant streams. Garsdale first; then the mass of Rise Hill towers ahead, and we go straight through on the level, in a long tunnel at nearly 60 m.p.h. Then comes Dent, a typical north-country station, with the village, whose name it bears, many hundreds of feet below in another deep valley. One thinks of winter days in those mighty dales when the villagers had to struggle up to the station to catch the local train when they went marketing in Settle or Hawes! High on the hillside to the left of us lay a double line of snow fences to catch drifting snow, and lessen the chance of obstruction on the railway.

Now the scene, and the locomotive running were alike approaching a climax. The head of Dentdale is ringed with high mountains; the railway crosses one ravine on a lofty viaduct built in the native gritstone—Arten Gill; another viaduct can be seen ahead, and beyond it a black dot on the mountain-side—the northern end of Blea Moor tunnel. Our compound engine has got that big train fairly rolling by now; we sweep across Denthead viaduct at 63 m.p.h. and now, high up on the great mountain-side we are approaching, the line of the tunnel beneath is pinpointed by two ventilating shafts, from both of which a plume of white smoke is drifting. We plunge into the long tunnel. The great Tasmanian engineer, Sharland, who built the line, made no concession to natural obstacles. Despite the toughness of the rock, the water, the underground springs, he bored straight through and almost on the level. Water is always dripping in the tunnel. The cab glasses became spattered as with rain, and still we roared on, at only a fraction below 60 m.p.h. Then ahead of us the vapour and smoke hanging in the tunnel suddenly cleared, and we saw the south exit, only about a quarter of a mile ahead; and in that amazing 'frame' getting larger every second, was the distinctive profile of the finest of the mountains of Craven, Ingleborough. Now that diesel railcars run over this route passengers may also enjoy this glorious sight; but at the time of which I am now writing it was a sight reserved for the men on the engines.

We were, however, rapidly switching from one thrill to another. At the southern end of Blea Moor Tunnel the long descent to Settle Junction begins—14 miles of it, nearly all graded at 1 in 100. No wonder that in referring particularly to the upward direction the enginemen call it 'The Long Drag'. But the track is little removed from straight, and once out of Blea Moor Tunnel the acceleration is terrific. High speeds, so beloved of the man with the stop watch, present no difficulties here! At first our driver did not touch the controls.

We tore over Ribblehead viaduct at 72 m.p.h. and were soon doing nearly 'eighty' on a splendid track down the wide open dale. But then he did adjust the controls, but to restrain rather than hustle the engine. We were well on time on this trip and 75 to 80 m.p.h. was enough. But the sheer joy of careering downhill through such grand country, with so little effort, and sweeping through short tunnels, rock cuttings and beside all the natural obstacles that once lay in the path of the constructing engineers was exhilarating beyond measure. But even so, 80 m.p.h. was far from the safe limit on that line. Some years later, on a raw winter's afternoon the rail conditions were so bad coming up from Carlisle that several minutes had been lost to Aisgill. There was no stop at the summit, for we were under maximum load; but once through Blea Moor Tunnel the driver made the most of the long descent, and speed reached 88 m.p.h. at one point.

Another vivid memory of the 'Settle and Carlisle' is of a winter's occasion when I was riding north from Leeds on the morning Edinburgh express. We had a few tons over maximum load, and 'orders being orders' we had a pilot—again a 7 ft. Class '2' superheater. With plenty of engine power we made short work of The Long Drag, and as usual there was plenty of interest in the running. Clouds were scudding across from the east, bringing showers of icy rain; little streams were spouting down many a gully and mist was riding across the mountain crests. Having come up the bank with no lower speed than 45 m.p.h. we dived into Blea Moor Tunnel; it was just as wet and horrible as ever, and we burst out again on to that high track overlooking Dentdale. I watched the leading engine, swaying and rolling as she took curve after curve; it was not the dangerous lurch, or continued hunting, but the easy buoyant ride of a swing. With screaming whistle she led us into Rise Hill Tunnel; out again at 70 m.p.h. on to that dizzy ledge above Garsdale to the highest water troughs in England. The fireman on the Class '2' lowered his scoop; the tender was evidently fuller than he thought for in seconds the tank overflowed, and we on the train engine were smothered. Involuntarily I ducked, for the water came over in a solid cascade and hit our cab glasses with a roar rather than a splash. This time our pilot was going through to Carlisle, and having topped Aisgill summit we went thunder and turf down to Appleby.

The cynics might dismiss my exhilaration at this wild progress, amid the elemental ferment of a mountain storm, as mere romantic hysteria, engendered by sentiment over a couple of obsolete and very inefficient forms of motive power. But if one such could be tempted away from his armchair into hanging on to a wild swaying compound, or an old Class '2' tearing through Hawes Junction over the summit and down to Kirkby Stephen in the teeth of a storm such as we met that day he would probably agree that there is more in railroading on the 'Settle and Carlisle' than mere statistics of ton-miles, drawbar horsepower hours, or the aggregate assistant engine mileage.

When travelling as a passenger I have had the occasional '90' over this route, but until comparatively recent times one of the fastest runs ever made, taking full advantage of the gradients and the superb alignment dates back to the very beginning of the period of this book—the year 1902. The train was the 9.30 a.m. Scotch Express from London and with a load of 320 tons the train was necessarily double-headed from Leeds up to Aisgill. The train engine was a Class '3' 4-4-0, generally known as the 'Johnson Belpaires', as being the first Midland express engines to have that type of firebox. In my school days at Giggleswick they were not often seen north of Leeds. They detached the pilot at Aisgill, and then there commenced a positively headlong descent towards Carlisle. Mallerstang signal box, $3\frac{3}{4}$ miles from the restart, was passed at 70 m.p.h. and then over the next 14·1 miles to Appleby the average speed was $81\frac{1}{2}$ m.p.h. At Ormside viaduct a full 90 m.p.h. was attained, and eventually the complete 48·6 miles from Aisgill to Carlisle were completed, start to stop, in 41 min. 55 sec..

I have passed a long way through my memories of the Midland Railway in the North Country without mentioning the engines that for so many years bore the brunt of the heaviest passenger work on the 'Settle and Carlisle', the '999' class 4-4-os. These engines were Class '4', rated equal in load-hauling capacity to the compounds, and in my time in the North used exclusively north of Leeds. They were fine looking engines, built by R. M. Deeley to compare the relative merits of compound and single expansion locomotives of the same boiler capacity. Whether Deeley himself ever came to form any conclusions is doubtful, for he found the revolution in management that I have referred to earlier so distasteful that he resigned. Only ten of the '999' class were built; but they did much excellent work for over twenty years on the principal expresses. Despite being Class '4' they often needed double-heading, for the Class '4' load was only 240 tons. When I was first at school, during the war years, there was only one day Scotch Express over the Midland Railway, and she used to come through Settle in the early afternoon. I cannot remember the exact time. The engine was always a '999'.

One of my most interesting recollections of these engines is of an occasion after the war when the whole family was travelling to Leeds, en route to Bridlington. The train from Carnforth was stopped by signal at Settle Junction, and looking from the carriage window I saw that all signals were off for a train taking the main line to Carlisle. It turned out to be the morning express from Leeds to Glasgow. Now Settle Junction lay at the lowest point of a 'Vee' in the gradient profile. 'The Long Drag' begins immediately, but there is a descent from the high ground east of Hellifield and drivers of Scotch Expresses used to take advantage of this to put on a spurt and take a flying run at the long bank. When the train we were held for came it was indeed a thrilling sight, with one of the beautiful Johnson unrebuilt 4-4-os (Class '1') piloting a '999'; and were they going — ! I did not count the number of coaches, but they had a long train, and by the combined roar of their exhausts they were fairly charging 'The Long Drag'. From the slightly lower level of the 'Little' North Western line we had a splendid sight of them.

In the many contacts I have subsequently made with Midland men in my professional life, and in pursuance of the hobby of railways I have come to realize the stresses and strains that the revolution in management placed on many of those who had to run the trains; in retrospect it can be seen as no more than the beginning of a complete metamorphosis that was eventually to engulf the entire British railway system. To the honour of all concerned however, little, if anything of those internal stresses and strains were evident to passengers, at any rate in the North Country. The carriages were immaculate inside, and externally the superb crimson-lake livery on carriages and engines alike was usually spotless. Among schoolboy enthusiasts too the Midland was a hot favourite. Partisans, who lived in Bradford and Leeds, ridiculed the judgment of those who favoured the Lancashire and Yorkshire, the North Eastern or the Great Northern. As for me, the comings and goings of the Midland were enough to make my firm boyish allegiance to the North Western waver, just a little, while earlier memories of the Great Western were slipping rapidly into the background.

CHAPTER NINE

The railways of Leeds

FOR SOME YEARS from 1916 onwards the City of Leeds was a nodal point in my travels. While there was only one way across country from Carnforth, that by the Midland through Hellifield and Skipton, Leeds for us became a 'grand junction', whence we continued north, east, or south. In those days it was a place of absorbing interest for a railway enthusiast. The trains of no fewer than five of the pre-grouping companies entered the city; and although they were not all to be seen at the same station, as then at York, or even more at Carlisle, the three stations were close enough together to make observation fairly easy. Coming in by the Midland we arrived at 'Wellington'; but the 'New' station was alongside, where the North Eastern and London and North Western trains arrived. The Great Northern shared the rather cramped Central station with the Lancashire and Yorkshire. And to arouse feelings of acute nostalgia I have notes of seeing 34 different classes of passenger locomotive in and around the three stations: 10 Midland; 10 North Eastern; 8 North Western; 3 Great Northern and 3 Lancashire and Yorkshire. Other observers may have seen more, but my own score was a feast indeed.

We could not always go direct to Leeds from the 'Little' North Western line. At the end of the school term all boarders dashed away to catch the earliest trains for home, and the eastbound train that stopped at Giggleswick about 8 a.m. was bound for Bradford. Just as Manchester businessmen commuted daily to Blackpool, Southport, and even Llandudno, with the celebrated 'club' carriages put on to the crack trains for their exclusive use, so Bradford men lived at Morecambe, and before World War I a beautiful club carriage was run for their pleasure. Bradford was in a curious and anomalous position so far as railways were concerned. Its geographical position, set deep among hills just aside from the broad highway of Airedale gave it a 'branch line' position, that was certainly not in keeping with its growing status as a city. The Midland main line to the north passed by a mere 3 miles away from its centre, and the branch made a triangle junction at Shipley. On that morning train from the west those of us who were bound for Leeds had to change at Shipley, and continue, much to my pleasure, on a corridor express destined for London.

The cities of Leeds and Bradford were keen rivals in many things, and the railway position of Bradford rankled with a great many of its citizens. For the 'branch line' status prevailed also on the other railway approaches. The Lancashire and Yorkshire came in from a junction with the Manchester–Leeds line at Bowling Junction again only $1\frac{1}{2}$ miles away, and the Great Northern came into the same terminal station, Exchange, via Mill Lane Junction. As long previously as 1898 the Midland had obtained Parliamentary sanction for a scheme to put Bradford on an alternative main line to Scotland, by construction of a new line coming in from the south roughly parallel to the Lancashire and Yorkshire line from Low Moor, and then tunnelling under the city centre and emerging at the Midland station in Foster Square. The company would then have had the facility of running some of its Scotch Expresses via Leeds and some via Bradford, in a similar way to the conditions existing farther south in the case of Nottingham and Leicester. It would have avoided the need for running the Bradford to London expresses via Leeds, and made them more competitive in speed to those of the Great Northern. It would also have relieved some of the congestion that occurred from time to time in the Wellington station at Leeds.

Nevertheless the Bradford Corporation, anxious as they were to see their city on the Midland main line were well enough aware of the hazards of driving a railway tunnel beneath the very centre of business and administration. There were also risks in respect of the water supply; and the Midland Railway only secured the passage of their Act on condition that they accepted liabilities in respect of possible interference or damage to certain vital water supplies. My uncle was then Town Clerk, and I have many of his records of this interesting period. By the year 1907 nothing had been done to begin construction of the new line, and the Midland management, entering into the throes of their own 'revolution' evidently felt they had enough on hand without getting involved in the building of a risky new tunnel under Bradford. So they presented to Parliament an Abandonment Bill. The city was instantly aflame with indignation. A deputation headed by the Lord Mayor, the Town Clerk and several eminent councillors went to Derby and argued the case with Guy Granet, the redoubtable General Manager of the Midland. Rather than have the prospect abandoned the Corporation was prepared to go most of the way towards relieving the railway company of the water liability clauses; and on that basis an agreement was hammered out. The delegation returned in triumph, and *The Yorkshire Daily Observer* of 16 February, 1907 contained a long article covering the proceedings that had been concluded, and under the sub-heading 'New Main Line to be Proceeded With'. It included a large-scale map showing the route of the new line. But from that time the whole project seems to have dropped completely out of the picture. The Midland certainly did nothing, and in my uncle's records there is nothing to show that the Corporation pursued the matter any further! The affair does however leave one to make some interesting speculations as to how railway history in the West Riding would have been changed by the construction of the line, and in no area more so than around Leeds.

The London expresses by the Midland route that originated at Bradford, Foster Square, were mostly worked by the handsome little Johnson 0-4-4 tank engines between Bradford

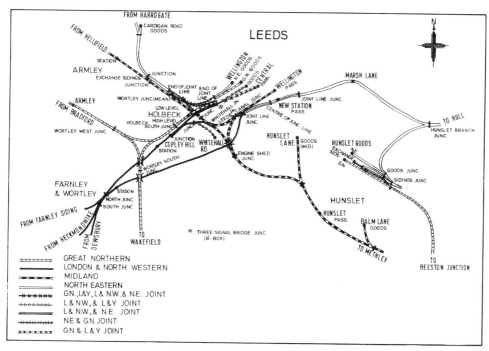

MAP 2: THE RAILWAYS OF LEEDS: EARLY 1900S

and Leeds, and at Leeds Wellington almost every variety of Midland passenger engine was to be seen. The only conspicuous absentees were the beautiful bogie 'singles', which did not normally work north of Leicester or Nottingham, except on trains destined for Manchester via the hilly route over Peak Forest. South of Leeds the Scotch Expresses were usually worked by the compounds, and around 1918 to 1921 they ran through to St. Pancras, with the men lodging in London overnight. The pioneer engines of this famous class, Nos. 1000 and 1001, were stationed at Leeds. I believe they had always been so quartered, from their first introduction in 1902 with all the early Johnson refinements and their double bogie tenders. They were then numbered 2631 and 2632; but in their original form, though magnificent engines when managed by experts, they were found a little too complicated for the average driver. R. M. Deeley simplified their control, and rather watered down their performance in the process. In their superheated form they were nevertheless very good engines—good enough for the L.M.S. to build another 190 of them after grouping.

In Leeds, also, one saw the through Bristol expresses, some of which left Leeds just after a southbound Scotch Express. The latter would probably run non-stop to Trent, and thence to Leicester, while the Bristol train would provide a very convenient connection for passengers from the far north to Sheffield and Derby. The Midland did its best to tempt Scottish passengers off the West Coast Route by running through carriages to Bristol from

both Glasgow and Edinburgh; but at the time of which I am now writing these were conveyed only on the night trains. Many of the Bristol trains were hauled by the Class '3' 4-4-os. A number of these were stationed at Derby, and worked both north and south, on this North to West of England route. I was reminded of Midland through carriage facilities in those years just after World War I by an old school friend who has always lived in the Somersetshire countryside, south of the Mendips. Although he, like the rest of us, had to change at Shipley to get to Leeds by that early morning train from Giggleswick, he then got a through carriage from Leeds right to his home station, Evercreech Junction. This was a service from the Midland to Bournemouth, via the Somerset and Dorset Joint Line from Bath, and was the forerunner of one section of the much-lamented 'Pines Express', of L.M.S. and early British Railways days.

My own earliest expeditions beyond Leeds were to the north, and strange though it may seem for as far back in railway history as 1916 and 1917, they were by road. In the later years of his Town Clerkship in Bradford my uncle had moved house to Harrogate, and he used to commute daily. He had not long previously taken to motoring, and a hired driver used to take the car, with the whole family on board to meet the evening Midland train at Otley, whence it had travelled via Shipley and the Guiseley line. But in motoring from Harrogate to Otley one gained a fine impression of the North Eastern lines making for Harrogate. The most spectacular feature of the landscape was the great Crimple Viaduct stretching right across the valley, and cutting under it at right angles on the south side was another very straight line. This was the one-time Leeds Northern which, to avoid heavy gradients that would have been needed to reach the high altitude of the centre of Harrogate, skirted the hills by going to the east, and located its 'Harrogate' station at Starbeck, about a mile away and at the foot of the hill. Thence the Leeds Northern went straight on to Ripon and Northallerton.

The line crossing the Crimple Viaduct was originally a branch from the York and North Midland Railway, constructed at about the same time as the Leeds Northern, and coming up from Wetherby on very heavy gradients of 1 in 86 from Spofforth and 1 in 91 across the viaduct itself. After the amalgamation of the various lines into the North Eastern Railway in 1854 the inconvenience of having two stations in Harrogate was eventually obviated by the construction of a short loop from the Leeds Northern whereby trains could swing round in a full right-angle, and climb over the viaduct into the high level station; and the line from this was extended down the hill to rejoin the old Leeds Northern line about

21. LOCOMOTIVES AROUND LEEDS

(a) A Class 'J' 7 ft. 7 in. single wheeler, No. 1522; the first engine on which the author rode on the footplate.
(b) A Class 'Q' 7 ft. 4-4-0 No. 1902, distinguished from all other N.E.R. locomotives by the clerestory-roofed cab.
(c) L.&.Y.R. One of Aspinall's original 2-4-2 tanks built 1895, still in service 1950.

$1\frac{1}{2}$ miles to the north. It was a fascinating sight to watch trains making their way slowly round the curving link between the two lines to Crimple Junction and then puff up the steep gradient over the viaduct. There were two alternative ways from Leeds to Harrogate. The longer one, and the most awkwardly graded was via Wetherby, and this formed part of a direct line from Harrogate to London. In pre-war years the Great Northern operated a through express to Harrogate via this route, while in the grouping era the L.N.E.R. for a time had a non-stop Pullman train between Harrogate and King's Cross. It was on this that engines of Great Central design first made their appearance in Harrogate, and were serviced overnight at the North Eastern sheds at Starbeck.

The shorter route from Leeds to Harrogate was that of the Leeds Northern, and it was one of particular interest to me for its inclusion, en route, of the great Bramhope Tunnel. How much men of my generation are indebted for their railway education to those coloured picture postcards of the Locomotive Publishing Company! Long before my family moved north I had a picture of one of the huge North Eastern 'R1' class 4-4-0s emerging from Bramhope Tunnel; but although I saw its approaches on those motor-car journeys to Otley, it was not until I was spending part of the holidays with some school friends in Leeds that I cycled to Arthington Junction, and defying all warnings about trespassing made my way along the cutting sides to the actual tunnel entrance. What a splendid façade it is, with its finely proportioned castellated towers. One saw various types of North Eastern 4-4-0 on the through trains from Leeds to West Hartlepool, but the engines that most took my fancy then were the very handsome 3-cylinder 4-4-4 tanks used on the faster trains that terminated at Harrogate.

To see North Eastern motive power in its full variety however one needed to go no farther than the platforms of the 'New' station. There were four classes of 4-4-0, obviously of the same 'family', but progressively larger in size the designations of which could conveniently be read on the buffer beam—'F', 'G', 'M' and 'Q'. They were most graceful engines, always spotless in their pale green livery. Between them they worked the bulk of the North Eastern longer-distance passenger trains from Leeds. One saw occasionally too the larger 4-4-0s of Class 'R', which although dating from 1899 had mostly been improved greatly in performance by the addition of superheaters. The North Eastern Railway had made it a point of policy to apply superheating to a large number of its older engines, and by the time I saw them, from 1918 onwards, practically all the earlier 4-4-0s of Classes 'F', 'G', 'M' and 'Q' had been so equipped. To my disappointment I never in those years saw one of the huge 'super' 4-4-0s of the 'R1' class. That picture postcard of Bramhope Tunnel had fired my imagination! But if I had known it one of them regularly worked the morning Leeds–Glasgow express as far as Newcastle. I was never about at the time to see this train, or the corresponding return service which came into Leeds late in the evening. Two engine classes which had perhaps a greater appeal than any others, among those of the North Eastern working into Leeds were the celebrated 'Tennant' 2-4-0s, and the 7 ft. 7 in. 4-2-2 'singles' of Class 'J'. I cannot say I ever saw one of the latter engines in Leeds itself, but they were familiar sights in the East Riding, as I shall relate in some detail in the next chapter. Before World War I however the 'J' class had a very special function on the railways of Leeds.

I have referred to the special businessmen's trains run from the great cities of the north to popular seaside residential towns; well, the North Eastern certainly played this traffic card for all it was worth, running fast evening expresses from Leeds to both Bridlington and to Scarborough, and also from Sheffield to Bridlington. The loads of these trains were not heavy, but the scheduled speeds were high, and they were an ideal haulage proposition for a single-wheeler. The 'J' class were among the most powerful of all British 'singles'; they had originally been built as two cylinder compounds, but before the end of the nineteenth century they had been rebuilt as two cylinder simples and fitted with W. M. Smith's patent piston valves. The Leeds to Bridlington train was booked to cover the $63\frac{1}{2}$ miles in 73 minutes, non-stop, an average speed of $52\frac{1}{4}$ m.p.h., while the Scarborough service involved running the $67\frac{1}{2}$ miles in 75 minutes. The loads were usually no more than three or four coaches, and those little engines fairly 'flew'. I will not enlarge upon their running at this stage because it was mainly performed in territory covered by my next chapter. Neither will I dilate upon the splendid little 'Tennant' 2-4-os, which at the time of which I am writing were essentially East Riding engines. Still within my ken they certainly worked frequently into Leeds.

Turning now to happenings at the Central station, although there was a direct connection into this terminus from the Leeds Northern Line I am not aware of regular North Eastern passenger train workings. The station itself was the joint property of four companies, for in addition to the two regular users—the Great Northern and the Lancashire and Yorkshire— the North Eastern and the London and North Western were also part owners. The Lancashire and Yorkshire ran a cross-country service to Manchester and Liverpool passing through Halifax and making connections from Bradford at Low Moor. These trains were usually worked by the Aspinall inside-cylindered 'Atlantics' which, with their coupled wheels of no less than 7 ft. 3 in. diameter, always seemed to me to be most unsuitable engines for a line with such heavy gradients. Almost off the platform end from Leeds Central the gradient was 1 in 100, and after half a mile it changed to 1 in 50. However these engines worked on the line for many years, reinforced by the equally elegant 7 ft. 3 in. 4-4-os. Some of the local trains were hauled by 2-4-2 tank engines, but at the time of my observations the Lancashire and Yorkshire was not one of the most favoured among the railways of Leeds.

My first visit to Leeds Central was not for the purpose of travelling at all. During my school days I had to go into Leeds to have my appendix removed, and when I was getting reasonably mobile again the stations were near enough to the nursing home for me to do an occasional spell of train-spotting. I went to the Central to try and see something of the Great Northern. I had read that before the war the famous Ivatt 'Atlantics' worked on the fast London expresses, and particularly the evening 'flyer' which ran non-stop from Wakefield to King's Cross. But during the war the locomotive workings had been changed, and the London expresses all changed engines at Doncaster. This meant that the 'Atlantics' were no longer working into Leeds. The most familiar engines were a class of tall super-heater 4-4-0s, which somehow never gained a place among my top favourite locomotives. I have always thought it strange that the Doncaster drawing office which, under Patrick Stirling's guidance, produced such beautiful designs of 2-4-0, 2-2-2, and 4-2-2, and which built such a combination of mechanical efficiency and elegant proportion into the Ivatt 'Atlantics' should have made such a poor job, aesthetically at any rate, of the 4-4-0s con-structed during Ivatt's time. There is, however, little doubt that Ivatt never intended the 4-4-0 to be a standard express locomotive type for the line, in the same way that the London and North Western, and Midland Railways relied upon it. He succeeded Patrick Stirling in 1896, and before two years were out he had the first-ever British 'Atlantic' on the road. The 4-4-0s seem to have been produced as stop-gaps, and some of them rather looked like it! This is not to say that they could not do good work. The big superheater versions were put on occasionally to deputise for 'Atlantics' on the main line expresses north of Grantham, and they produced many an excellent run. It is certainly true that the scheduled speeds were not very high, even in pre-war days; but that was not because of any inability of the locomotives to keep time. The superheater 4-4-0s of the '56' class, which were the first Great Northern express passenger engines I ever saw, had all the characteristic Doncaster details of design in the Ivatt era: built-up chimney, large dome, the Ramsbottom safety valves encased in a very neat and small mounting, and the short open-sided cab. While on the large-boilered 'Atlantics' these features were blended into a beautifully homogenous effect, on the '56s', with the chimney and dome made taller they looked a mere agglomera-tion. The effect was made worse by the raising of the running plate high above the driving wheel bosses.

Another class of locomotive which then worked into Leeds on passenger trains was the large-boilered Gresley two-cylinder 'Mogul', of the '1640' class. During the war, while the standard green livery was maintained on purely passenger engines, including the suburban tanks, the goods engines were finished in dark grey, with the letters and numbering in white, lined in black. The '1640' class Moguls, later so well-known as L.N.E.R. Class 'K2' were not frequent sights in those days; but they used to work into Leeds from Doncaster on some of the London expresses. Although so plain in their grey livery, compared to the very fine style of the passenger engines, they were most impressive machines. It is remark-able to recall that they were one of only two classes of locomotive then working into Leeds having outside Walschaerts valve gear. All the Midland engines had inside gear, and the North Eastern without exception used the Stephenson's link motion. The only other 'Walschaerts' engines then coming regularly into Leeds were the London and North Western 4-cylinder 4-6-0s of the 'Claughton' class, the workings of which I will describe later. In view of the almost universal employment of outside Walschaerts gear in the latter days of steam traction on British Railways, in the north country at any rate, the very sparse extent of its early penetration is remarkable.

The Lancashire and Yorkshire presence at Leeds Central, exercising running powers over the Great Northern for the last $9\frac{1}{2}$ miles from Bowling Junction, needs some further comment. One of the most important constituents in the early railway merger that formed the L. & Y.R. was the Manchester and Leeds. It was one of George Stephenson's lines, and he could be relied upon to find an easy route, if there was one. Now Leeds is fairly encompassed by hills, and although he was planning a finely graded line down the valley of the Calder, from Todmorden, through Mytholmroyd to Mirfield, there was some very hilly country on the direct line to Leeds. Stephenson had already built the North Midland Railway coming up from Derby, through Chesterfield, and curving into Leeds from a south-south-easterly direction on a practically level track. If instead of heading direct for Leeds over the hills from Mirfield the line from Manchester was continued down the valley, not only would it put Wakefield on this new main line, but it could end in a junction with the North Midland at Normanton, and reach Leeds by the exercise of running powers. So the eastern end of the 'Manchester and Leeds' was at the picturesquely named Goose Hill Junction, where it joined the North Midland just to the south of Normanton. While this line became heavily used in the traffic expansions of the Lancashire and Yorkshire, in the direct access it gave towards York and Hull, it was inconveniently roundabout for Leeds itself; so when the branch line through Halifax to Bradford was constructed, running powers over the Great Northern into Leeds were readily arranged.

There was every reason for the Lancashire and Yorkshire to shorten its route from Leeds to Manchester, because from quite early days it was in competition with the London and North Western; and having mentioned that giant among English railways it is time to return to the New Station to view some of its activities. It was not only in respect of the Leeds–Manchester service that the Lancashire and Yorkshire and the North Western were in competition. Both were in partnership with the North Eastern in running a through express service between Liverpool and Newcastle. The North Western trains from the west came through Leeds, where they changed engines; but on the rival route they skirted Leeds altogether, and travelling via Wakefield the L. & Y.R. engines went through to York. The North Western had a very difficult run of 43 miles between Leeds and Manchester. True to the general geography of the area trains leaving Leeds were immediately involved in hard climbing up to Morley, beyond which the high ridge between the Aire and Calder valleys was pierced by the two-mile long Morley Tunnel. This, incidentally, had one of the most distinctive entrances to be seen anywhere in the country. There was no classic, or castellated façade; the massive profile of the elliptical arch of the tunnel was extended outwards from the face of the hillside, and smoke-blackened from the locomotive exhausts in countless decades of heavy traffic it looked positively awesome in the bleak surroundings.

This line of the North Western intersected the old Manchester and Leeds main line for 3 miles at Mirfield, where running powers were exercised over the L. & Y.R. But that intersection became something of an embarrassment to both companies, and to avoid Mirfield, and keep important through traffic clear of the teeming West Riding towns of Dewsbury, Batley, and Morley, and their local business, the North Western built a new line, on still heavier gradients, going through Heckmondwike and Cleckheaton, and climbing on gradients of 1 in 77 and 1 in 80 to a summit point at Birstall. Thence came the worst of all descents into Leeds, continuously at 1 in 70 for $3\frac{1}{2}$ miles, through the $1\frac{1}{2}$ miles of Gildersome Tunnel. Gradients or not, however, this became the principal express route for those cross-country trains of the L.N.W.R. that did not stop between Huddersfield and Leeds. It was certainly a mighty pull for North Western engines taking on the heavy Newcastle–Liverpool restaurant car expresses at Leeds, and being faced with this incline, all within the first seven miles of a 'cold' start! Use of the Cleckheaton line lengthened the overall distance from Leeds to Manchester by $1\frac{1}{2}$ miles, and despite gradients—and there were far longer ones beyond Huddersfield—it was not unusual to do the $44\frac{1}{2}$ miles between Leeds (New) and Manchester (Exchange) in the level hour.

When I did my first train-watching at Leeds the principal North Western express engines on the job were the inside-cylinder superheater 4-6-os of the 'Prince of Wales' class: extremely competent engines in any kind of service, but ideal for dealing with banks like those between Leeds and Heckmondwike. One saw also those wonderful superheater 4-4-os of the 'George the Fifth' class, the work of which I have extolled in chapter five, while on the lighter trains the non-superheater 'Precursor' class 4-4-os, and the 4-6-o 'Experiments' were familiar sights. In somewhat earlier days, before the time of my personal observation but within the period of this book the Webb 4-cylinder compound 4-4-os of both the 'Jubilee' and 'Alfred the Great' classes worked into Leeds. Although sluggish engines on a fast run, as between Euston and Crewe, they had plenty of strength for a bank, and found a niche in these severe conditions for several years. At one time there were a few duties on which London and North Western engines went beyond Leeds, and handed over the through trains to the North Eastern at York; but this practice had ceased when I made my own first observations. At Leeds, of course, North Western engines had an added attraction, in that they were, at that time, the only named engines entering the city.

One of the most interesting North Western locomotive workings into Leeds in the years at the end of World War I concerned certain 4-cylinder 4-6-os of the 'Claughton' class. The excellent performance and immaculate condition of most locomotives in the pre-grouping era is often attributed to their having their own regular crews, who had opportunities for taking personal pride in the machines they consistently worked. The details of 'Claughton' working into Leeds around 1920 provides striking evidence that this state of affairs did not always exist, even among crack locomotives and crews. At that time there were 60 engines of this class, and two of them, No. 250 *J. A. Bright*, and No. 2042, then unnamed, were allocated to the Manchester shed Longsight, a depot entrusted with the running of many of the principal Manchester and London expresses. But these two engines were put on to a very different kind of duty, which involved their being away from their home shed for 24 hours. The two engines worked this particular round on alternate days. This is what was involved.

The first engine left Manchester in the late evening, and worked to Crewe. There it was turned, and took on the 12.30 a.m. night mail through to Leeds, via Stalybridge and Huddersfield. Then the Longsight men booked off and lodged. At 10.30 a.m. next morning, in charge of Farnley (Leeds) men it took an express to Liverpool, and returned to Leeds on the 2.40 p.m. Newcastle express, working as far as Leeds. There the Farnley men booked off after running this Manchester engine 77 miles each way across country. Finally at 10.40 p.m., just as the second engine of the pair was starting out from Manchester, the first engine took the 10.40 p.m. night mail from Leeds to Crewe. It returned from Crewe to Manchester with an early morning local train. The night's work totalled up to 100 miles, so that the total round amounted to 350 miles. But the important thing to appreciate was that these two engines were on the job week-in, week-out, and far from having regular crews they were run, in turn, by every driver and fireman in the top link, not only at their home shed, Longsight, but also at Farnley. It is true it was a prestige job, and at that time it was the only duty at either shed that was allocated to a 'Claughton'; but even so, those two engines were very much 'common user' units, in respect of their manning, if not their duties. When I travelled from Leeds to Crewe by the night mail some seven years later it was still a Longsight 'Claughton' job.

The engine sheds around Leeds were not in very favourable places for an onlooker to see what was going on. The North Western, at Farnley, were nearly two miles out near the junction of the Morley and Cleckheaton lines. The Midland were the most visible, from the main line to London, and better still from North Western trains coming in on the Viaduct line, which crossed the Midland in full view of the sheds. The Great Northern sheds were at Copley Hill—perhaps the most inaccessible of them all. The North Eastern depot for both locomotives and carriages was located well out of the city at Neville Hill Junction, $1\frac{1}{2}$ miles east of the New Station on the line to York and Hull. What a massed parade of locomotives those four sheds could have mustered between them. I have mentioned only passenger engines, but one has only to look at the map of the district, and see the multiplicity of goods stations to appreciate something of the traffic that then flowed into and out of Leeds by railway: Cardigan Road; Whitehall Road; Wellington N.E. Goods; the Great Northern, and the L.N.W. and L.Y. joint at Central station; Hunslet Lane, and Balin Lane, on the Midland; and the Great Northern and North Eastern stations in Hunslet, with their exchange sidings. Those were great days for train watchers. How much more closely we would have watched, and how much more detailed would have been our note taking if we had then realized how soon it would all begin to disappear!

CHAPTER TEN

East and North Riding

FOR SEVERAL YEARS after World War I Leeds New Station was the gateway to our summer holiday haunts. It is true that we had to travel half across England to get there; but the Furness Railway was then home country, and the Midland eastwards from Carnforth savoured too much of school. But when we crossed from Wellington into the New station at Leeds it was like casting off the shackles of duty; and the railway lines that led to the various resorts on the Yorkshire coast were then a positive Valhalla for the locomotive historian. I must confess that in those days I would like to have seen more of the really big engines of the North Eastern Railway; but I photographed everything that was to be seen on the line at Bridlington, Scarborough and Whitby, and although the quality of those old 'snaps' left practically everything to be desired in their clarity, I kept most of them and today they can certainly tell a tale. At Bridlington a remote cart track led to the lineside at the sheds, and in those far off days a camera—albeit only a 'Box Brownie'—was as good as a shed pass to those friendly enginemen, and their fatherly old foreman; and I had not been there long, before I was over the fence, and given the freedom of the yard.

My very first journey on a coast-bound train from Leeds set the standard. It was a Saturday in August, and with the luggage for a month's stay we piled into the Bridlington train where we could, into a North Eastern non-corridor clerestory carriage. With vast numbers of people milling around, having got seats we had perforce to stay put. There was no going up to the front to see what kind of engine we had on. I cannot say I remember much of the actual journey. It was a hot, drowsy afternoon, and my main recollections are of a rather jogging motion of the carriage, and of going very fast at times, and very slowly at others. Not until we reached Bridlington did I discover to my great surprise, that our engine had been one of the little 'Tennant' 2-4-0s. This certainly prepared me for the profusion of 'middle aged' passenger engines that formed the mainstay of the North Eastern in the East Riding. We had actually travelled over a route of much historic interest, which like many through lines of the pre-grouping era had been built up piecemeal. The first stretch, the 21 miles of the 'Leeds and Selby' was one of the oldest railways in the country, and was actually opened to traffic in 1834; but until 1890 there was no through continuation to Bridlington. One had to travel on from Selby to Hull, change there and continue northwards up the 'branch' through Beverley and Driffield. This was another very early line, having been built in the height of the 'Railway Mania', and opened in October 1846.

The network of lines projected and built during this time, when George Hudson was at the zenith of his power and prestige was remarkably comprehensive. But one link in the direct line remained open for many years. The 'Hudson' expansions had pushed the line over the level country eastwards from Selby to Market Weighton, but there remained the high ridge of the Wolds between this railhead and the Hull and Bridlington branch; and by tradition the recognized way to Bridlington was via Hull—at least by members of the older generation of travellers. I remember vividly how the first post-war family holiday was proposed, in Bridlington. My father knew the local manager of a very well-known firm of travel agents, and one day he came home to tell of the rather complicated route we had to take, via Hull! At that stage in my historical railway reading I was quite unaware of the past history of this group of lines, and the idea of going via Hull had never occurred to me. A little digging into timetables revealed the welcome fact that there were through trains from Leeds, and we did in fact journey from Barrow-in-Furness to Bridlington with only one change of carriage. The last link in our route, from Market Weighton on to Driffield, was originally known as the 'Scarborough, Bridlington and West Riding Junction Railway'— one of those high sounding titles that expressed the function rather than the geographical extent of a railway. This line was barely fourteen miles long, and it touched neither Bridlington nor Scarborough, still less the West Riding! It was opened in 1890, and worked from the outset by the North Eastern.

It was no wonder that little 2-4-0 of ours went slowly at times, for immediately after leaving Market Weighton the line climbs for nearly four miles at 1 in 95–100 to the crest of the Wolds, at Enthorpe. Then we went bucketing downhill to that finely named station, Middleton-on-the-Wolds. There is a good story about Middleton to be told when I come to a still more rural line in these parts—the one from Driffield to Malton. At Driffield one is down to level country once more, and the railway there was once a four-way junction like Market Weighton. The line coming up from Beverley and Hull was much busier than the cross-country 'link' we had traversed from Selby, and at that time Bridlington was a passenger, goods, and locomotive station of considerable importance. The station itself was confusing to my parents, but to me, of course, it was the running sheds that mattered, and I have already told how I found them.

At that time there were no fewer than six varieties of vintage express passenger loco-motives working into Bridlington. Four of these were of the classic Worsdell 4-4-0 'family'; with variations of coupled wheel diameter, cylinder and boiler capacity, but all unmistakably of the same breed. The 'F' class had started life as two-cylinder compounds on the Worsdell–von Borries system, and the 'G' class, the 'Waterbury's' were originally 2-4-0s. The magnificent 'M' class, which so distinguished themselves in the Race to the North in

1895, originally had outside steam chests, while the 'Qs' could always be distinguished by the clerestory roofs to their cabs. When I knew them they had all been modernized by the addition of superheaters, and provided an outstanding example of the equipping of relatively small, and otherwise obsolescent engines to prolong their useful life. These four classes were indeed the mainstay of the passenger service in the East Riding at that time. For ready reference the basic dimensions of those four classes are tabulated.

N.E.R. THE OLDER 4-4-0S

Class	F	G	M	Q
Cylinders				
dia.	18 in.	18 in.	19 in.	19 in.
stroke	24 in.	24 in.	26 in.	26 in.
Piston valve *dia.*	$7\frac{1}{2}$ in.	$7\frac{1}{2}$ in.	$8\frac{3}{4}$ in.	$8\frac{3}{4}$ in.
Heating surfaces				
tubes	795 sq. ft.	728 sq. ft.	775·4 sq. ft.	775·4 sq. ft.
firebox	112 sq. ft.	98 sq. ft.	123 sq. ft.	123 sq. ft.
superheater	263 sq. ft.	270 sq. ft.	288 sq. ft.	288 sq. ft.
Grate area	17 sq. ft.	15·16 sq. ft.	19·8 sq. ft.	19·8 sq. ft.
Coupled wheel				
dia.	6 ft. 8 in.	6 ft. 0 in.	7 ft. 1 in.	7 ft. 1 in.

As superheater-equipped Classes 'M' and 'Q' were virtually identical, but in their original form the 'Q' class had slightly larger cylinders.

Technicalities and dimensions apart, the entire family were most stately, and beautifully kept engines. The North Eastern had not found it necessary to simplify, or make austere its pre-war locomotive livery, and that rather pale 'leaf green', with its smart black and white lining, red line on the running plate valance, and its fine coat of arms on the tenders looked splendid. The large brass casings over the safety valves were always well polished, and no less so were the cast number plates carried in the middle of the driving wheel splashers. Although it did not need much experience to distinguish the four constituents of this 4-4-0 family things were made easier for the beginner because the class was painted in small white letters beneath the number on the buffer beam. With that collector's urge that persists in so many of us I naturally began to try and fill in the gaps in the entire alphabet of North Eastern locomotive classes. There were no published registers of such things on the majority of railways at that time. Only the Great Western had an official list on sale, although there was the monumental work of C. Williams, at Crewe, to delight supporters of the L.N.W.R. But it was great fun attempting to compile the N.E.R. classification from lineside 'spotting', and I returned home from that month in the East Riding with 15 out of the 26 letters 'in the bag'. The fact that there were variations and subdivisions of several classes did not matter. I found also that certain older classes, like the Tennant 2-4-0s were

22. NORTH EASTERN TRAINS

(a) One of the ponderous Class 'W' 4-6-2 tanks setting back on to a Whitby train at Scarborough.

(b) Scarborough to Liverpool Express, composed of L.N.W.R. stock near Chaloners Whin Junction, south of York, in 1913. Engine No. 1207 Class 'R'.

known by their numbers, and had no distinguishing letter; but this all added to the enjoyment of the game.

The 'Tennants' were delightful little engines. Jack Hill's exquisite painting of a shed scene at Bridlington in 1919, which shows one of them standing between an 'F' class 4-4-0, and one of the 'C' class 0-6-0 goods is based on one of my own photographs. They used to take turns on the Leeds stopping trains; but at a slightly earlier time there were some of the still older '901' class in the East Riding. These were the Fletcher 2-4-0s of 1871, modernized a little in their appearance by the fitting of boilers similar to those of the Tennants. Although they had coupled wheels as large as 7-ft. diameter they were able to put in a large amount of most useful branch line work. I never saw any of the '901' class myself around Bridlington. How I encountered one of them at Tebay in 1923 is another story. The Tennants differed from the traditional North Eastern style of locomotive lineament and finish by having cut-away cabs, after the style of Patrick Stirling on the Great Northern Railway, and having the initials N.E.R. on their tenders, instead of NORTH EASTERN, with the coat of arms between the words. But although protection from the weather was much more sparse than on engines of the 4-4-0 'family' the 'Tennants' were always great favourites with the men— but no less so than the '901' class. They were so essentially 'right' in all their mechanical features; they had a soft beat, they ran smoothly and fast, and although they could not be unduly hustled from a station start, once they were going they ran to some purpose.

In 1919 there was yet another express passenger class working regularly through Bridlington that holds a special place both in locomotive history and in my own personal memories. Very early in that family holiday we found our way along the cliff path that led out towards Flamborough Head, and equally soon I found that only a slight detour from that path led to a level crossing on the railway that continued north from Bridlington to Scarborough. The signalman there was as friendly as the men at the engine sheds, and he told me that a train would soon be coming 'up the bank'. Up the bank indeed, for immediately on leaving Bridlington the line climbs for $5\frac{1}{2}$ miles continuously at 1 in 92 to reach the high ground inland from Flamborough Head. It is, I think, significant of the way in which old engines were then taken for granted that I was not unduly surprised at what so soon came up the bank. It was a 'J' class 7 ft. 7 in. single-wheeler. She was labouring somewhat on the heavy gradient, and my photograph shows a train of five bogie coaches and a horsebox. I did not fully appreciate at the time what a 'scoop' I had secured. The engine was No. 1518, and was one of several working in the area in that summer, and one that I shall always particularly remember was No. 1522. But before indulging in any personal reminiscences however, I must relate the very interesting history of the class.

It was in 1886 that T. W. Worsdell built his first two-cylinder compound passenger engine for the North Eastern Railway. It was a 2-4-0, but in the following year he developed this design into his first standard express type, the 'F' class 4-4-0. Three years later in anticipation of the opening of the Forth Bridge, and of heavier traffic to Scotland he built the 'J' class of single-wheelers, also as compounds, and these engines at once displayed a remarkable capacity for weight pulling, and high speed. The first engine of the class attained a speed of 90 m.p.h. shortly after her construction, and the second one, that which I photographed near Flamborough in 1919, gave some quite outstanding outputs of power during trials conducted between Newcastle and Berwick. These engines did not remain long as compounds, and in 1895 they were converted to simple engines, with W. M. Smith's patent piston valves, and direct drive Stephenson link motion. While they had originally been brilliant performers as compounds the complication of certain features of design had led to running troubles, and as converted in 1895 they were restored to much of their excellence, but at the same time becoming far more reliable on general service. It was in this condition that they were running in 1919. In the previous chapter I referred to the fast evening trains from Leeds to the coastal resorts, before World War I. The 'J' class engines were regularly used on these services, and some interesting records have been preserved.

Engine No. 1524 had the 4.47 p.m. to Bridlington, with a four-coach train weighing 105 tons. She got a bad road as far as Selby, being twice heavily checked by adverse signals, and taking $27\frac{3}{4}$ minutes to cover the first 20·7 miles. Then she got going, and on the level towards Market Weighton got up to 65 m.p.h. She had to slow drastically over the junction at Market Weighton, to 25 m.p.h. and thus got a bad start to the ascent over the Wolds; but on the stiff climb to Enthorpe the little engine accelerated to 42 m.p.h. and then went galloping down to Driffield at 72 m.p.h., only to be stopped by signal just beyond. But for this, time would have been kept, despite the initial hindrances, and the 63·4 miles from Leeds into Bridlington were completed in $75\frac{3}{4}$ minutes, $2\frac{3}{4}$ minutes late. The details of this pre-war journey however, show that it was not so illogical as might be imagined to use 4-2-2 engines, with 7 ft. 7 in. driving wheels on the kind of duties I saw. An engine that can take a four-coach non-corridor train up a bank of 1 in 92–100 at 42 m.p.h. was an excellent general service unit for light secondary trains. And then there was No. 1522. One day when I was at the shed she came in, to turn, water, and prepare for another trip; and once again that 'Box-Brownie' did the trick. I was invited to climb up, and ride round the yard while the various duties were performed, and so No. 1522 became the first locomotive on which I rode on the footplate—not a very long or fast ride, but it was a beginning! That year was almost the end of the career of those fine little engines. By the end of 1920 they had all been scrapped. But on reflection, what a galaxy of North Eastern locomotive history the Bridlington yard presented in those years immediately after the war.

Continuing north over the hilly road to Scarborough one came among an even greater variety of locomotives, both more powerful, and some even more ancient, than the 'regulars' at Bridlington. It was at Scarborough that I first saw one of the big 'R1' class 4-4-0s. There has often been speculation among students of locomotive history as to why Wilson Worsdell reverted to the 4-4-0 type in 1908 after having built very large 'Atlantics'. There was no question of building 4-4-0s for secondary services. For upwards of two years the ten engines of the 'R1' class monopolized the principal Anglo-Scottish trains between York and Edinburgh, and it was the 'Atlantics' that moved 'one down' as it were. There is no doubt that the first batch of 'Atlantics' did not come fully up to expectations, and although the two four-cylinder compounds built on W. M. Smith's system were extremely good engines,

Worsdell seemed disinclined to incur the additional expense of their construction for a standard type. Apart from these two, the most successful North Eastern express locomotives so far had been the 'R' class 4-4-os, a very powerful development of the 'family' so much in evidence at Bridlington; and one can sense that Worsdell felt that a further enlargement would amply pay off. It certainly did. The 'R1' class was designed for hard work with heavy trains, and they immediately showed an ability to lift a big load cleanly off the mark, and get rapidly up to 60 or 65 m.p.h. No more was then needed. At first they were not super-heated, and had the high boiler pressure of 225 lb. per sq. in.; this was reduced to 180, when they were superheated in the time of Vincent Raven as chief mechanical engineer.

Again, however, one could well be inclined to cast technicalities to one side in recalling the 'look' of these most impressive engines. If they were set alongside the largest and most powerful British 4-4-os of the day—a North Western 'George the Fifth', a Midland com-pound, and a Caledonian 'Dunalastair' of the fifth or superheated series—I do not think there is much doubt which would 'win' on the score of sheer grandeur of appearance. An outline drawing would go some way towards making the choice, even before one had viewed their respective colours; but then add the beautiful 'leaf-green' livery, with all its embellishments, two forms of the N.E.R. coat of arms—one on the leading wheel splasher and one on the tender—and to crown all that huge brass casing around the safety valves, and one is inclined to think that North Western 'Blackberry black', Midland 'lake', and even Caledonian blue would drop into subsidiary places! By the year 1916, when I did my first 'spotting' on the North Eastern the 'R1s' had been displaced from the principal Anglo-Scottish workings; but those stationed at Leeds worked into Scarborough, as well as to Newcastle, and great sights they were in the fine countryside of the East Riding.

Scarborough could be an exciting place for all railway enthusiasts, especially when excursions from other railways worked right through with their own engines. The Great Central, in particular, seemed to specialize in this kind of operation, and one recalls the memorable occasion when a trip was worked from Manchester to Plymouth, with one engine. One day when the family made a day excursion from Bridlington to Scarborough we arrived to find an excursion from the Great Central had come in just ahead of us. The coaches were an assorted lot, but at its head was one of the supremely beautiful Robinson 'Atlantics'—a 'Jersey Lily'—in all the glory of the Great Central turn-out. I obtained

23. N.E.R. LOCOMOTIVE DEVELOPMENT

(a) No. 1269: an engine with a history! Originally one of Bouch's freakish 'Ginx's Babies', 4-4-os of 1871. Was first one of class to be rebuilt as a conventional 2-4-0 in 1874, and then did more than forty years main line work in condition shown.
(b) The Raven 3-cylinder 4-4-4 express tank engine of 1913, used on the Leeds–Harrogate fast trains.
(c) The very successful 3-cylinder 'Z' class express passenger 'Atlantic' engine, first introduced in 1911, of which there were eventually fifty.

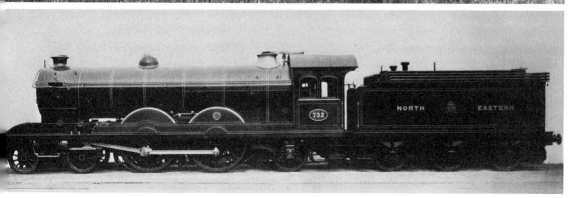

parental leave, rather grudgingly I recall, to take an earlier train as far as Seamer Junction, where the coastal railway diverges from the main line to York, and get some snaps, and sure enough I successfully 'copped' the 'Jersey Lily' on her return journey. But this is primarily a chapter about North Eastern engines and I must not dilate upon this, my very first encounter with 'The Amazing Great Central!' But before actually leaving Scarborough another interesting feature of the contemporary scene must be mentioned. At Bridlington there was, in my days of observation, a complete absence of tank engines. I had seen many North Eastern types around Leeds, but to Scarborough came the 'Whitby tanks', rather large and ponderous 4-6-2s of Class 'W' that had not enjoyed the best of reputations in their early days. I snapped one of them on my way to Seamer Junction on that evening, but through sheer bewilderment missed the supreme photographic opportunity of the trip.

The station platforms were ideal for photography. The sky was clear, and the evening sunshine almost broadside to the line, and I had great hopes of getting a really big engine on the down through express from King's Cross. The signals were eventually pulled off and I steadied the camera on a seat, for my hands were trembling with excitement. But as the train came into sight I began to stare with unbelieving astonishment at the oncoming engine. It was not an 'Atlantic', nor an 'R1'—not even one of the 4-4-0 'family' becoming so familiar to me at Bridlington. It was something far quainter to my eyes, and in a fit of boyish disgust I put the camera aside as the four-coach corridor express swept through. And so I missed a McDonnell 4-4-0, and failed even to note its number. At that time I had not yet read of the intensely human story and the embittered labour relations that surrounded the introduction of those engines at Gateshead in 1884. The engine I let pass in 1920 was one of only four that then remained of the class of 28. In my earlier book *Steam Railways in Retrospect* I have told something of the unhappy McDonnell interlude at Gateshead.

Travelling to Whitby was something of an adventure in those days. Again Leeds New Station was our point of entry to the North Eastern, and again force of circumstances compelled a Saturday journey. Until a certain occasion during World War II I think I can only recall one journey in so crowded a train. We managed to get four seats, and near a window too; but in that non-corridor carriage we managed to wedge six people aside, and have another four or five sitting on suit-cases in between our knees. The train seemed to stop everywhere! And at York many more carriages were added. Peering from the window I had noticed that the engine was an 'F' class 4-4-0, and with that load we were not making very rapid progress. I have little recollection of anything interesting seen at York that day— only masses upon masses of people, and a very slow start, as our elderly engine slipped repeatedly in trying to get its big load under way over the series of diamond crossings at the north end of the station. We had travelled across country from Barrow, and with the excessive crowding after Leeds even I was beginning to get tired of railway travelling. Furthermore, the weather was bad and in continuous rain the country did not look its best. Even so nothing could dim the beauty of that winding stretch in the deep valley of the Derwent, past Kirkham Abbey and Castle Howard, and I recall how, in the wet humid air the exhaust steam from the engine hung behind us in a long motionless trail above the track, round those curves. So we came to Malton, where there was a lengthy stop.

It was many years later that I travelled over the cross-country branch line from Driffield, but the recollection of that trip in an inspection saloon from Hull, leads me on to the colourful subject of the splendid railwaymen who used to work these deeply rural lines. They were, and still are a rare mixture. I have already written of Leeds engines working to Scarborough. Equally many of the enginemen, guards, and other railway staff came from families that had lived for generation after generation in the countryside and included many who had been in the service of the landed gentry. The gulf that still exists between the attitudes to the countryside of these two types of railwaymen was most amusingly brought out in an incident that occurred on the main line between Malton and York. It was told by a friend who at one time held very high office on the railway at York, but who has now retired. Well, they were bowling along one snowy morning when suddenly there was a bang; all the brakes went on, and feathers came in through the heating and ventilating louvres. They all got down, and gathered round the engine. A pheasant, in the suicidal way pheasants have, had flown across the track just as the train was at hand, and had been hit by the stand-pipe of the brake hose. The driver was a Leeds man, and didn't mince his words or his dialect: 'Bluidy bird put bluidy bra-a-ke on and we're stopped!' But the guard—a 'feudal' gentleman from Malton—looked at the feathers, and then said: 'Eeh, do you know what you've been and gone and done, that's one of Lord Middleton's pheasants you've been and gone and killed!'

I have been a long time in leaving this 'feudal' country, on our marathon journey to Whitby, and by this time we had collected a second engine to help in the long climb over the moors of the North Riding. The pilot was an 0-4-4 tank engine, of Class 'O', the regular local passenger type on the line between Malton and Whitby, as I found to my disappointment later. We wound our way over those rain-swept moors and came down precipitous gradients into the valley of the Esk, and so eventually, into the cramped little terminal station by the riverside in Whitby. The arrival platform, as I remember it, was just about long enough to take an 'O' class tank and a four-coach train. The scene just after our arrival can be better imagined than described. With two engines, and a tender engine into the bargain, only about two-and-a-half coaches got berthed alongside the platform. The rest of that long train was outside; and remembering how packed it was and how impatient we all were to get to the end of that tedious journey no one stood upon ceremony. Doors were flung open and passengers jumped down on to the track in their hundreds. There was a low retaining wall beside the arrival line, and it seemed that a goodly proportion of the population of Whitby was lined along that wall watching the fun. The rain had ceased, but pools of water lay everywhere, and I remember my parents' horror when our own massive trunk—for a month's stay—was unloaded into one of the deepest of these pools!

As a railway centre at that time in history Whitby was disappointing in its striking lack of variety of locomotives in use. There was a time, as the camera of Dr. T. F. Budden has so brilliantly recorded, when all shapes and sizes of North Eastern tender and tank locomotives jostled each other in its confined yards, but it was very different just after the war. There seemed to be only one passenger train in the day that was hauled by a tender engine; that arrived about tea-time, and the engine turned, and went southwards soon afterwards. I was old enough then to have a walking permit, on the track; but I tramped around to little purpose, except for one day. I was walking rather disconsolately back to the station when I was hailed by the crew of a nondescript-looking 0-6-0 goods engine. They were a friendly and enthusiastic pair, and more to please them than anything else I photographed their engine. The intricacies of North Eastern locomotive history took some mastering, and at that early stage in my studies 'Class 1001' on the buffer beam meant, I am afraid, nothing to me. But I had, that day, made some amends for letting that McDonnell 4-4-0 pass me at Seamer Junction. Engine No. 1275 which I had photographed at Whitby was one of the very celebrated Stephenson long-boiler type, and had been built for the Stockton and Darlington Railway in 1874. She was historic enough to be restored to her original condition to run in the magnificent pageant of locomotives at the Railway Centenary celebrations in 1925, and today she reposes in all her original glory in the Railway Museum at York.

If this line from Malton was lacking in locomotive variety so equally was the coast line, which came up from Scarborough over a succession of fearsome gradients and equally hair-raising curves. It crossed the deep valley of the Esk just outside Whitby Town station, on a lofty viaduct and trains on the Scarborough–Saltburn service used a different station, Whitby West Cliff. With one exception, all trains on the coastal route were hauled by the Class 'W' 4-6-2 tanks. Compared to the beauty of line and elegant finish of other North Eastern passenger classes they always seemed to me rather dull engines. They looked grubby, and no one seemed to care for them. They started life in 1907, as 4-6-0s. Wilson Worsdell somewhat naturally wanted maximum adhesion for climbing those gradients, which included one holy terror of a bank between Fyling Hall and Ravenscar, of 1 in 37 for over three miles. But it was found that their small coal bunkers carried insufficient fuel for a through trip, and in enlarging the bunker it was found necessary to add a pair of carrying wheels at the rear end. I used to see them threshing their laborious way up the banks with trains of four or five flat-roofed bogie coaches, and I was not surprised when one of the drivers remarked that they were 'more like dredgers than engines'.

On the last of my pre-grouping visits to Whitby there was an afternoon train from the north that was worked by Darlington shed, and one of the new 3-cylinder 4-4-4 tanks of Class 'D' was usually on that job. She came off the train at Whitby West Cliff, and returned about an hour later. These were most imposing engines, and the men loved them, because they were so free and smooth running after the 'W' 'dredgers'. One might question whether the 4-4-4 was an ideal wheel arrangement for such a difficult route; but the loads were not heavy and these new engines hauled them competently enough. With my walking permit I had ample opportunity to walk round and photograph them while they were waiting the return working at Whitby West Cliff. Nearly forty years later I met them again when I was doing some footplate work from Scarborough; but by that time they had all been converted from 4-4-4s into 4-6-2s, without, I may add, any diminution in their freedom and smooth running. That, however, is not a story of pre-grouping days.

After our gruelling experience of Saturday travel en route to Whitby the family decided to forego one day of the holiday and return on a Friday. There were two minor disasters on the way, but both were no more than indirectly connected with railways, and the main thing about the journey from Whitby to Leeds, on the North Eastern, was the excellent opportunity it gave for observing a little of the working at York. Our train connected with the up 'Flying Scotsman', and while standing at the platform we had a fine view of her sweeping round the curve from Clifton Junction, rattling over the crossings at the north end, and running in to stop at the south end. The engine was one of the beautiful 3-cylinder 'Atlantics' of Class 'Z' and at the far end of the station I could see a Great Northern 'Atlantic' waiting to take over. York vied with Carlisle in the number of different railways that worked in. Both tied, in having the locomotives of six major railways; and while Carlisle had one extra railway in the little Maryport and Carlisle, York regularly saw the arrival, or passage at one time of the carriages of four companies whose engines did not normally appear. The regulars at York, so far as engines were concerned, were the Great Northern, Great Eastern, Great Central, Midland, and Lancashire and Yorkshire—in addition of course, to the North Eastern; and there were carriages of the London and North Western, London and South Western, Great Western, and North British.

CHAPTER ELEVEN

Herbert Nigel Gresley

FROM A VERY early age the Great Northern 'Atlantics' were among my favourite 'pin-up' engines. I was sorry not to see any of them in Leeds on my earliest North Country train-watching expeditions. But I did not have to wait long. On our return from holidays at Bridlington we had, for some reason, to change at Selby. Where the train from Bridlington went to I have no idea; but the major point was that in waiting for a train from Hull to Leeds we had about three-quarters of an hour on Selby station at a time when the main line was busy with East Coast traffic. I use the term East Coast here in its railway rather than its geographical sense, in referring to the Anglo-Scottish main line from King's Cross to Edinburgh and the North. In that waiting time of ours no fewer than five expresses went through, all drawn by Great Northern 'Atlantics'. There were two up trains in succession that both stopped at Selby, and on the down line nothing less than the Flying Scotsman, running on one of those busy Saturdays in three parts. With speed reduced for the swing bridge just north of the station those down expresses were ideal subjects for photography.

Favourites those Great Northern 'Atlantics' may have been, not only with very youthful admirers but with everyone who had to run them, right up to and including Sir Nigel Gresley himself, but it is not always realized that there were *ten* varieties of these famous engines. Certainly four of these varieties were represented by no more than a single locomotive, but they existed all the same, though not all at the same time. These varieties are shown in the accompanying table.

128

G.N.R. LARGE-BOILERED ATLANTICS

GROUP 1: THE TWO CYLINDER SIMPLES

Engineer	Type	Cylinders dia. stroke	Valves	Boiler pressure p.s.i.	Superheaters No. of elements	h.s. sq. ft.
Ivatt	1	$18\frac{3}{4} \times 24$	slide	175	—	—
Ivatt	2	20×24	piston	150	24	427
Gresley	3	$18\frac{3}{4} \times 24$	slide	170	24	427
Gresley	4	20×24	piston	170	24	427
Gresley	5	$18\frac{3}{4} \times 24$	slide	170	32	568
Gresley	6	20×24	piston	170	32	568

GROUP 2: THE SPECIALS

Engineer	Engine No.	Date	Variety
Ivatt	292	1905	4-cylinder compound
Ivatt	1421	1908	4-cylinder compound
Gresley	279	1915	4-cylinder simple
Gresley	1419	1923	Standard engine, but fitted with booster

The full story of the development, from the building of the first example of variety No. 1 at Doncaster in 1902, to the conversion of engine No. 1403 to variety 6 in 1919, is an epitome of locomotive progress in itself. None of the 'specials', even including the rebuilt 1419, with booster, had any appreciable effect upon the main process of evolution.

In the construction of engine No. 251, in 1902, H. A. Ivatt not only carried the process of reversing his predecessor's practice to extremes, but generally flouted the general trend of British locomotive development. Until then, with the marked exception of the Caledonian, the tendency had been to use relatively large cylinders, and boilers that would have been considered ridiculously inadequate by Continental and American standards, but which did very well, because of the exceptionally high quality of coal available for railway use in England, and which permitted the maintenance of high rates of evaporation from small fireboxes and small heating surfaces. Furthermore some engineers deliberately used large cylinders, so that they should be worked economically, at well below the maximum output of power that their cubic capacity would have made possible with more generous supplies of steam. Ivatt did exactly the reverse. The boiler he designed for engine No. 251 had the largest diameter of barrel, and the greatest heating surface that had then been seen on a British locomotive. It is true that it was very nearly matched in the following year by Wilson Worsdell's 'V' class 'Atlantic' on the North Eastern; but then Worsdell put on 20-inch by 28-inch cylinders, in contrast to Ivatt's $18\frac{3}{4}$-inch by 24-inch. The cylinder

volume was $33\frac{1}{2}$ per cent greater on the North Eastern engine. Cylinders 19-inch diameter by 26-inch stroke were common in Great Britain at that time for 4-4-0 locomotives with a total heating surface barely two-thirds of that of the Great Northern 'Atlantics'.

The outcome of these proportions was that the Great Northern 'Atlantics' in their original form never seemed able to use the vast quantities of steam that could be generated in their boilers. Things were made worse by the steam and exhaust ports in their balanced slide valves having areas that were not only small in themselves, but small in relation to the piston areas. They were seriously restricted in this respect compared to contemporary express passenger engines of the Great Western, London and North Western, and Caledonian Railways. But in the second decade of the twentieth century on the railways of Britain the prime object lesson was of the value of the high degree superheated steam on locomotives required to work heavy loads at high speed. It was daily being demonstrated by the 'George the Fifth' and 'Claughton' class engines on the London and North Western. But when Ivatt applied superheating to a new batch of 'Atlantics' he reduced the boiler pressure from 175 to 150 lb. per sq. in.; and although he put on larger cylinders, and piston valves in place of the balanced slide valves on the earlier engines the performance was not greatly improved. Gresley succeeded Ivatt as locomotive engineer of the G.N.R. in 1911, but his earliest attentions to the locomotive stock were all towards the provision of improved designs for freight traffic. But some rebuilding of the earlier Ivatt 'Atlantics' with super-heaters was carried out, and in making these changes the boiler pressure was fixed at 170 lb. per sq. in. Some of these rebuilds retained their slide valves while others were fitted with 20-in. by 24-in. cylinders, and piston valves. These rebuilds constituted a kind of half way house, between the Ivatt engines, and the final development that came in 1919.

It was then that No. 1403, previously an Ivatt non-superheater type, was not only rebuilt with large cylinders and piston valves, but the superheater introduced was much larger, containing 32 elements, and having a heating surface of no less than 568 sq. ft. This again was larger than that of any other British passenger locomotive at the time; but the extreme fluidity of the highly superheated steam, coupled with the good design of piston valves fitted in conjunction with the 20-in. diameter cylinders enabled large quantities of steam to flow freely through what were still relatively small cylinders. This made it possible to haul heavy loads at speeds considerably higher than would have been thought possible—on the basis of the nominal tractive effort of the locomotives. Gresley had, in fact, completely

24. VINTAGE G.N.R. EXPRESSES

(a) In 1909: the 4.45 p.m. stopping train, Peterborough to Lincoln near Werrington Junction, hauled by Stirling 'straightback' 2-2-2 No. 234, and mostly six-wheeled stock.

(b) Up Anglo-Scottish express near Potters Bar hauled by small-boilered Ivatt 'Atlantic' (1898 design) No. 950

(c) Cambridge express near Hadley Wood, hauled by Stirling 2-4-0 No. 883 (rebuilt with Ivatt domed boiler) and Ivatt 4-4-0 No. 1383 —again nearly all six-wheeled stock.

transformed them, and produced one of the truly outstanding locomotives of the age. Such was the advantage of high-degree superheating that although the entire class was eventually fitted with 32-element superheaters not all of them received the additional refinement of piston valves. In later years, when the opportunity came to make a number of journeys on the footplate, I found the slide valve engines extremely fast and 'willing' units, though not quite up to the remarkable standards set by those having 20-inch diameter cylinders and piston valves. At the time I saw them first, at Selby in 1919, the majority of the Great Northern 'Atlantics' working on the Anglo-Scottish trains were in the intermediate stage, with 24-element superheaters. One at least that I photographed in 1920 on a southbound train was still non-superheated.

While achieving this remarkable success in the modernization of the Ivatt 'Atlantics' Gresley was also paying much attention to the freight locomotive stock. There was need for faster goods services, and the experience of other railways had shown the suitability of the 2-6-0 type for this kind of duty. Gresley was one of those able engineers, who not only knew a good thing when they saw it, but knew how to adapt it to the needs of their own railway. He developed the Ivatt 0-6-0 into his own 2-6-0, and built a class of large 2-8-0s to give enhanced power for the heavier and slower freights hitherto worked by Ivatt 0-8-0s. Both these new designs had the characteristic Doncaster look about them. Gresley, although trained at Crewe and having worked for a time on the Lancashire and Yorkshire Railway, was intensely loyal to the traditions of the Great Northern. It was not in his nature to proclaim his individuality to the world by new painting styles, or radical departures in design practice. He put the two-wheeled leading 'pony' trucks on his new freight engines to improve their riding, and the only other change was to outside cylinders and the Walschaerts radial valve gear instead of the Stephenson link motion. Gresley was an all-round railwayman of the highest calibre and the outside valve gear no doubt appealed to him, in its enabling all the 'works' to be serviced without the need for getting the engine over a pit, or for a man to crawl beneath. Hitherto, the only Doncaster-built engines with outside valve gear had been the four-cylinder compound 'Atlantics' Nos. 292 and 1421.

In the meantime developments elsewhere in England were attracting Gresley's attention. As a Crewe man he had naturally been deeply interested in the outstanding success of Bowen-Cooke's express locomotives with high-degree superheat, and his own colleague on the East Coast route, Vincent L. Raven of the North Eastern, was standardizing locomotives with three cylinders. The very graceful 'Z' class 'Atlantics', briefly mentioned in the fore-going chapter, were proving most successful and economical in hauling the Anglo-Scottish expresses north of York. But the North Eastern remained steadfastly faithful to the Stephenson Link Motion. Gresley once said publicly that it was a matter of tradition—that in the land of the Stephensons, it was natural that the indigenous form of valve gear should be used. Not necessarily, because the link motion, with skilful attention to detail design was capable of providing a highly efficient distribution of steam, quite apart from any sentimental reasons for using it. Detail design apart however, there was the physical fact that the North Eastern three-cylinder engines had a set of valve gear for each cylinder, and while two of those cylinders were outside, all three sets of valve gear were between the frames. This was just the kind of condition Gresley was setting out to avoid in using the Walschaerts gear on his new Great Northern 2-6-0s and 2-8-0s.

While his favourable impression of the three-cylinder locomotives on the North Eastern Railway was being weighed up against his dislike of having motion work between the frames his attention was drawn to an arrangement being developed on the Prussian State Railways, where a number of three-cylinder locomotives were being fitted with a conjugated arrangement of this valve gear whereby the valves for the central cylinder were actuated by a system of links from the two outside cylinders. There was no motion work inside the frames. This was just the kind of mechanism Gresley was looking for; but war conditions precluded the obtaining of any detailed information about it, still less of its performance in service. But Gresley put the Doncaster drawing office on to it, and in 1915 a similar arrangement was worked out, for application to one of the large 2-8-0 mineral engines. Again because of war conditions the opportunity to build an engine incorporating this gear was not immediately forthcoming, and it was not until early in 1918 that a trial could be made. The new engine No. 461, was extensively publicized in the technical press. *The Railway Magazine* had a colour plate, from an 'F. Moore' oil painting, and Charles S. Lake, technical editor of *The Railway Gazette*, gave a long account of a test of the engine's performance on a 1,300-ton coal train between Peterborough and London. I was still at school at the time, and I shall always remember the disgust of a young friend, who had strong partisan feelings towards the Midland Railway, on opening *The Railway Magazine* for March 1919, and seeing a report of that test. He exclaimed: 'They seem quite pleased with this potty Great Northern engine!'

But not all the locomotive world was as impressed as the railway press. The arrangement of the conjugated valve gear, which was undoubtedly complicated, came in for a good deal of criticism. A letter from H. Holcroft of the South Eastern and Chatham Railway fairly 'started something'. He revealed that some years previously when he was in the drawing office at Swindon he had worked out the design of a conjugated valve, and gone to the extent of making a working 'live steam' model locomotive incorporating it. The arrangement had been brought to the notice of G. J. Churchward, and on his instructions it had been patented. It was a much simpler arrangement than the German layout, adapted by Doncaster to the new 2-8-0 engine No. 461. Gresley was intensely interested. At that time Holcroft had been seconded from his normal duties on the S.E. & C.R., to supervise a depot of the wartime Railway Executive Committee at Purfleet, and Gresley called him into consultation, and even went to the extent of inviting him to join the staff of the Great Northern Railway; but although this did not eventuate, the next Gresley three-cylinder locomotive had the greatly simplified layout of the conjugated valve gear devised in the first place by Holcroft, and it became the standard arrangement for all high-powered locomotives on the G.N.R., and, subsequent to the grouping, on the London and North Eastern Railway for the next twenty years.

The first Doncaster engine to have the simplified gear was certainly a machine to set all

the tongues wagging. For some time there had been rumours that a 'super' locomotive was under construction, and at first those with their ears to the ground, but without inside information, varied in their speculations as to whether the new engine was to be a 'Pacific', or a 2-6-2. And then, early in 1920, engine No. 1000 made her bow—'merely an enlargement of the existing Moguls' as one disenchanted commentator put it. This was a perfectly true description of the new engine, but what an enlargement! She had three cylinders, and the conjugated valve gear, but the boiler had the largest diameter yet seen on any British locomotive. Hitherto 5 ft. 6 in. had come to be regarded as the British maximum—not necessarily the largest that *could* be mounted, but a diameter that had actually been the largest for upwards of twenty years. Engine No. 1000 had a 6-ft. diameter boiler, and the effect was impressive beyond measure. This boiler did not have the wide shallow firebox of the 'Atlantics', because with the 2-6-0 wheel arrangement the box had to be narrow, and fairly deep. It was nevertheless a prolific steamer. It had to be, for the cylinder volume on these remarkable engines was 36 per cent greater than that of the piston-valve 'Atlantics'. Ten of these engines were built in 1920.

The Great Northern was certainly setting the pace in its locomotive development in those immediate post-war years. The new Gresley three-cylinder engines may not have been many in number, but their novelty caught the imagination. It must be confessed however that the most significant development of all—the fitting of 'Atlantics' with 32-element superheaters—escaped the attention of all contemporary commentators. There was plenty of praise bestowed on the day-to-day work of these engines, referred to collectively as 'the superheater Atlantics'; but over the variation and evolution of their 'innards' not a word was written. By the year 1920, however, Gresley was poised on the threshold of an even greater development. It is perhaps inevitable that anyone writing retrospectively of the Great Northern Railway of that period should tend to concentrate upon locomotive matters, because the career of Gresley was always one to excite the attention of publicists, and equally of that band of railway enthusiasts that had become devoted to the G.N.R. But I am writing not only of this period during which he was locomotive engineer. Before he succeeded Ivatt in the post he had been carriage and wagon engineer of the company, and in this latter post he had brought his imaginative genius to the design of some of the most distinctive carriages running in Great Britain in this period.

Just before the turn of the century a startling change had been made in Great Northern main line passenger coaches. Until then non-corridor six-wheelers had predominated, even on the crack Anglo-Scottish and Leeds expresses; and although the company had been the

25. G.N.R. LOCOMOTIVE DEVELOPMENT

(a) Ivatt's superheated 4-4-0 of 1911, as painted in L.N.E.R. colours, in 1923.

(b) The second of the very famous Gresley 'Pacifics', No. 1471—later L.N.E.R. No. 4471 *Sir Frederick Banbury*, built Doncaster Works, 1922.

(c) The first Gresley 'Mogul', the small boilered 'K1' class of 1912.

first in the country to introduce dining cars these latter were completely self-contained, and not connected by vestibules to the rest of the train. The dining cars themselves were magnificent vehicles, spacious, lofty with high clerestory roofs, and when the new main line coaches were introduced, with corridors throughout the clerestory type of roof was retained. They, too, were superb, They ran on six-wheeled bogies, and were massively constructed in the traditional teak of the Great Northern, but adorned with a profusion of gold lettering, and the coat of arms magnificently rendered. They were naturally heavy, weighing 35 to 36 tons apiece, but at first this did not greatly matter. The time schedules of most of the express trains were not unduly sharp, and the faster ones were mostly of light formation.

Elsewhere in England train loads were on the increase and Gresley, who was as conscious of the locomotive position as of his own immediate responsibilities as carriage and wagon engineer, set out to produce carriages that should be at least as luxurious as the earlier clerestory-roofed stock but much lighter, and thereby enabling the locomotive to haul longer trains without extra coal and water consumption. The result was the highly distinctive bow-ended stock, used both on the Leeds and on the Anglo-Scottish expresses. These coaches had high elliptical roofs, but the ends, instead of being square to the length of the body, were bowed, and the roof ends were tapered down in sweeping curves to a height no more than that of the top of the gangway connection. It was a form of streamlining, in that it eliminated completely the flat ends of the carriages, which could, on a vehicle of maximum height, present a pocket to set up strong air resistance. Quite apart from the outward shape, Gresley modified the internal design in a number of different ways to reduce weight. Externally the Great Northern tradition was fully maintained, with the varnished teak-panelled sides, and roofs that were treated with white lead paint. Naturally they did not stay white for long; but white or grey the turnout was always extremely smart.

The North Eastern also built a number of coaches for East Coast joint services, and these, while also having a varnished teak finish, had almost flat ends. The Great Northern built a number of the bow-ended coaches for the London–Newcastle service, and these were lettered 'GN & NE'. They were used on the crack 8 a.m. up from Newcastle, and the 5.30 p.m. down from King's Cross. At the time I was making my first observations of East Coast express workings, the Anglo-Scottish expresses were often made up of a mixture of the Gresley bow-enders, and the earlier 12-wheeled clerestory-roofed coaches. Whatever the loads might have been in the early years of the century they were heavy enough in 1919–20, and 'Atlantic' engines were regularly called upon to haul loads of about 450 tons, often much more. In Stirling's day the rule had been 'one train, one engine'. Double-heading was forbidden. But with the introduction of heavier rolling stock in 1897–99 the old single-wheelers could not cope, and they often had to be used in pairs. Once the 'Atlantics' were on the road the old rule was reinstated and some tremendous loads were taken with one engine during the war years, when the train service was much decelerated. With the speeding up that followed the end of the war a slight concession was made in giving 'Atlantics' assistance from King's Cross out to Potter's Bar in cases of exceptional loading.

A development of great significance took place in connection with the 1907 carriage building programme on the Great Northern Railway. There were a number of six-wheeled corridor coaches running on the East Coast service. These had rigid axles at each end, and side play to the middle axle. They were fairly long, for six-wheeled coaches, and were inclined to ride 'hard', and not infrequently roughly, on curves. To improve their riding Gresley took two of them, and mounted them together as a twin-articulated unit. The axle-guards, scroll irons and so on were removed, and the pair—close connected at the middle—were supported on three four-wheeled bogies, one at each end, and one at the middle supporting the point of junction between the two coach bodies. One of these latter was a 5-compartment 'third' and the other a 4-compartment 'first'. The articulated twin unit was put into regular service between King's Cross and Edinburgh in 1907, and proved a great success, gaining immensely in flexibility and ease of running as compared with the previous individual six-wheelers. Gresley patented the arrangement, and it formed the basis of some striking developments in coaching stock design on the London and North Eastern Railway.

Before grouping took place however the articulated principle had been ingeniously developed for a purely Great Northern service. In 1921 Gresley applied the principle to the construction of a 'quintuple' restaurant car set from the King's Cross–Leeds service. This consisted of five vehicles, namely 'first' brake; 'first' dining-car; kitchen and pantry car; 'third' dining car; 'third' brake. These five vehicles, which would ordinarily have needed two bogies each, had, by use of the articulated principle, only six between them. Thus not only was great smoothness in riding obtained but there was a considerable reduction in weight, by elimination of four bogies. Although this quintuple set formed a 'train' of its own it was, of course, no more than the basic formation of the heavy expresses between London and the West Riding. The seating on the first and third 'brakes' at each end of the set would not have provided enough for London–Leeds traffic alone, let alone for Bradford, Halifax, Hull, and Harrogate. The quintuple set, which ran on the 10.10 a.m. express from King's Cross was reinforced by many extra coaches through to different destinations in the West Riding. It did, however, provide the restaurant car accommodation for the whole train. It proved to be the only quintuple unit built; but many triplet sets were built after the grouping.

While Gresley was endeavouring to reduce the burden on his locomotives by building lighter carriages he proved one of the foremost protagonists of the policy of building loco-motives of maximum power. I have written at some length of how the capacity of the Ivatt 'Atlantics' was enhanced by the use of high-degree superheating. I was very amused not long ago in browsing through some contemporary literature to find an engineer-correspondent of one of the technical journals appraising the work of these engines, which he described as of 1902 design, modified only by the addition of superheating. 'Only' indeed! Modified almost out of recognition, would have been a truer comment, if one qualified the word superheating by adding 'high degree'. Then Gresley had strengthened his motive power stud by the addition of the ten splendid 3-cylinder 'Moguls' of the '1000' class, the

performance of which gave valuable additional data in the haulage of very heavy passenger trains.

The logical development of the boiler and wide firebox arrangement of the 'Atlantics', combined with the haulage capacity of the 3-cylinder 'Moguls' was of course a 'Pacific', and sure enough the first two Gresley locomotives of the type were completed at Doncaster in the last year of existence of the Great Northern Railway. I had left school and commenced my engineering studies in London, when the two new engines 1470 *Great Northern* and 1471 *Sir Frederick Banbury* were put into traffic, in the spring of 1922. Although in later life the Gresley 'Pacifics' in their several subsequent varieties became very familiar to me, and I rode many thousands of miles on their footplates, I shall never forget my first sight of one of them at King's Cross, in 1922. My unspoken thought was whether so colossal an engine was really necessary. It was No. 1471 then unnamed, and standing at the head of the 'Flying Scotsman' in King's Cross station. At an adjoining platform was the relief 9.50 a.m. train, with only one coach less, and headed by an 'Atlantic'. But when the winter service came on both 'Pacifics' were taken off the Anglo-Scottish trains, and put on to the West Riding services, as between King's Cross and Doncaster, and on those trains they took some tremendous loads with complete success.

Those first two 'Pacifics' were true Great Northern engines. Although the type afterwards became acknowledged as an L.N.E.R. standard its origin should not be forgotten, and those first two engines at first bore the beautiful Great Northern livery. Their numbers were rendered in small transfer figures on their cab sides; they carried the letters G.N.R. on their huge 8-wheeled tenders, and their underframes were painted a brownish red, as on the 'Atlantics'. Like the Ivatt 'Atlantics' they did not attain their final form at first. There were some very important developments in L.N.E.R. days. But the basic design was there, and in it the Great Northern Railway bequeathed to the railways of Britain one of the greatest passenger locomotive designs of the grouping era. I always feel that it was a great pity that one of those two pioneer Gresley 'Pacifics' was not restored to the original condition, for preservation, and painted in Great Northern colours. The obvious engine for such an honour would have been the first of them all, No. 1470 *Great Northern*. But after Gresley's untimely death in 1941 his successor in the office of Chief Mechanical Engineer on the London and North Eastern Railway seemed anxious to reverse much of Gresley's policy, and one act of his, that outraged the feelings of railway engineers far beyond the ranks of purely Gresley men, was his choice of No. 1470 for a drastic rebuild into a horrible looking

26. GREAT NORTHERN: VARIETY IN TRAINS

(a) Leeds and Bradford Express in Hadley Woods, hauled by superheated 'Atlantic' No. 1442.

(b) Newcastle express, during the 1921 coal strike, hauled by new 3-cylinder 'Mogul' No. 1003, near New Southgate.

(c) An Adams 4-4-0 of the North London Railway working a Broad St.–Potters Bar train on the G.N.R.

'misfit'. This rebuild postulated a principle that he was anxious to extend; but it could so easily have been applied to one of the less significant engines of the class. The virtual destruction of the pioneer Great Northern 'Pacific' was really inexcusable.

The Great Northern was a railway of immense individuuality and yet those 'Atlantics' that I saw and photographed at Selby in 1919, and 1920, were actually on foreign ground. The beautiful painting that Jack Hill has prepared from one of my old snaps shows this clearly enough, in the design of the signals. These are of the North Eastern pattern, and indeed the East Coast expresses have been running over fourteen miles of North Eastern metals by the time they pass Selby. From a very early stage in the operation of the East Coast joint service York was the point of changing over from Great Northern to North Eastern engines. Doncaster would not normally be a stopping station, and the arrangement worked gave engine runs of $82\frac{1}{2}$ miles from Grantham to York, and 80 miles from York to Newcastle. The North Eastern signals were of a distinctive pattern, working in a slot in the post; but the Great Northern were much more so, being of the centre-balanced or 'somersault' type. How this design originated, and was later taken to South Wales, and then to Australia and New Zealand is a longer story than can be told here; but it was a veritable hall-mark of the Great Northern—as much so as the bow-ended corridor carriages, and those amazing 'Atlantic' engines.

CHAPTER TWELVE

The pageant of Carlisle

IT NEEDS NO more than a glance at a contoured map of Great Britain to appreciate why Carlisle has been a major traffic junction from times extending far back beyond the beginning of railways. And after the significance of the Border had passed away, from a strategic point of view, roads, and then railways, from all directions in Northern England, and Southern Scotland converged upon Carlisle. And yet in the very beginnings of the railway age there was an echo of history, in that the first two railways to enter Carlisle came in under the shelter, as it were, of the Roman Wall. First of all there was the Newcastle and Carlisle, the first line to be built across England, which was opened throughout in 1838. Carlisle however had its first trains in 1836, when the western end of this important cross-country line was opened. Then from the west came the Maryport and Carlisle, the first section of which was opened into Carlisle in 1843. The Newcastle line made its passenger terminus at London Road, and the Maryport company, entering the city in a north-easterly direction swung round in a quarter circle to use the same station. But these purely North Country projects were barely under way before Carlisle became the focus-point of railway planning on a far more extensive scale, fostered directly by the London and Birmingham, and Grand Junction Railways, which were anxious to see a line of railway communication established between London and the major Scottish cities.

So, in 1846, there came the Lancaster and Carlisle, and in 1847 the Caledonian. Before those lines were actually built there had been much discussion, and some bitter controversy as to the routes to be followed. On the Lancaster and Carlisle project George Stephenson was at one time consulted, and he had recommended going round the Cumberland coast, to avoid the heavy gradients that would be involved in going through mountains. In the north, Glasgow interests favoured an extension of the Glasgow, Paisley, Kilmarnock and Ayr Railway, and an approach to the south through Nithsdale. Other interests having in view serving Edinburgh as well as Glasgow favoured a route up Annandale, and over the Lowther Hills into Upper Clydesdale. As finally agreed, Joseph Locke was the engineer for both railways, and he took the Lancaster and Carlisle over Shap Summit, and the Caledonian up Annandale. But rival Glasgow interests lost no time in projecting their own line south-wards from Kilmarnock, and they made junction with the Caledonian at Gretna. In 1850 the G.P.K. & A. and its associates changed their name to Glasgow and South Western, and although exercising running powers over the Caledonian over the last $8\frac{1}{2}$ miles from Gretna Junction to Carlisle they nevertheless became lifelong rivals, and a constant 'thorn in the side', until both were eventually absorbed into the London, Midland and Scottish Railway in 1923.

Although the Caledonian had been more or less forced to grant running powers to the Glasgow and South Western to enable the latter company to reach Carlisle they did not make things any easier for them once they had arrived. Passengers by through trains frequently wondered if the G. & S.W. had any engine sheds in Carlisle, and if so where they were. That most famous of pre-grouping railway photographers, F. E. Mackay, told me how he once spent a whole afternoon walking the tracks looking for those sheds, and failed to find them. It so happened that there was no train detaching, or picking up an engine that would have given him a clue. It is not surprising he was baffled, because they were located at Currock Road, on the Maryport and Carlisle line, and most discreetly tucked away out of sight. The third major Scottish company arrived in Carlisle in 1862, by the completion of the Border Union line of the North British, from Hawick, to complete the famous Waverley Route to Edinburgh. At that time the only outlet to the south was over the Lancaster and Carlisle, which from 1859 had been leased by the London and North Western. The final development in this extensive build-up came in 1876 with the completion of the Settle and Carlisle line of the Midland Railway. The chronology of the build-up was therefore thus:

1836 Newcastle and Carlisle (to Greenhead only)
1838 Newcastle and Carlisle throughout
1843 Maryport and Carlisle (to Wigton only)
1845 Maryport and Carlisle completed
1846 Lancaster and Carlisle
1847 Caledonian, to Glasgow and Edinburgh
1850 Glasgow & South Western, to Glasgow via Kilmarnock
1862 North British, Waverley Route to Edinburgh
1876 Midland, Settle and Carlisle

The Newcastle and Carlisle became part of the North Eastern Railway in 1862, and from then until the end of 1922 there were six major, and one less-major railway companies running into the Citadel passenger station at Carlisle, though there were a number of separate goods stations.

Such was the historical background to the pageant of train working that could be enjoyed from the station platforms. It has attracted and fascinated generation after generation of railway enthusiasts. I know men now well beyond middle-age who have spent long vigils during the night observing the tremendous flow of traffic immediately before the Twelfth

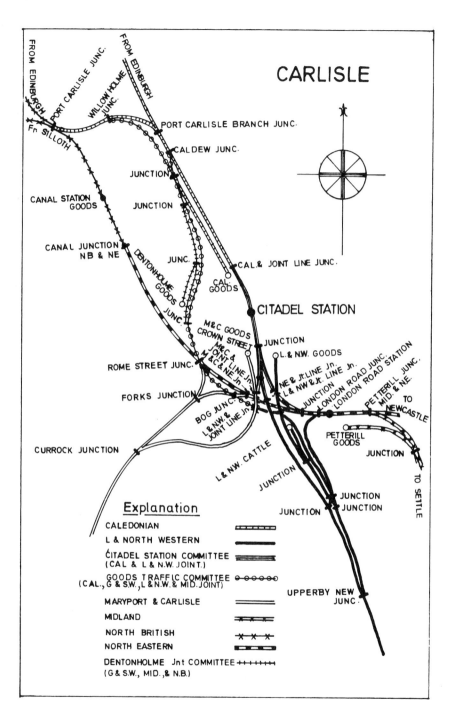

MAP 3: CARLISLE: PRE-GROUPING OWNERSHIPS

143

of August, noting engines, loads and punctuality; and every train on its way to Scotland would be changing engines, so that there would be English and Scottish engines to each. On the night of 10 August, 1900, for example, 13 Scottish expresses were dispatched within the space of four hours. Quite apart from special occasions, the normal timetable in the summer of 1900 included a total of 259 trains to be dealt with at the station every 24 hours. This total was made up as follows:

Railway	Through Express	Local
L.N.W.R.	43	18
Caledonian	35	10
Midland	23	12
Glasgow & South Western	17	15
North British	15	19
North Eastern	—	36
Maryport & Carlisle	—	16

Some of the North Eastern trains in the above summary were express in themselves, but they terminated at Carlisle. But statistics apart the *colour* of that pageant takes some imagining today.

The highly individual designs of locomotives on the different railways were a study in themselves. At the turn of the century there could not have been 4-4-0 engines less alike in outward appearance than the Caledonian 'Dunalastairs', the Johnsons of the Midland, the Worsdell family of 4-4-0's on the North Eastern, or the latest North British, which looked a cross between the products of Dugald Drummond, with the twin lock-up safety valves on the dome, and the cut-away cabs of Patrick Stirling on the Great Northern. And then the colours! Midland lake; North Eastern leaf green; 'milk-chocolate' brown of the North British—a colour that partook of a distinct greenish hue in some lights; the soft blue-green of the Glasgow and South Western, and the bright apple-green of the Maryport and Carlisle. Then there were North Westerns in their scores. They may have been black; but what a black, and among the most highly groomed and burnished of any engines entering Carlisle. I have left until last the Caledonians, for they really were in a class by themselves so far as colouring was concerned. The limpid sky-blue had not begun to appear, and they all bore the 'official' Prussian blue. It was magnificently set off by the purple-lake under-

27. CARLISLE: MIDLAND 'SCOTCH' TRAINS

(a) London Express ready to leave, hauled by Johnson 2-4-0 No. 228 and a '999' class 4-4-0.

(b) Glasgow express approaching from the south: engine No. 997, with a very heavy load.

(c) On the G. & S.W.R. side- express from Glasgow passing Rockcliffe, hauled by Manson 4-6-0 No. 497, as rebuilt by Whitelegg.

frames, and the little touches of individual adornment put on by the drivers. In those days all Caledonian express drivers had their 'own' engines, and they vied with one another in the smartness of the turn-out.

Among connoisseurs of locomotive design practice there were some who perceived, or thought they perceived, a rivalry between the companies that amounted to little more than 'one-up-manship', or a policy of 'keeping up with the Joneses'. It is surprising to what an extent this interpretation of events has persisted in the writings of men who became well known for carefully balanced views on North Country railway matters. One comment regarding the introduction of 4-6-0 locomotives on the Glasgow and South Western may be quoted: 'The rival Caledonian having produced its huge Nos. 49 and 50, capable of taking practically any Caledonian train single-handed, the G. & S.W. directorate evidently thought that their prestige was in danger. So Manson prepared designs for a 4-6-0.' If this was actually the case the news of the construction of the Caledonian engines at St. Rollox, and details of their design, must have leaked out some time before their actual completion. Otherwise it would have been quite impossible for the Glasgow and South Western Railway to have designed a new engine *after* the first appearance of the Caledonians, placed a contract with the North British Locomotive Company, and had ten engines in traffic within four months! Yet such were the dates on which the two classes appeared, both within the first six months of 1903. There can be little doubt that the two projects were quite unconnected, particularly as the two Caledonians were built for trials, whereas Manson, on the G. & S.W., had built a production batch of ten, straight off the drawing board.

If it had been a question of prestige the G. & S.W. had been very slow in waking up to it. The Caledonian had jumped several strides ahead of them in 1896 with the production of the first series of 'Dunalastairs', and the margin had been successively increased in the two following years with the second and third series of those ever-famous 4-4-0s. Even before the appearance of the great 4-6-0s, 49 and 50, the 'Dunalastair III' class was vastly larger and more powerful than Manson's 'No. 8' class on the G. & S.W. The latter were splendid little engines in themselves; but they *were* so little! They usually worked in pairs on the Scotch expresses off the Midland line. Until the year 1902 the 'Dunalastair III' class was unquestionably the finest of all express passenger locomotives regularly working into Carlisle; but in that year it was the Midland, of all unexpected companies, that stepped into the limelight, with a design so much in advance of the 'Dunalastair III' as to claim premier membership of the 'Twentieth Century Big-Engine Club' of Carlisle. This was the very celebrated Smith–Johnson 3-cylinder compound 4-4-0. The first two engines of this class, Nos. 2631 and 2632, were stationed at Leeds, and at first worked exclusively on the Carlisle road. In contrast to the slender, supremely beautiful appearance of Johnson's earlier engines, both 2-4-0 and 4-4-0, which had hitherto been the standard motive power for the Midland Scotch Expresses at Carlisle, the new compounds created a positive sensation by their massive, albeit still graceful appearance, and their huge double-bogie tenders. It was not long before the railway fraternity of Carlisle, both professionals and amateurs,

learned of some well-nigh sensational performances by these engines over the heavily
graded Settle and Carlisle line. It was an odd twist of railway management policy that
resulted in these superb pacemakers of 1902 being watered-down in their maximum
capacity, and never improved upon during the remaining independent life of the Midland
Railway.

Despite their excellent work, which was fully reported in the engineering press of the day,
the Midland compounds 2631 and 2632 appeared to have been outclassed by the introduction of large 4-6-0s on the Scottish lines in 1903. Certainly both the McIntosh and the
Manson engines were much larger. The Caledonian 49 and 50 could be described as a
tremendous 4-6-0 version of the 'Dunalastair III', and it was rightly considered as the most
powerful express passenger design on any British railway at that time. The tractive effort
had been increased from 18,350 to 24,990 lb., and the total heating surface of the boiler and
firebox had gone up from 1,540 to 2,323 sq. ft. They were extremely simple in their design,
and massively constructed, while in the dark-blue livery, and purple-lake underframes the
appearance was impressive almost beyond words. The Glasgow and South Western 4-6-0s,
which came rapidly off the assembly-lines at the Atlas Works of the North British Locomotive Company soon afterwards were also most handsome engines, though some considerable distance behind in tractive power. Manson seems to have had certain weight restrictions
placed upon him, because things were cut rather fine in the structural design of these
engines. From the outset they always seemed to be handled on a light rein, in contrast to
the all-out pounding meted out to Caledonian engines. They were taken gently up the
banks, frequently double-headed, and then allowed to fly downhill. Maximum speeds of
over 80 m.p.h. were much more frequent on the G. & S.W. than on the Caledonian at that
period.

For three years the two 'super' Caledonians, and the Mansons held the limelight at
Carlisle; and the reader may well now be wondering what the London and North Western—
the 'Premier Line' of all Britain—was doing all this time. The Anglo-Scottish traffic over
the West Coast Route was incomparably the heaviest of all passing through Carlisle, and
until 1905 the L.N.W.R. had no express passenger 4-6-0s. Up to that time the traffic was
operated by a miscellaneous, though fascinating assortment of engines, ranging upwards in
tractive power from the tough little 2-4-0s of the 'Precedent' and 'Whitworth' classes,
through various Webb three-cylinder compounds, to the latest 4-cylinder compound 4-4-0s
of the 'Alfred the Great' class. None of them showed any consistent reliability, except for
the little 2-4-0s; and these latter were minutely small for the traffic of the early 1900s.
Nearly every train was double-headed, and there was little comradely spirit between
enginemen of the two partners in the West Coast services. The Caledonian men, on their
powerful 'Dunalastairs'—not to mention 49 and 50—developed a tremendous superiority
complex towards the men who brought the trains in from the South. The tractive effort of
the North Western 'Alfred the Great' class was actually greater than that of the new
Midland compounds, but there was literally no comparison between their respective performances. In 1904 the locomotive position on the L.N.W.R. had been greatly improved by

28. CARLISLE: THE CALEDONIANS

(a) A Conner 2-4-0 No. 52, originally built 1871 and used on local
    trains in the early 1900s.

the introduction of the 'Precursor' class of simple 4-4-0; but not many of those engines
could be spared for the Carlisle road, and for the most part the running department had to
carry on as best they could. With nearly every train needing two engines there was often an
acute shortage of power; and it is recorded that on one occasion southbound expresses were
kept waiting in Carlisle, because there were literally no engines in the sheds capable of
taking them forward.

In the summer of 1905 the first of the new 'Experiment' class began working north from
Crewe. They have been described, a little unkindly perhaps, as 'a rather half-hearted
attempt' at a main line 4-6-0 passenger engine. For a line carrying the traffic of the North
Western an engine having a tractive effort of only 18,600 lb., compared with 20,350 lb. on
the G. & S.W. 4-6-0s and 24,990 on the Caledonian 49 and 50, did seem very much on the
small side; and the first five engines of the class, which worked almost exclusively on the
Carlisle road in 1905, did not produce any outstanding feats of performance in their first
months. Nevertheless, many more were built from 1906 onwards, and for upwards of five
years they remained the top passenger class of the L.N.W.R. at Carlisle. In sheer size they
were positively dwarfed by two new Scottish classes that entered the Citadel station first in
1906, and before anything larger or more powerful had emerged from Crewe the membership of the 'Big Engine Club of Carlisle' had been further increased by the regular visits of

148

(b) The 'Cardean' class 4-6-0 No. 907, of 1906. This engine was damaged beyond repair in the terrible Quintinshill disaster of 1915.

North Eastern 'Atlantics' from Newcastle. The two new Scottish entrants during 1906 were the modified version of the Caledonian 49 and 50, as represented by the '903' or 'Cardean' class, and the North British 'Atlantics'. The 'Club' then consisted of the following:

Date	Railway	Type	Class	Wt. without tender *tons*	Tractive effort *lb.*
1902	Midland	4-4-0	Compound	59·5	13,900
1903	Caledonian	4-6-0	49 & 50	70·0	24,490
1903	G. & S.W.	4-6-0	'386'	67·1	20,350
1905	L.N.W.R.	4-6-0	'Experiment'	65·8	18,600
1906	Caledonian	4-6-0	'Cardean'	73·0	22,667
1906	North British	4-4-2	Reid Design	74·8	23,500
1906	North Eastern	4-4-2	'V'	72·0	23,300

If one were asked to point to one locomotive class that marked the culmination of the ultra-simple form of design, that had become so characteristic of British practice in the nineteenth century the 'Cardean' class of the Caledonian would be the obvious choice. Inside cylinders, a low, straight running plate, deep splashers, and a most symmetrical outline, together with a complete absence of gadgets, combined with an enormous boiler to provide all the ingredients necessary to justify the choice. As for *Cardean* herself, engine No. 903, one could add a tremendous marine siren of a whistle—far richer, and far more distinctive than the famous Caledonian 'hooter', with which many enthusiasts of a later generation became familiar when it was standardized on the L.M.S. in Sir William Stanier's time. *Cardean* became, and still is, something of a legend in Scottish railroading. Except when she was in for repairs she worked the 2 p.m. up Scotch 'Corridor' express from Glasgow down to Carlisle, and went back with the corresponding express leaving at 8.13 p.m. in the evening. She was on that duty, with very few intermissions for upwards of ten years and for most of the time in the charge of one driver, David Gibson, of Polmadie shed, Glasgow. There were five engines of the class, but *Cardean* was the only one to bear a name. Engines 904 and 905 were stationed at Perth, while 906 and 907 were at Kingmoor sheds, Carlisle. The regular duties of these two latter engines were northbound on the early morning sleeping car expresses, and back with the morning southbound Anglo-Scottish expresses.

Many years ago a 'Pertinent Paragraph' in *The Railway Magazine* recalled the days of *Cardean* on the 8.13 p.m. from Carlisle, and the scene after the London and North Western engine had coupled off: 'A handsome combination *Cardean* made with the seven cars of the "two o'clock", all twelve-wheelers of a special design, and some of the smoothest riding stock that has ever run over West Coast metals. And so, on a typical winter's night at Carlisle, with half the city—or so it seemed—making the Citadel Station the venue of its evening promenade, and *Cardean* the centre of attraction, the same ritual would be gone through after *Cardean* had backed down: the fireman, usually high up on the great tender, would wave to and fro an improvised torch consisting of an oilcan, whose spout contained a blazing wick of oily waste, to show to officials farther down the platform that the brake test had been made satisfactorily; then would come a thrilling blast on the great foghorn that *Cardean* carried in place of a whistle, and the shapely form of the "two o'clock" vanished into the night.'

Although the 'Cardean' class were bigger and heavier engines than 49 and 50 they had, as the foregoing table showed, slightly less tractive effort, having cylinders one inch less in diameter; but for heavy load haulage they were the better engines. By the time *Cardean* was built the lighter blue livery had come into vogue. The story goes that it 'crept in' un-officially, when the paint shop found they could make the expensive Prussian blue go a little further by mixing some white with it. The result was so beautiful that it was adopted as the standard livery. All the same, the engines in Prussian blue had an immense dignity about them.

The second addition of 1906 to the pageant of splendid locomotives seen regularly at Carlisle was the North British 'Atlantic'. So far as gradients were concerned, the 'Waverley Route' to Edinburgh was undoubtedly the hardest of any leading from Carlisle, either northward or southward. There were two formidable summits to be climbed, Whitrope in the Cheviots, and Falahill on a spur of the Lammermoor Hills. One might have thought six-coupled engines were essential, with the heavy Midland Scotch expresses; but the Waverley Route, like the East Coast main line between Edinburgh and Dundee, was so beset with curves that the civil engineer made a strong plea for the use of the 'Atlantic' type rather than the 4-6-0. After all 'Atlantics' were in general use on the East Coast Route south of Edinburgh. And so the locomotive engineer, W. P. Reid, produced his huge 'Atlantics'. So far as dimensions were concerned they bore a remarkable similarity to the 'V' class of Wilson Worsdell, on the North Eastern; but the boiler was pitched a little higher, and in consequence the chimney and dome were so dwarfed in height as to look little more than buttons! These great engines immediately became great favourites with the spectators of the pageant at Carlisle. They were all named, and it was usually contrived that those with local names worked on the Waverley route, such as *Liddesdale*, *Abbotsford*, *Hazeldean*, *Teribus*, *Tweeddale* and *Holyrood*. In Carlisle they made a striking, but equally impressive, contrast to the blue engines of the Caledonian, and the greens of the Glasgow and South Western.

The working of the big North Eastern 'Atlantics' into Carlisle, previously mentioned, has sometimes been written down as mere showmanship, since no trains on the cross-country route from Newcastle required such large and powerful engines. Certainly they showed the North Eastern 'flag' to some purpose, among the great engines of the Scottish companies. In actual fact however the North Eastern was very mileage-conscious in the utilization of the principal express locomotives. All the Gateshead top link engines were double manned in the course of a single day's work—very much in contrast to the large engines of the Scottish companies. The majority of these would do a round trip from Carlisle to Glasgow and back or Carlisle to Edinburgh and back, and that was all—about 200 to 220 miles in the day. But with the North Easterns, it was not enough to go from Newcastle to Edinburgh and back, 250 miles; they must then be remanned, and go to Leeds and back, or Carlisle and back. This largely explains how such big engines as the 'V' class Atlantics appeared in the Citadel station. In later years the Gresley 'Pacifics' from Gateshead shed did the same.

The pageant of Carlisle was however not confined to the latest and largest engines, and some of the smaller ones provided examples of great and historic interest. I have already mentioned the 'No. 8' class 4-4-0s on the Glasgow and South Western. The still older 4-4-0s of Hugh Smellie's design were also regular visitors. These were a direct derivative from the days of James Stirling, at Kilmarnock. They had the Stirling family's cab, cut away as on his brother Patrick's Great Northern engines; and while having domeless boilers they had a simple mounting for the Ramsbottom safety valves in the middle of the boilers. These Smellie 4-4-0s were not the most handsome of Scottish engines, but they were supremely swift runners. Some of the Caledonian locals from Carlisle were worked by ancient outside-cylinder 2-4-0s of Ben Conner's design, that made the 2-4-0s of the Midland and the London and North Western look quite modern by comparison. The use of 2-4-0s as express train pilots had largely ceased on the Midland by 1910 and thereafter, but on the North Western the little 2-4-0 'Jumbos'—an affectionate nickname for the whole

family of 6 ft. and 6 ft. 6 in. engines of the 'Whitworth' and 'Precedent' classes—were piloting main line expresses until well after the grouping, in 1923.

The years from 1902 to 1910 saw big changes on the Midland trains running into Carlisle. Johnson's magnificent compound engines proved too complicated for the average driver to manage, and in simplifying their controls their maximum capacity was considerably reduced; and when further engines of the type were built by Johnson's successor they were mostly used south of Leeds. As I have told in an earlier chapter the brunt of the work on the Settle and Carlisle line was done by non-superheater 4-4-os that had been rebuilt from Johnson's engines, with larger boilers. But from 1910 onwards the real metamorphosis in train working at Carlisle came on the London and North Western Railway. That year, into the stately precincts of the 'Big Engine Club' came Bowen-Cooke's outstanding 4-4-os of the 'George the Fifth' class. These engines, inside-cylinder 4-4-os, did not look very big alongside such engines as *Cardean*, the North British 'Atlantics', and the North Eastern 'V' class; but those new L.N.W.R. engines were clocking into Carlisle on time, having hauled trains of 350 to 390 tons unassisted over Shap. They could be seen setting out for the south with equally big loads, and no pilots.

It was inevitable that comparisons were made. From Carlisle the three major summit points are at Aisgill, on the Midland, Beattock on the Caledonian, and Shap on the North Western. The Citadel station stands about 65 ft. above sea level, and the following table shows the average inclinations faced by the locomotives of outgoing trains.

Railway	Summit	Altitude in ft.	Distance from Carlisle (*miles*)	Average Gradient
Midland	Aisgill	1151	48·3	1 in 235
Caledonian	Beattock	1015	49·7	1 in 277
L.N.W.R.	Shap	915	31·4	1 in 194

The Caledonian had by far the hardest individual obstacle, because on the Beattock bank proper the gradient varied between 1 in 88 and 1 in 69 for a solid ten miles, and it followed a lengthy gradual pull up from the Solway Firth. Even *Cardean* used to take rear-end banking assistance with the minimum load of the 'two o'clock'—about 300 tons. Going up to Shap the North Western's worst pull was 7 miles continuously at 1 in 125. Coming north

29. CARLISLE: MORE SCOTTISH TYPES

(a) A North British superheated 0-6-0 (W. P. Reid design), became L.N.E.R. Class 'J.36'.

(b) One of the first N.B.R. 'Atlantics', No. 880 *Tweeddale*, as originally built, non-superheated.

(c) G. &. S.W.R. A Manson 'No. 8' class 4-4-0, No. 78, on Stranraer to Carlisle boat express passing Gretna Junction.

certainly there was the Shap incline itself with its 4 miles at 1 in 75. But there is a good deal more than mere inclination, and Shap could be 'charged' at a speed of about 65 m.p.h. Nevertheless those L.N.W.R. 4-4-0s were doing a mammoth job from 1910 onwards, especially seeing that their Midland rivals were limited to a maximum unpiloted load of 230 tons.

The 'George the Fifths' were no more than a beginning on the West Coast Route. The superheated version of the 'Experiment' class 4-6-0s—the 'Prince of Wales' class—followed in 1911, and then in 1913 came the 'Claughtons'. There was no question of comparisons from that time onwards. The 'Premier Line' of Great Britain was running into Carlisle with locomotives that, on the basis of scientifically recorded horsepower output, were the most powerful in the whole country, let alone the narrower field of the railways running into Carlisle. I must not dwell unduly upon the 'Claughtons' in this chapter, for I shall have much to write about them when I come to Shap itself, in chapter sixteen. But to see them start a maximum load train southbound from the Citadel station was indeed a sight. The North Western had the hardest immediate start. I have told earlier how the Newcastle and Carlisle was the first railway to arrive in the city, and while its passenger station was on London Road, and east of the present station the line was continued westward, on a branch to reach the canal, and it was over this branch that the Maryport line originally came in. So, when the Lancaster and Carlisle was projected the earlier line lay athwart their path; and in the way of old railways arrangements were made to cross it on the level. As traffic developed this was, of course, an intolerable situation for the London and North Western, and a viaduct was built to cross the North Eastern line. This needed a short gradient of 1 in 110 almost from the platform end, in order to gain the necessary altitude, and up this gradient the North Western engines used fairly to blast their way.

The Midland came into Carlisle by running powers over a short length of the North Eastern line and expresses leaving for the south had a short falling gradient to reach the lower level of the North Eastern line. Commentators also remarked frequently on the rapidity of Caledonian starts. So they ought to have been, for there is a descent at 1 in 100 for nearly half a mile from the very platform end! But that gradient could cut both ways, as I once saw for myself just before the grouping. One could see huge trains from the north coming into Carlisle hauled by one 4-4-0 locomotive, and even the latest 'Dunalastairs', superheater equipped, were not the equal of the 'George the Fifths', let alone the later North Western engines. These very heavy Caledonian trains had most likely been double-headed up to Beattock summit from the north. There a stop would be made to put off the pilot, leaving one 4-4-0 with a 50-mile downhill run to Carlisle. Well, one day when I was at Carlisle the 10 a.m. from Glasgow to Euston—now known as The Royal Scot—approached right on the heels, as it were, of the Waverley Route train for St. Pancras, and it was stopped by signal right on that 1 in 100 gradient leading up into the Citadel station. The engine was a superheater 'Dunalastair IV', but she had such an enormous load that the L.N.W.R. had *two* 'Claughtons' waiting to take it up to Shap. Of course the one Caledonian 4-4-0 was hopelessly stuck on that 1 in 100 gradient, and could not restart. After one or two fruitless struggles her crew sent out an S.O.S. and, after a few minutes, the two waiting 'Claughtons' were waved back through the station and coupled up to the stranded 'Dunalastair'. The noise as the two of them lifted the Caledonian engine and its train out of the predicament was worth going many miles to hear!

Mention of trains arriving close upon each others' heels leads me to tell of the situation that sometimes occurred at the south end. In view of the volume and complexity of the traffic it is remarkable that there were—and still are—only three through platform lines. Two of these were unidirectional, and only the central one could be used in either direction. At the south end, however, trains could approach from the Midland and London and North Western lines simultaneously. There was often some close running between the rival Scotch expresses. The 9.30 a.m. from St. Pancras used to come in at much the same time as the Edinburgh portion of the 10 o'clock from Euston, while in pre-war days there was similar conjunction between the 1.30 p.m. from St. Pancras, and the famous 'two o'clock' from Euston. In the mid-afternoon, when the two morning expresses from London were due the celebrated railway photographer of that era, F. E. Mackay spent several afternoons in the hope of getting the two trains running 'neck and neck' into the station. The nearest he got to it was of the Midland train rounding the curve up from the North Eastern line, with the North Western just discernible in the distance on the viaduct crossing the canal lines. The North Western train, 'Claughton' hauled must have come in pretty sharply, because in his photograph of the latter the engine had gained sufficiently on its rival to be abreast of the Midland dining car.

Before ringing down the curtain on the pageant of Carlisle, in pre-grouping days I must not forget the gay little engines of the Maryport company. My first introduction to them had been during the war, when one of them worked the up evening mail down the Furness line as far south as Millom. I shall always remember the first sight I had of that train. One had grown used to the iron-ore red engines of the Furness Railway, and then suddenly to see this brilliant green apparition was to make a stranger rub his eyes. The most familiar passenger engines were of the 0-4-2 type, with coupled wheels 5 ft. $7\frac{1}{2}$ in. diameter, but none of them had been built more recently than 1895. They were nevertheless kept well up to date for the modest passenger requirement of the company, and added yet another colour to the kaleidoscopic effects in Carlisle. The 'green' of the Maryport and Carlisle engines was quite different from the other greens to be seen in the Citadel station, being much brighter, and heading towards the startling malachite green adopted for the Southern Railway locomotives in Bulleid's time. In a photograph the carriages had the 'black and white' appearance of the London and North Western stock, but actually the bodies were dark green, and the upper panels white, with a faint touch of green in it. The prosperous little company certainly added its quota of individuality to the pageant of Carlisle.

CHAPTER THIRTEEN

Rivals on the Clyde coast

THERE ARE FEW among us, even the most liberally minded of travellers, who do not have their favourite routes; and where the Firth of Clyde was concerned in pre-grouping days, and Glaswegians were heading 'doon the watter' the heat of partisanship between those who favoured the 'Sou'-West' and those of the Caley at times reached temperatures excelled only by the supporters of 'Hibs' and 'Hearts', or other similarly inclined contestants. A friend of my younger days, a farmer down in Wessex, had some family connections with shipbuilding on the Clyde, and every year he spent part of his holidays staying with his relations near Greenock. He was a keen railway enthusiast and some fifty years ago made some very interesting contributions to railway literature; but to the end of his long life there was only one way to Greenock for him: West Coast from England, and then by the Caledonian. Although he had wide interests in other parts of Great Britain, for him the Glasgow and South Western Railway might not have existed! People who lived on the spot were well enough aware of the 'enemy', depending upon whose side they were on; and it is quite astonishing how frequently the old fires were raked into a fresh blaze, even after the two companies had for long been brought together within the L.M.S. system. There is a story told of the anxious November of 1936. At Ayr two ex-G. & S.W. men were talking:

'I hear', said one, 'that the King is to abdicate.'
'Ay, they tell me there's a Caley man getting his job.'

All else apart, when it came to scenery the 'Sou'-West' was incomparably supreme in its approach to the Clyde. In a 'Rhapsody by way of Introduction to the Firth' George Blake has written 'The train, suddenly gathering speed, began to race downhill from the uplands about Kilmalcolm to sea level, a drop of fully 400 feet in four miles or so. The line was precariously cut into the side of the hills that rose nearly sheer from a water's edge studded with the uprights and gantries of shipyards, and it seemed to those who saw the carriages swaying down the incline and also to those who travelled in them that the 9.35 a.m. out of St. Enoch's must, like a spent rocket, hurtle at length into the sea: so vertiginous is the drop in that section of the old Glasgow and South Western Railway. . . .'

156

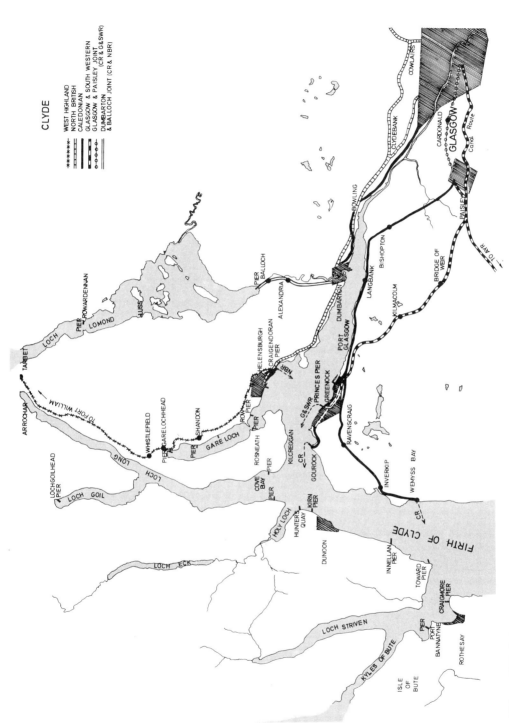

CLYDE

WEST HIGHLAND
NORTH BRITISH
CALEDONIAN
GLASGOW & SOUTH-WESTERN
GLASGOW & PAISLEY JOINT (CR & G&SWR)
DUMBARTON
& BALLOCH JOINT (CR & NBR)

MAP 4: THE FIRTH OF CLYDE: RAILWAYS AND SHIPS

It is rare that a non-technical writer understates the facts where railways are concerned; but while his '400 ft.-drop' is near enough, the precipitous descent is nearly six miles long, and the nearer it gets to the water's edge the steeper it becomes! The Caledonian got into Greenock first, and took a quick cut to the riverside on easy gradients through Bishopton and Langbank. The 'Sou'-West' with an eye to developing some residential traffic, went over the hills, through the little town of Kilmalcolm. Going towards the coast there is a long climb almost from the point where the main line is left near Paisley, though the gradients are not so severe as those climbing from Greenock to the summit point near a tiny little signal box called 'Upper Port Glasgow'. The bare statistics of running over this line do not give much impression of breathless haste, for the very fastest time-schedule over the 25 miles from St. Enoch to Princes Pier was 37 minutes, inclusive of a brief stop at Paisley. But when the difficult nature of the route was considered the congested start to Paisley, the long climb up to Upper Port Glasgow, and the need for caution on the final stages of the descent into Greenock it involved some hard work for the little engines employed right up to the time of grouping. In any case, with incredibly smart working of the steamers these trains provided a service in three minutes under the even hour from Glasgow St. Enoch to Dunoon, on the far side of the Firth of Clyde.

Some of the best locomotives ever to run on the Glasgow and South Western Railway were used on the Greenock service. Hugh Smellie and James Manson both built small-wheeled versions of their main line express 4-4-0 for the Clyde coast. The main line engines had to run fast, and were given coupled wheels 6 ft. 9 in. diameter. The main problem on the Clyde services was the need for rapid acceleration, and an ability to climb the heavy gradients. These were more difficult on the homeward run towards Glasgow. Right off the platform end at Princes Pier the gradient becomes 1 in 70, through a succession of tunnels, and that 1 in 70 continues for an unbroken $3\frac{1}{2}$ miles. Then there is an easing to 1 in 98 for the last two miles of the climb. In the reverse direction, although the total vertical rise is the same it is spread over $8\frac{1}{2}$ miles, and although speed has to be reduced a little when diverging from the Ayr main line there is a mile of sharp descent before the climb to Upper Port Glasgow is commenced, and one can therefore take a run at it.

Hugh Smellie's 4-4-0s designed for this road had 6 ft. 1 in. coupled wheels, and were always known as the 'Wee Bogies', to distinguish them from the 6 ft. 9 in. main line engines. The 'Wee Bogies' were grand little machines, loved by all who had to use them; but in the period of which I am now writing they had largely been superseded on the more important jobs by Manson's 'Greenock bogies'. Both classes had cylinders of the same size, namely $18\frac{1}{4}$ in. diameter by 26 in. stroke; but the Manson engines, having larger boilers, and a higher working pressure were considerably the more powerful. A run I had with one of these engines showed how admirably they fulfilled the hard task for which they were designed. They were first introduced in 1895, but they were so much on top of the job that they virtually had the Greenock road to themselves for the best part of thirty years. At the time I made this particular journey the engine was over twenty-five years old. We came ashore from one of the steamers to find a load of 175 tons—quite a train for such a combination of elderly engine and very severe road. We started without a suspicion of hesitancy, or slipping, and gathered speed steadily on the 1 in 70 gradient through those grisly tunnels beneath the town of Greenock. Up that precipitous hillside she went pedalling away, and at the top of the 1 in 70 the speed was 25 m.p.h. The easing of the gradient to 1 in 98 brought a sharp increase in speed to $28\frac{1}{2}$ m.p.h., but when we reached the summit, $5\frac{3}{4}$ miles from Princes Pier we had been $14\frac{3}{4}$ minutes on our way—ample evidence of the severity of that start. Then we went flying down the bank towards Paisley, with speed rising to a steady 73 m.p.h., and the $17\frac{3}{4}$ miles to the stop there took $28\frac{1}{4}$ minutes.

A present-day reader might, by this time, be wondering just what all the hurry was about on these Clyde coast services. Why, for example, should it have been necessary to get from Glasgow to Dunoon in less than an hour? Surely another five or ten minutes would not matter! If one was touring, or journeying to the outer shores of the Firth for a holiday it would certainly not matter. The traveller would be glad to drink in the beauties of the scenery on the way. But in the latter part of the nineteenth century, just as some of the more affluent London businessmen lived at Brighton, as Manchester men came in from Southport or Blackpool, and the rich merchants of Leeds lived at Scarborough or Bridlington, so Glasgow folks began to live on the Clyde. Clusters of choice villas grew up on the shores of the Gareloch, round the Holy Loch, at Dunoon, and even as far afield as Rothesay and the Kyles of Bute. The Glasgow and South Western Railway, and the Caledonian—rivals from their very inception—were not slow in taking up the challenge of competition, for what looked like becoming a highly profitable commuter service. Many people had summer or week-end villas, others lived on the coast all the year round. It was not only the two great rival railways that were involved; the North British was in it too, though one felt that choice of route would to some extent be dependent upon where one worked in Glasgow. While it is true that 'crossing the City' was never the problem it is in London, if for example, one's train terminates at Waterloo and the office is near Euston. But in Glasgow the North British running along the north bank of the Clyde never got caught up in the speed fever to quite the same extent as the two 'enemies' on the south side.

On the Dunoon run the Caledonian always had a certain advantage over the 'Sou'-West'! The railway route was much easier, and the fact that Gourock pier was nearly two miles farther from Glasgow Central than Princes Pier was from St. Enoch was really an advantage. It was that much nearer to Dunoon, and in a combined rail and steamer service the less distance that had to be covered by water was an advantage. But the Caledonian never rested on this particular advantage. The Gourock boat trains were run at breakneck speed, to such an extent that regular travellers petitioned the railway company for some deceleration. With the Caledonian, there was no question of running the trains with superannuated 'Wee bogies'. Polmadie shed was required to provide a 'Dunalastair' for the crack evening run to Gourock, whatever the demands of the main line service might be; and as the trains grew heavier the locomotive superintendent, the great John F. McIntosh, built a new class of 4-6-0 locomotive specially for the job. While the 'Sou'-West' was relying entirely on the little 'Manson bogie' 4-4-0s McIntosh put St. Rollox works on to the building of a small-

wheeled version of the great 'Cardean' class for the Gourock run. The main object of building these big engines was to secure very rapid acceleration from rest, and from slacks, and so keep the fast overall schedules without having to resort to the high maximum speeds that were necessary with the smaller engines. They were known as the '908' class, and their status was emphasized through two of them being named.

Only a very few Caledonian engines were named. There was the *Dunalastair* named after the estate of the chairman of the company, and *Dunalastair 2nd*, the first engine of the second batch of those engines. There were one or two engines named after personalities, and then of course there was *Cardean*, named after the Perthshire estate of Edward Cox, the deputy chairman. In the '908' class, engine No. 911 was named *Barochan*, the residence of the chairman of the company at the time the engines were built. It lay on the Firth of Clyde, near Langbank, within sound, if not sight, of the line to Gourock, and it was naturally arranged that engine No. 911 *Barochan* should work regularly on the Gourock trains. At times of busy traffic all sorts and conditions of engines were pressed into service on the Clyde Coast trains, including 0-6-0 goods engines. The Caledonian had a fine distinction in the utilization of its goods and mixed traffic engines. Those for use purely on goods were not fitted with the Westinghouse brake and were painted black. The Westinghouse-fitted engines, which were of course the only ones that could be used on passenger trains, were painted blue. Despite the use of 0-6-0 engines on special occasions it was nevertheless something of a surprise when McIntosh built a small class of four 0-6-0 engines, in 1912, specially for the Clyde Coast *passenger* services. With superheated boilers, and ample dimensions all round, they were brisk, powerful engines; yet with coupled wheels no more than 5 ft. 0 in. in diameter they were hardly ideal for a service that required maximum speeds of well over 60 m.p.h. Their construction, however, merely tended to highlight the continued stagnation in engine design for the Clyde services on the Glasgow and South Western Railway.

During World War I the line from Glasgow to Gourock partook of a new importance. The inner reaches of the Firth became a naval anchorage. Ocean liners fitted out as transports brought the troops of our overseas allies in their tens of thousands. Far heavier trains had to be run than the 'neck-or-nothing' commuter trains to Dunoon, on which no more than two minutes was allowed for the transfer from train to boat. McIntosh had retired in 1914, and his successor, William Pickersgill, went in for outside cylinders on his six-coupled engines. In 1917 he received authority to have twelve new engines for the Clyde Coast built by the North British Locomotive Company. These handsome engines could be broadly described as a tank engine version of the '908' class, with outside cylinders, except that the new tanks were superheated, had slightly larger cylinders, and a lower boiler

30. CLYDE COAST TANK ENGINES

(a) Pickersgill 4-6-2, Caledonian Railway.
(b) North British of earlier vintage—0-4-4 No. 94.
(c) Robert Whitelegg's G. & S.W.R. express type, No. 543, of 1922.

pressure. The tractive effort was 20,704 lb. They were ideal engines for the heavy wartime traffic, and afterwards, when there was a partial return to normality, they took over the ordinary service to Gourock to the exclusion of practically every other class. While those post-war trains did not have to run so hard as of old the 4-6-2 tanks certainly skipped along very freely with them. It was rather curious that Pickersgill designed and built a 4-6-0 main line engine just before the 4-6-2 tanks. The two designs seemed obviously of the same character, in their use of outside cylinders, and other features hitherto new to the Caledonian. The main line engines proved to be dreadful sluggards, although very strong on a bank; and yet the 4-6-2 tanks, which had smaller coupled wheels were altogether more lively.

Some of our family holidays, after the war, were spent at Rothesay, and journeying thence we used the Caledonian route to Wemyss Bay. There was no direct competition on this service. The Glasgow and South Western had no nearer port to Rothesay than Princes Pier, and from there steamers took the route via Dunoon. It was a good thing for the Caledonian and its passengers that racing was confined to the Gourock line, because the 10 miles of the Wemyss Bay line were even more hilly than the 'Sou'-West' between Princes Pier and Paisley. One cannot get away from the shores of the Firth of Clyde without climbing, and climbing it is with a vengeance, immediately upon diverging from the Gourock line just beyond Port Glasgow, at Wemyss Bay Junction. The gradient is at once 1 in $67\frac{1}{2}$, and those fine 4-6-2 tank engines used to tell us all about it once they were over the junction. The railway climbs high above Gourock, giving a magnificent panoramic view over the firth, with Gourock almost at one's feet, steamers plying in many directions, the mountains of Argyll away to the west, and right opposite, rising behind the hills on the northern shores, the distinctive summit of Ben Lomond. The heavy pounding beat of the engine is music in the ear of the railway enthusiast, until it suddenly ceases ready for the stop at upper Greenock. The restart from there had to be made right on the 1 in $67\frac{1}{2}$ gradient, but the summit is reached less than a mile beyond, and then it is mostly downhill running through high tumbled country, inland from the firth. The last time I made this run was in the cab of one of the modern electric trains—impressive in its mastery over severe gradients, but lacking the immense *character* of the laborious steam working of old.

Quite suddenly, or so it always seemed, we came down to water's edge again, and into one of the most beautiful railway stations I have ever known. The Caledonian was a rare mixture, when it came to stations. There were grand ones, like Glasgow Central and Edinburgh Princes Street; there were pleasant, and very busy smaller ones like Stirling, Callander, and Gleneagles, and then the 'shacks', headed by the prize example of them all, Glasgow Buchanan Street. But Wemyss Bay was like none of these; and although on the water's edge it derived nothing from the outlook from its steamer piers. The trains came in to this terminus on a gentle curve, and just beyond the buffer stops was a spacious, beautifully light concourse, entirely roofed with glass, and decorated profusely with hanging baskets of geraniums. Somehow, it was managed to keep that concourse and its glazed roof clean; but what delighted those who had time to look up and see it was the superb design of that roof, and how the light steel girder-work was curved and blended towards the central feature of the circular booking office, and then extended to graceful arches over the entrances to the platforms. In that concourse one was no more than vaguely conscious of the trains; and the firth and the steamers were completely out of sight. There was probably method in this. The Firth of Clyde is no different from the entire West Highland seaboard of Scotland in its fickle weather. I remember one holiday at Rothesay when there were only two days in a month when we did not have rain. It was not a sustained deluge, but days of quick intermission of bright skies and sudden downpours; and the sheltered central concourse at Wemyss Bay station was very welcome when waiting for the steamers. Of course, on the principal runs from Glasgow the Rothesay steamer was usually waiting; but that one broad jetty had space enough for five steamers to berth at once, and there were many connections, up and down the coast.

Even when one landed on the Isle of Bute the railway atmosphere was still strong, and Rothesay pier was a veritable 'York' or 'Carlisle' of the Clyde steamer services. Glasgow and South Western, and Caledonian steamers berthed alongside each other; the North British were there too, with their steamers named after characters in the Waverley Novels, duplicated in nearly every case by names on their 'Scott' class of locomotives. One saw also the steamers of the non-railway owners, mostly engaged on summer tourist runs through the Kyles of Bute and into the western sea-lochs. But of these the most important, to which even the railway steamers made obeisance was the veteran paddle steamer *Columba* run by MacBrayne's. The *Columba* was, however, much more than a glorious vintage specimen of a nineteenth-century paddle steamer. She carried the Royal Mail. All this was long before the days of commercial air services, and many of the 'main' roads in the Western Highlands were little better than cart tracks. So the mail went by water, and from various ports of call, out in the 'back of beyond', smaller steamers provided connecting services. During the summer the *Columba* left Glasgow, Bridge Wharf at 7.11 a.m. It was typical of the insistence placed upon regular time-keeping to have that odd minute, instead perhaps, of the more obvious 7.15. I believe it was timed originally to provide connection with the West Coast Postal special from Euston, which arrived in Glasgow shortly after 6 a.m. But I regret to add, however, that even in the days of the North Western, and of the Caledonian, the time-keeping of the 'Postal' was not always immaculate, and I believe most of the English mail for the west was conveyed to Gourock by train, and put on to the *Columba* there.

The *Columba* itself was an institution in western Scottish transport, recognized far beyond the purlieus of Glasgow, or indeed of Scotland itself. The uncle of mine, of whom I have written in chapter nine of this book, had travelled widely even before the turn of the century, and had enjoyed the *Columba*, so much so that after World War I, when he was retired and living in Sussex and a holiday at Rothesay was contemplated, he went north by a not-very-convenient night train from Euston so as to arrive in Glasgow in good time to catch the *Columba* at 7.11 a.m. from Bridge Wharf, and sail the whole way down the Clyde to Rothesay. What my aunt said afterwards about that night journey from Euston does not, however, bear repetition! MacBrayne's also carried the mails into the northern fiords of the

31. PRESERVED SCOTTISH VETERANS
The Caledonian 4-2-2 No. 123 and G.N.S.R. 4-4-0 *Gordon Highlander*
on a Stephenson Locomotive Society Special at Killochan, (Stranraer
Line) in 1962.

firth, by another of their graceful paddle steamers, the *Iona*. This connected with the
Columba at Gourock, and also, of course, collected any appropriate English mail that the
Caledonian Railway had brought down from Glasgow by train; then she sailed for
Lochgoilhead. Unless one happened to be staying in Gourock the run of the *Iona* was not
an easy one to fit into a day excursion, and from Rothesay it was much more convenient
and profitable to use the North British Railway steamers.

North of a line from Greenock and Gourock to Dunoon, the North British had the
country and the intricate waterways to themselves. The 'commuter run' so far as Glasgow
citizens were concerned, came down the north bank of the Clyde, through Clydebank,
Bowling and Dumbarton, and terminated at Helensburgh; but the steamer services were
operated from a combined rail and steamer station at Craigendoran, just a little short of
Helensburgh itself, and as finely equipped as Gourock and Princes Pier. The North
British certainly entered the fight for the Dunoon traffic as keenly as the other two; but
Craigendoran was not exclusively a steamer terminal on the railway, and the train-to-
steamer allowance on the hottest competitive runs could not be cut below three minutes.
Nevertheless that was sharp enough, to walk from the station platforms to the steamer
berths; and as on the rival trains of both Glasgow and South Western, and Caledonian, no
luggage was allowed! But to a visitor rather than a commuter the great charm of the North
British services in these areas of the Firth of Clyde lay on the non-competitive tours, to the

many little piers on the Gareloch, and into the real Highland fastnesses of Loch Goil and Loch Long.

Before venturing into these farthest recesses of the Firth of Clyde, which were served by the North British by train as well as by steamer, I must retrace my steps to the starting point; because the North British terminus in Glasgow, Queen Street, near neighbour of the primitive Buchanan Street of the Caledonian, was—and still is—something of a 'character' among British railway stations. There were then, as now, two parts of Queen Street. One is a terminus, at the foot of an even more precipitous incline than that which used to lead into Buchanan Street. The only consolation is that there is no large goods depot alongside. So far as the West Highlands are concerned it was only the through trains to Fort William that went from the terminal part of Queen Street, and had to claw their way up through the long tunnel to Cowlairs on a heavier gradient than any they were subsequently to meet in the mountains. The coast trains went from the 'Low Level', which is rather like a Scottish version of some of the 'semi-daylight' stations on the Inner Circle in London, and where the tracks are exactly at right angles to those in the 'terminal' part of the station and far below them. What with the smoke of hard-worked locomotives, and the grime of half a century of intensive use, Queen Street provided as unlikely a starting point for a delightful journey as could possibly be imagined.

In contrast to the practice of the Glasgow and South Western, and of the Caledonian until Pickersgill designed his big 4-6-2s, the North British used mainly tank engines on the Clyde Coast run. W. P. Reid, who built the 'Scott' 4-4-0s, and his splendid 'Atlantics' for the main line expresses had some handsome 4-4-2 tanks on the Helensburgh trains. Like all other North British engines, with the exception of the 'Atlantics', they had inside cylinders. There were three groups of passenger services working in this area north of the Clyde: the fast residential and boat trains to Craigendoran and Helensburgh; the long distance trains going through to Fort William, and in most cases conveying carriages for Mallaig, and a local service between Craigendoran and Arrochar. The junction with the West Highland line is just east of Craigendoran main station, and as the former immediately begins to climb at 1 in 57 there is a separate high-level platform. The local service between Craigendoran and Arrochar used to be worked from the main, or low-level part of the station, and the two-coach train would back out of the junction before starting on its run over the West Highland line proper.

The beautiful scenery of the Gareloch could be seen to fine effect from the little local train from Craigendoran to Arrochar. One of the Reid 4-4-2 tanks used to nip along pretty smartly between stations with its two-coach load, stopping at Upper Helensburgh, Rhu, Shandon and then Garelochhead. There was no competition here, but that did not mean there was any lingering by the wayside. One point that always used to impress me was the speed at which drivers on this line approached the stations, whether it was the two-coach Arrochar local or the 'sleeper' with through coaches from King's Cross and St. Pancras. The North British like the Caledonian, used the air rather than the vacuum brake, and those old drivers were certainly experts in getting a rapid, albeit very smooth station stop. The final stretch of this most picturesque local run beside the Firth of Clyde is indeed breathtaking in its scenic beauty. Even with no more than two coaches the North British 4-4-2 tank engines made plenty of noise about the start from Garelochhead. The gradient is 1 in 54, then 1 in 60, and then suddenly the line came to a little station—nothing more than a platform—called Whislefield; and there far below was Loch Long. Though not having the added excitement of high speed it is perhaps the most dramatic piece of railway in the whole area of the Firth of Clyde. The loch is 300 feet below, winding sinuously among the mountains, and right opposite is the entrance to a still-narrower fjord, Loch Goil. The very suddenness of its appearance makes this scene leave a most vivid impression. One saw, on occasions, one of the red-funnelled North British steamers paddling its way—a tiny little craft, as seen from above, leaving the characteristic twin trail of white foam in its wake.

This memorable picture was no less entrancing when seen in reverse. We were sailing up Loch Long one day, and had just turned from the entrance to Loch Goil and were heading for Arrochar. The unmistakable sound of a steam engine's whistle attracted my attention, and I looked up the hillside on our right to see a train up on the West Highland Line. It looked just such a tiny toy as the ships appeared from the elevated viewpoint of the railway. It happened to be one of the through express trains rather than a local, and even from that far-off vantage point I could see that the engine was one of W. P. Reid's 'Glen' class 4-4-0s. Strictly speaking, they had no connection with the Clyde Coast services, apart from traversing the line along the north bank from Glasgow to Craigendoran; but one really cannot leave the North British of this era without something more than a mere passing mention of those outstandingly successful 4-4-0 engines. As Smellie, Manson, and Dugald Drummond had built smaller-wheeled variants of their main line passenger engines for use on the Clyde Coast, so Reid built a smaller-wheeled version of his 'Scott' class—not for the Clyde Coast but for the very severe conditions of the West Highland. The 'Glen' class was the result, and a finer hill climbing engine has never run the rails in Scotland, or in England either for that matter. It was a great sight to see them taking the junction at Craigendoran, and then go barking fiercely up the 1 in 57 gradient towards Upper Helensburgh. It was still more thrilling to *hear* them tackle the long and difficult gradient up Glen Falloch—but this is straying beyond the precincts of this chapter.

When a semblance of normality returned to the Clyde Coast after World War I the evidence of a new broom at Kilmarnock was apparent in the locomotive stock of the Glasgow and South Western Railway. Peter Drummond, who had succeeded Manson as locomotive superintendent in 1912 died in 1918, and in his place the directors appointed Robert Whitelegg. Now Whitelegg had been locomotive superintendent of the London, Tilbury and Southend Railway, when that line was taken over by the Midland in 1912. He was not the man to accept a subordinate position, and had resigned. He had just previously introduced some large 4-6-4 tank engines, for the very intense commuter service of the L.T.S. line, and when he assumed office on the Glasgow and South Western his thoughts turned to the same type of locomotive, not for the Greenock line but for the longer-distance residential trains from Glasgow, to Ayr, Fairlie, and Ardrossan. Five of these huge and impressive engines took the road just before the grouping; but history strangely repeated itself. In 1923 the Glasgow and South Western was virtually 'taken over', becoming completely subservient so far as future locomotive practice was concerned to one or another of the English constituents of the London Midland and Scottish Railway. And so for the second time in his life Whitelegg resigned, leaving behind him a newly-introduced 4-6-4 tank engine class. What happened to his 'Baltics' on the Glasgow and South Western afterwards is carrying the story beyond the period of this book, and beyond, of course, the life of the G. & S.W.R. itself; and so with this brief mention of them I must end this chapter.

CHAPTER FOURTEEN

Aberdeen awa'

IN THE YEARS 1907 and 1908 the air was thick with rumours of railway amalgamations and 'working agreements' in Great Britain. Apart from those journalists who swooped on rumours for their novelty and for sheer lack of other copy, there were others who took a more professional view of the proliferation of train service facilities that had taken place since the turn of the century. One such, writing in *The Railway Magazine* in 1908, commented thus: 'For the last three summers, the question has simply been: Where is it all to end? Much of the waste of locomotive power, caused directly by the running of powerful engines on very light trains has been indirectly due to competition, for while the tendency has very naturally been to construct engines capable of dealing with the maximum loads that can be hauled on one train, the needs of the moment have too often dictated some further duplication of express services and the running of lighter, not heavier, trains.' There were rumours of arrangements between the London and North Western and the Midland, to cut out some wasteful competition, and the daily press got wind of this, and some journals splashed headlines reading: 'One night train instead of three to Scotland'. In his blissful ignorance this particular scribe probably imagined there was only one train each from Euston, St. Pancras, and King's Cross. Oh sweet simplicity!

Had he known it, however, he was propounding the germ of the present-day principle whereby train services are 'rationalized', or 'streamlined'—whichever catchword suits one's particular fancy. Up to the end of the 1920s one had the choice of three routes from London to Aberdeen; now there is only one. Despite the forecasting of the daily press of 1908, any arrangements made between the companies did not extend to cutting out the many competitive through train and through carriage services on the Scottish routes. Of these, those of the Midland were among the most interesting, and to a younger generation it may seem surprising that the Midland ran through carriages from St. Pancras to Aberdeen, and to Inverness. One might imagine that the main object in the operation of such services was to give through facilities for large towns on the routes that were not served by either the East or West Coast trains, such as Leicester, Nottingham, Sheffield and Leeds. Yet in actual

32. ABERDEEN AWA'—BY CALEDONIAN

(a) Down express goods train near Stanley Junction, hauled by McIntosh superheater mixed traffic 4-6-0 No. 181.

(b) Larbert Station, showing local train hauled by Conner 7 ft. 2-4-0 No. 30.

fact the number of through passengers from London was surprisingly high. The Midland was a very popular line, and there were many who preferred to spend a little longer on the journey to get the comfort of the Midland carriages, and its fine scenery on daytime runs.

The Midland management had every reason to foster its services to Scottish destinations north of Edinburgh, for it was a partner in the ownership of the Forth Bridge, with the North British, North Eastern and Great Northern. It was very heavily committed financially. The Forth Bridge Company guaranteed its shareholders a dividend of 4 per cent per annum, in *perpetuity*, and the liability for providing the necessary funds to pay that dividend was shared by the four railway companies, in the following proportions: North British, 30 per cent; Midland $32\frac{1}{2}$ per cent; and the Great Northern and North Eastern $18\frac{3}{4}$ per cent. The Midland was thus the largest individual guarantor. One feels that the other two English companies must have chuckled to themselves when this proportion was agreed upon, because the amount of through traffic that came on to the Midland line from over the Forth Bridge must from the very outset have been a very small fraction of that going into England by the direct East Coast Route. Everything to and from the Midland had to pass over the Waverley Route from Carlisle to Edinburgh, and then be re-marshalled into the first convenient North British train. I used to see the Midland through carriages that had left St. Pancras at 9.15 p.m. the previous evening coming through Stonehaven at about 11 o'clock in the morning, on the same train as the carriages off the 10.25 p.m. from King's Cross. I often wondered if anyone made the through journey from St. Pancras.

Even before World War I events were very gradually moving away from the intense competition between the East and West Coast companies that had led to the great Race to the North, in 1895. There was a natural rationalization of Scottish services taking place without any formal arrangements. The East Coast was very gradually assuming the ascendancy so far as Aberdeen was concerned, with the West Coast taking the greater share of the Inverness and Far North traffic. In two respects the West Coast remained supreme through the period of this book, and indeed without question until the nineteen-fifties. These two respects were the conveyance of the Royal Mail, by the world-famous special postal trains between Euston and Aberdeen, and at least once a year the conveyance of the King and Queen, en route for their annual summer visit to Balmoral. So far, however, I have been considering traffic to Aberdeen from south of the border. In Scotland itself there was a time when rivalry between the North British and the Caledonian threatened to develop into 'race' techniques; but this particular rivalry was short-lived, and an 'arrangement' was concluded that eliminated what could have been a most wasteful competition.

The Caledonian route to Aberdeen, from the south, leaves the main line to Glasgow at Law Junction and by-passes the crowded area of Motherwell. But the junction layouts north of Motherwell are such that trains for Aberdeen, or Glasgow for that matter, can take either route. The racing trains of 1895 naturally went via Holytown, and after resumption of normal running the famous 8 p.m. tourist express from Euston continued to run non-stop between Carlisle and Stirling. There is some complicated railway geography north of Holytown, and a fascinating field of study for those who delight in delving into the early history of individual pieces of line. But so far as through running is concerned the north main line, engineered so splendidly by Joseph Locke, meets the line from Glasgow at Glenboig. There is a triangle junction here whereby trains from the south could turn to the left, and descend from Robroyston into the Buchanan Street terminus of the Caledonian. There was a large goods station adjoining, and some of the most important express goods trains from the south terminated there. I write all this in the past tense, for in recent years the entire Buchanan Street complex of the Caledonian has not only been closed, but completely demolished and swept away. While one can regret the passing away of old individual activities there are not many tears to be dropped over the disappearance of Buchanan Street station itself!

The headquarters offices of the Caledonian Railway were nearby, but the station itself was an extraordinarily drab collection of 'shack' buildings, short platforms and thoroughly inconvenient track layout. To meet the competition of the North British, in the early 1900's some magnificent new trains were put on, but the Glasgow station from which they started was, even in those days, enough to put anyone off! And then there was that tunnel, less than half a mile from the buffer stops and rising steeply on a gradient of 1 in 79. The heaviest trains used to start, draw clear of the platform, while a rear-end bank engine buffered up. Then the cavalcade used to pound up through the tunnel, and past the dismal little station of St. Rollox, and out into a succession of highly industrial suburbs. There were three miles of heavy 'grind' until the level line was reached at Robroyston. St. Rollox— one might have thought to see something of the works where Caledonian engines were built and maintained—but there was barely a glimpse. The only consolation for a partisan was to know that the North British had an even worse start out of Glasgow!

Despite the rather dismal surroundings there were some splendid engines to be seen at Buchanan Street. The sheds for engines on the north road were at Balornock, near to St. Rollox works, and although they rarely met face to face there was no little rivalry between the enginemen there, and at the other large shed, Polmadie, near Rutherglen, which provided for the English trains and the Clyde Coast services. By the way, for those who do not know the accents of Glasgow the pronunciation of that shed name is *Pol*-ma-*dee*, with the emphasis on the first and last syllable. The great 4-6-0 locomotive No. 50, one of the pioneers of 1903, was stationed at Balornock, and worked on the Aberdeen trains as far as Perth. For some years she was driven by a great character in the person of James Grassie, with whom I was once privileged to ride on the footplate—but alas, not on No. 50, but after the grouping on a Midland compound. The working of the Aberdeen trains out of Buchanan Street was shared by the '908' class 4-6-0s, which with their 5 ft. 9 in. coupled wheels were ideally suited to the heavy gradients between Buchanan Street and Perth. In the last years of the Caledonian, however, there was a disposition to use 4-4-0 locomotives on nearly all express trains, and to concentrate all 4-6-0s, except the 'Cardean' class and 49 and 50 on to fast freight workings. It was then that rear-end banking from Buchanan Street up to Robroyston became common.

Of what might be termed the industrial section of the Aberdeen main line of the Calea

b

c

d

33. ABERDEEN AWA', BIG ENGINES AND SMALL

(a) N.B.R. Atlantic No. 509 *Duke of Rothesay*.
(b) N.B.R. Holmes 4-4-0 No. 769, in 1922, as rebuilt.
(c) N.B.R. A little Drummond survival at Dunfermline: 4-4-0 tank No. 1426.
(d) C.R. One of the McIntosh 'Oban' 4-6-os No. 53 at Stirling.

donian I have the liveliest recollections in connection with the running of the West Coast Postal Special. This train used to divide at Carstairs, and the Carlisle engine, which was usually a 'Dunalastair IV', continued with the Aberdeen vans non-stop to Stirling. From the locomotive point of view the load was at its lightest on this section, but there was some pretty smart work in the sorting vans. There were many places where mails were delivered at full speed, by the traductor apparatus, and two in particular came very close together. A heavy dispatch for the Falkirk district was set down at Carmuirs West Junction, and less than a mile farther on came Larbert. The speed of the train was usually well over 60 m.p.h. in this area, and the sorter in charge of the traductor apparatus had to fix the Carmuirs bag, judge to a split-second the moment for swinging it out to deliver into the lineside net, then after it was gone reload the arm, and be ready for the Larbert dispatch in a matter of twenty seconds or so. I have had the privilege of watching it done from the inside of the van, and it was one of the 'slickest' pieces of work I have ever seen. Those massively re-inforced mail bags are no light weight to move quickly!

With Stirling and its collieries, industrialism is finally left behind, and the Aberdeen road climbs up the glen of Allan Water, past Dunblane to the high moorland plateau that rises gradually towards Gleneagles. The use of 4-4-0 engines, in the later Caledonian days, sometimes involved rear-end banking from Stirling, for the Dunblane bank is nearly six miles long with gradients varying between 1 in 78 and 1 in 100; but with those trains that did not make a station stop at Stirling, unless the engine was in difficulties, or very heavily loaded it was quicker to take a run at the bank, and risk speed getting down to little more than 20 m.p.h. at the top, than to stop at Stirling, wait while a bank engine buffered up in the rear, and then re-start. It was not until near the end of Caledonian days that Gleneagles got its present name. Originally it was Crieff Junction. But when the huge and luxurious hotel was built nearby, for the golfing fraternity, something had to be done, and the name was taken from the wild glen that leads southwards from the railway just to the west of the junction—Glen Eagles. Once over the railway summit in this neighbourhood, drivers of northbound expresses could cease worrying. There is a fast descent down into Strath Earn, and Perth is reached in 150 miles from Carlisle.

In pre-grouping days, once away from Carlisle, and more particularly past Gretna Junction, the engines and trains to be seen from the carriage window would have been exclusively Caledonian, and West Coast Joint Stock; the famous 'white trains'. But coming into Perth the scene once again took on the diversity of Carlisle—not to quite the same extent so far as locomotives were concerned, but certainly in respect of carriages. Running in from the South one passed the Caledonian engine sheds immediately after emerging from Moncrieff Tunnel, and then came those of the North British. There one would see the graceful brown 4-4-0s of the 'Sir Walter Scott' class, all with names of characters and places immortalized in the Waverley Novels. If one was lucky there might be one of the big 'Atlantics' in from Edinburgh. Engine No. 901 *St. Johnstoun*, the patron saint of Perth itself, was a frequent visitor. Once arrived in the station, the variety of carriages to be seen almost equalled that of Carlisle. East Coat Joint Stock, and Midland came in on trains from

Edinburgh via the Forth Bridge; then there would be North British through carriages for Inverness, and above all the highly distinctive green trains of the Highland Railway. In the early years of the twentieth century the Highland was in the process of changing its engine livery; and it did so several times, not contributing to gaiety of turnout in the process. Peter Drummond had abandoned the very beautiful and elaborate style of David Jones, on his 'Castle' class 4-6-os of 1900; but with purple underframes, and black and white lining they still looked very smart. But as shown in Jack Hill's painting of *Gordon Castle* leaving Aviemore, facing page 176, at a later stage Drummond had changed to a plain unlined dark green, and although the engines were still beautifully maintained and finely polished up they undoubtedly lost much of their earlier distinction.

But we are 'Aberdeen Awa' ', and not bound for the Highland line, and are thus still in the stately hands of the Caledonian. And now, less than fifty miles ahead, is that place of dramatic memories, Kinnaber Junction. It is a sobering thought that in these days of 'route rationalization' one cannot travel to Aberdeen by this one-time fast express route, but is taken down beside the Tay into Dundee, and there funnelled into the East Coast Route. One can imagine with what horror proud Caledonian men would have dismissed the very idea that the stretch of line between Perth and Forfar, which for many years was the scene of the fastest regular running on the line, would be closed, and travellers between Glasgow and Aberdeen taken over the winding mountainous line along the coast from Montrose to Arbroath, with all its hindrances to fast running. Yet so it is today. But at the time of which I am now writing the great race of 1895 was a vivid personal memory of nearly all Scottish railwaymen; the Caledonian and North British seemed ever ready to take up arms again, whatever their English allies thought about it. Looking back upon the 'Race', now nearly eighty years ago, its pattern seems more like the style of some wild film, or television scenario, when two trains set out from London, and raced for 500 miles through the night for the junction where the two routes converged! As I knew it Kinnaber Junction looked a very ordinary, very 'innocent' signal-box, up on the hillside overlooking the Montrose Basin. In the prosaic days of the early 1920s East Coast trains, far from racing, were required to slow down to about 15 m.p.h. over the points; but when old 'Jamie' Grassie was running the 5.30 p.m. up from Aberdeen, and I was on the footplate with him, he took the points to the Caledonian line at practically full speed, and laughed heartily at the lurch that compound gave us.

The situation that developed between the Caledonian and the North British in 1906 was prefaced by the introduction of some very fine new coaching stock by both companies—a competition in amenities—and then came the big new engines. McIntosh allocated two of his new 'Cardean' class 4-6-os to Perth shed, and the history of 1903 was repeated in that the Caledonian building of great locomotives in ones and twos, was countered by a 'production batch' from the rivals, and again from the works of the North British Locomotive Company. For the N.B.R. took delivery in 1906 of no fewer than fourteen new engines of the 'Atlantic' type. Six of them were sent new to Aberdeen, and three others stationed in Edinburgh were allocated to the Aberdeen service. For the record, the Aberdeen engines were named *Aberdonian, Dundonian, Bon Accord, Thane of Fife, Auld Reekie* and *St. Mungo*. The second engine of the class, No. 869, was shortly afterwards renamed *Bonnie Dundee*. These were all very appropriate names, because the city of Glasgow came very much into the North British picture when competition with the Caledonian developed. The Edinburgh engines allocated to the Aberdeen road were *Dunedin, Waverley*, and not so appropriately, *Liddesdale*. This latter engine always seemed to work north of Edinburgh. She gave me a great run on the up King's Cross sleeping car express from Dundee to Edinburgh shortly after the grouping.

For a short time in that exciting summer of 1906 the North British scheduled the Edinburgh–Aberdeen run in the level three hours. This may not have seemed very enter-prising for a journey of only 130 miles, seeing that the fastest run in the 'Race' of 1895 had been made in 2 hr. 19 min. But knowing the line, with all its twists and turns, its sharp gradients and its awkward junctions I never cease to marvel at the time made by the East Coast racer on that last night—exactly level time over the 59 miles from Edinburgh to Dundee. Curves that are now restricted to 30 or 35 m.p.h. must have been taken at least at 50 m.p.h. to make the times they did; and while this might be dismissed as pure foolhardi-ness, in the white heat of a competition that had at most become a national sporting event there was just a little sound reason behind it. The 4-4-0 engines in use had a low centre of gravity, and were beautifully designed as vehicles. They rode superbly, and though heeling over on the curves were probably within the limit of safety—just! The record racing times were not the result of a sudden acceleration. The rivals had been working up to it gradually, and drivers finding they could negotiate the difficult parts of the line safely were, little by little, venturing ever faster. It would have been a different matter with the huge 'Atlantics' of 1906, with their high pitched boilers. Certainly no one was taking any risks, and in actual working the three-hour schedule between Edinburgh and Aberdeen proved a little too fast to be maintained. At the turn of the century the North British had a shocking reputation for time-keeping, or lack of it; and the fast, highly competitive Aberdeen trains were frequently delayed by faulty traffic working.

The journey to Aberdeen, whether from Edinburgh or Glasgow, was always much more exciting by the North British than by the Caledonian. The lines from the two great cities converged at Dalmeny at the very approaches to the Forth Bridge. I shall never forget my first crossing of the bridge on the footplate of a locomotive, which came in the early hours of a bitterly cold March morning. On our way north we had run through snowstorms: the wind howled in the ventilators of my 'sleeper', while snow and sleet spluttered against the window-panes. When we got to Edinburgh the snow fortunately had ceased, but it was still mighty cold at 4 a.m. when I climbed into the cab of the engine that was to take me forward to Dundee. The approach to the Forth Bridge was enthralling. Through rifts in the stormy sky the moon shone out and revealed great banks of snow-laden clouds over the sea. The mighty girders were silhouetted weirdly against the night sky; as we passed underneath, each cross member was lit up by the glare of the fire. Past Aberdour, where the line runs down to the shore the prospect across the Firth of Forth is tremendous, whether by day or night. One looks across to Edinburgh, and the distinctive heights behind it, and sees the Lothian coast stretching far out towards the open sea. By night—even shortly after four in the morning—the waterfront is a chain of a thousand lights. Then round a typical sharp curve, through Burntisland, and again we are heading directly north.

Riding one of those big 'Atlantics', fine steady engines though they were, and seeing the curves in the track, one thought inevitably of that incredible racing night. Our time from Edinburgh to Dundee was 80 minutes, and we had to run hard to keep it; that little 4-4-0 in the early hours of 22 August, 1895 did it in 59 minutes. One is bereft of any further ability to comment. After another half-hour or so of switchback road we swept through Leuchars Junction, and over the hilly ground beyond till suddenly another great prospect opened out—the Firth of Tay—and the lights of Dundee strung out in a long shimmering line on the farther shore. The Tay Bridge even in daylight is impressive only in its length and massive construction, and because of the shudder that involuntarily comes in recalling the tragedy of 1879 when the first bridge across the firth collapsed under a train. But by the time we came round the curve at Tay Bridge South Junction, and entered upon the bridge, those rifts in the sky had closed and it was intensely dark. Except in the middle there are no cross-girders. We were racing over an open viaduct across two miles of water. It was eerie, especially as we drew nearer to the Dundee shore, and our speed was if anything increasing. Then we came to the curve through Esplanade station, swung round to the right, and dived down to our stop in Dundee Tay Bridge Station.

When the 'Atlantics' were first introduced none of them were stationed at Dundee. The workings were so arranged that they ran throughout from Edinburgh to Aberdeen. In more recent times, however, and particularly when I first knew the line it was the regular practice for trains to change engines at Dundee. Although there were variations on some duties, most of the through expresses were hauled by Edinburgh-shedded engines between Edinburgh and Dundee, and by Dundee engines on the northern end of the line. The crack 'Atlantic' duties consisted of two return trips over each stretch, with a different driver and fireman on the early and late turns. A Dundee engine, for example, would take the down 'sleeper' from King's Cross and return on the 9.50 a.m., another London train, which included a through carriage for Penzance! Then this engine would be allocated to the down afternoon express from Edinburgh, and return finally from Aberdeen to Dundee on the up 'sleeper' for King's Cross. The engine on this 'diagram' covered 280 miles in the day, while the double-manned Edinburgh 'Atlantics' covered 236 miles.

By the end of World War I North British engines had partaken of a slightly different look. They still had the brown livery, but instead of having NBR on their tenders they had their numbers in large transfer figures in the middle, and the letters N and B on either side. The handsome engraved brass number-plates on the cab sides were removed. It must be admitted that North British engines had lost something of their old smartness of turn-out during the war years, and the 'brown' often had a somewhat mildewed appearance. But those large numbers on the tender sides were for the purpose of traffic control. The North British had installed a system of control similar to that used on the Midland Railway, and

(e) Highland Railway. Inverness to London sleeping car express leaving Aviemore with through portions, via the East Coast, Midland and West Coast Routes. The engine is no. 143 'Gordon Castle'.

JACK HILL

it had worked wonders with punctuality. From being one of the worst timekeepers in Great Britain, the North British in the years just after World War I was one of the most punctual lines in the country. The Caledonian also came into Dundee, from Perth along the left bank of the Tay. The 5 ft. 9 in. 4-6-0s of the '908' class, and even the two 'Cardeans' stationed at Perth used to work in; but although through carriages from Glasgow were run on some of the trains, it was something of a backwater so far as the main Caledonian services were concerned, and the big engines came down from Perth to fill in time between heavier main line duties.

The North British 'Atlantics', although of great power, were at first inordinately heavy coal burners. At that time they were not superheated; but the modification of their boilers to include superheating fairly transformed their work, and while they never had the opportunities for sustained heavy load haulage that came the way of their counterparts on the Great Northern, as powerful hill climbers they were unsurpassed among 'Atlantics'. The northern end of the Aberdeen road was a good place to see them at work. There was a lovely spot up on the cliffs above Stonehaven, where between the trains one could simply enjoy the wide prospect over the sea. Then up the bank, pounding away at about 30 m.p.h., would come one of these stately engines. Five out of the six originally allocated to Aberdeen in 1906 were still on this road at the time of the grouping. They had been joined by one of the later ones of 1912, *Highland Chief*, and one of the two built just after the war, the *Duke of Rothesay*. This last named was a magnificent engine. I had some memorable runs on her footplate. *Thane of Fife* was often on the second London 'sleeper'—the one that brought the Midland carriages from St. Pancras; and she was followed closely by the Caledonian train, bringing carriages from Euston.

There is a hilltop just to the south of Stonehaven crowned by a little monument; it was a favourite objective in a strenuous afternoon's walk, and from it the rugged coast of Kincardineshire could be seen stretching for some fifteen miles to the north. The trains out of Aberdeen had a stiff climb, and for several minutes the slowly drifting cloud of smoke could be seen, while the engines were being heavily fired on that ascent. The Caledonian 'Dunalastairs' may have been fast and powerful, but how they 'chucked it out' as the engineman's saying goes! I was reminded of the old comment of a test engineer belonging to another railway: 'the exhaust was very discoloured'!! Somewhere above the fishing village of Portlethen they reached the top of the bank and the heavy smoking ceased. Then we looked out for a first sight of the train itself, as it came to that exciting stretch of line almost on the cliff edge; there was a flash of bright blue, and we saw her skimming along. There were three trains up from Aberdeen in the afternoon: the 3 o'clock to Glasgow; then the 'Postal Special', which as far as Perth carried some passenger carriages, and then the North British for Edinburgh, always with an 'Atlantic'. The latter train, and also the 3 o'clock to Glasgow, stopped at Stonehaven, and while they stood for a minute or so, one could see a plume of white steam rising from the safety valves of the engine. The 'Postal' did not stop, and was usually going like the proverbial bomb.

Aberdeen Awa'! One journey will always remain in my memory. It was the continuation

(f) 'Lest we forget'; London and North Western Railway war memorial engine no. 1914 'Patriot' passes through Oxenholme on a March day in 1921, with the 9.30 a.m. express from Euston to Glasgow.

from Dundee of that occasion when I crossed the Forth Bridge on the footplate in the early hours of the morning. Our load was heavy enough for us to be double-headed from Dundee, and on the North British it was always the practice to put the regular engine in front, and the assistant next to the train. This always seemed to me a much more logical proceeding than the standard practice of two great English railways that did much double-heading. The North British had the regular, and obviously more experienced driver in front, whereas the North Western and the Midland put the little pilot engines in front. On this occasion our train engine, on which I was riding, was the *Duke of Rothesay*, and behind us was a 4-4-0 of the 'Scott' class, *Lady of Avenel*. Our driver was a grand old engineman, bursting with pride in his job, and delighted to have a visitor to whom he could display his craft. By the time we left Montrose it was daylight, a grey stormy dawn, but the clouds had cleared away enough to reveal some broad vistas over the country. We blasted our way up the bank to Kinnaber Junction, and then as we gathered speed the driver beckoned me to cross to his side of the footplate. As we neared the valley of the North Esk I saw the Grampians away to the west. After a night of snow they hung wraith-like across the sky, exquisitely beautiful in the greyness of this winter dawn. As we climbed the Marykirk bank the driver spoke of the passes leading over to Deeside and of the Royal deer forests around Balmoral. And then he added: 'I've driven the King seven times.'

34. BIG 4-6-0 LOCOMOTIVES AT PERTH

(a) One of the Smith 4-6-os built for the Highland Railway ('River' class), but transferred to the Caledonian.
(b) One of the two 'Cardean' class 4-6-os regularly working on the Aberdeen road, No. 905, at Perth.
(c) Christopher Cumming's *Clan Mackenzie*, Highland Railway, 1921.

CHAPTER FIFTEEN

The amazing Great Central

THIS UNIQUE RAILWAY, this audacious, unnatural growth, was always equally the admiration and the bewilderment of all interested in the development of transportation in England. As the nineteenth century drew towards its close one would have thought that the railway network extending from London to the North Midlands had reached the zenith of its proliferation. In the first 140-odd miles the three great trunk routes—London and North Western, Midland, and Great Northern—had not spread outwards to cover a belt of country more than forty-five to fifty miles wide; and if one did not mind a longer or more roundabout journey there were through trains from London, via Ely and the Fens to Lincoln, Doncaster and York, by the Great Eastern Railway, and via Oxford to Birmingham, Chester and Birkenhead by the Great Western, Yet, crash into this already crowded area came another main line. It was not something on the fringes, endeavouring to 'pick up the leavings', as it were, but an interloper weaving his way right through the very heart of the Midlands. It was not a new railway as such, but the well-established Manchester, Sheffield and Lincolnshire seeking new fields, and in so doing, 'turning every man's hand against him!'—every one of the great trunk routes, that was.

I have always felt that the Great Central Railway could be likened to a compact and flourishing rose bush, that suddenly starts to send out a very straight and strong briar. The rose gardener will immediately clip the briar at its source, lest its strong and unruly growth saps the strength of the main bush. But in the case of the Great Central it was the offshoot that was planned, cultivated, and constantly nurtured, with results that cannot have been to the liking of the shareholders of the original Manchester, Sheffield and Lincolnshire. But the Great Central, unlike some earlier British railway companies that had to scrape and save to the positive dilapidation of their equipment in trying to earn the most meagre of dividends, was so well run, and so splendidly equipped as to make it the admiration of all except the most rigidly hostile of partisans. A friend once referred to it as the 'Jekyll and Hyde' railway. It was 'Dr. Jekyll' to its customers—passenger and goods alike—and 'Mr. Hyde' to its shareholders. Up to the outbreak of World War I no dividend had been paid on the Deferred Ordinary Stock since 1889, and not a penny on the Preferred Ordinary since 1898. Yet, to the honour of the management, and to the fortitude and long suffering patience of the proprietors the railway, as a transportation concern, was one of the smartest and most enterprising in the kingdom.

From the moment of opening the London extension it was a case of 'total war' with the North Western and the Midland—and no wonder, seeing how the new line burst in upon their established territories. The Great Northern also was hostile. After all the old M.S. & L. had been glad enough to team up with the Great Northern in running a highly competitive service from King's Cross to Manchester, via Retford and Sheffield; and King's Cross can hardly have been very pleased when its one-time partner decided to go it alone, the whole way from Sheffield to London. With Sam Fay as general manager, however, the strong central strategic position of the Great Central appeared to offer immense possibilities for cross-country services, if not by complete trains, then at least by through carriages. The Great Central could not look to the Midland or the North Western for co-operation in this respect, but a vital link in the planning of the London Extension had been the construction of a short branch line from just south of Woodford to Banbury, on the Great Western north main line, and it was through this connection—built up to first class main line standards—that a remarkable series of cross-country services was built up. Whatever the attitude of the Great Northern may have been its northern partners on the East Coast Route were ready enough to co-operate, and so was the Lancashire and Yorkshire. It might have been imagined that in earlier days the old M.S. & L. and the L. & Y. might have trodden upon each others' toes in some areas; but although both covered considerable areas of Lancashire and Yorkshire their ways were remarkably separate. So with the Great Western and the London and South Western at the one end, and the Lancashire and Yorkshire and the North Eastern at the other, the Great Central, had, at one time, the following through services in operation:

Newcastle and Bournemouth*
Newcastle and Barry*
Southampton and Scarborough
Southampton and Glasgow (via Newcastle)
Manchester to Dover
Liverpool and Manchester to Yarmouth and Norwich*
Halifax to Ilfracombe
Bradford to Bournemouth

From the above it will be seen that the Great Eastern, to Norwich, and the South Eastern and Chatham, to Dover, were also involved.

I have an interesting family document that relates to the intensely-expansionist activities of the Great Central, and it relates to the year 1908 when the younger of my two sisters

* Through restaurant car expresses.

was born. Our relations in Bradford were anxious to see the latest arrival. We were then living in Reading, and a letter from my aunt arrived announcing that she was intending to call upon us for the afternoon. 'Don't prepare a meal' she concluded; 'We'll take luncheon on the train.' Coming across this letter in the family archives some years ago I was greatly intrigued; after all, Bradford to Reading for an afternoon call was a little unusual in 1908. So I looked up Bradshaw for the year concerned to find the trains by which they must have travelled. Coming south they would have left Bradford Exchange at 7.30 a.m. on a through express for Torquay, and travelling first over the L. & Y. line as far as Penistone. Then after coming down the Great Central main line, and switching over to the Great Western via the Woodford–Banbury link they reached Oxford. There the through carriages for Southampton and Bournemouth were detached, and reached Reading West at 1.30 p.m. Returning from the same station at 5.5 p.m. they had another through carriage for Bradford, with restaurant car, which was eventually attached to one of the London expresses at Leicester. By this they arrived back in Bradford at 11.5 p.m. What a day—and how dearly one would now like to know the types of locomotive employed on the various stages! Although I was one of the 'reception committee' at Reading West, being then of very tender years I cannot say I remember much about it.

My next personal contact with Great Central activities did not come until a dozen years later, and there is much to be said about the intervening years. If the enterprise of the Great Central was amazing in respect of new passenger services it was even more so with freight. Although the old M.S. & L. ran some smart passenger trains between Sheffield and Manchester, and although its engines had to run hard with the London expresses of the Great Northern, as far south as Grantham over the latter company's line, it was primarily a freight carrier, and particularly of coal. In the Barnsley area it was firmly entrenched in one of the richest coalfields in England, and its southernmost extent, in M.S. & L. days, lay in the North Nottinghamshire coalfields. The Midland already claimed the lion's share of the haulage from this area to London, with the Great Northern and the Great Eastern tapping a fair proportion eastwards. But to the Great Central management the most profitable hauls were over the Pennines to Manchester and Liverpool and, above all, for export to the Continent, via Grimsby. One can look back a little wistfully to the days when England had a vast export trade in coal to the Scandinavian and Baltic states, in exchange for which came equally vast quantities of Baltic pine—the finest-ever material for railway sleepers. By the beginning of the twentieth century however, Grimsby was becoming

35. THE GREAT CENTRAL

(a) A contrast in suburban tank engines: one of J. G. Robinson's superheater 4-6-2s of 1911, coupled ahead of a Parker 2-4-0.
(b) One of J. G. Robinson's small-wheeled 4-cylinder mixed traffic 4-6-0s, No. 461, photographed at Neasden, 1920.
(c) Heavy eastbound freight train, emerging from Woodhead Tunnel, hauled by standard 2-8-0 locomotive.

saturated. The traffic in coal and timber could be expanded only to the constriction of the other staple traffic—fish; and in the early 1900s Grimsby was the premier fishing port of the whole world. So the Great Central took the plunge; an entirely new port must be created for the export of coal and the importing of timber.

With the receipt and expenditure programme for 1905 showing a credit balance of a mere £15,000, compared with the £2 million of the Midland in the same year, the Great Central embarked upon the construction of the enormous new deep water dock at Immingham. On 12 July, 1906 Lady Henderson, wife of Sir Alexander Henderson, chairman of the company, cut the first sod, and six years later, on 22 July, 1912 the Dock was formally opened by King George V and Queen Mary. It was located six miles higher up the river Humber than Grimsby itself on almost virgin ground. There was unlimited space to lay out the dock, its approach railway lines, and all handling facilities on the most modern plan. There was nothing to restrict the layout in any way, and in the huge main dock the quays for loading export coal, for the importing of timber, and dealing with heavy miscellaneous cargoes were all kept completely separate. There were seven loading gantries for export coal, capable between them of shipping 5,000 tons of coal per hour; in the 170 miles of sidings leading to them there was accommodation for 11,600 loaded wagons. Apart from all this freight activity, the layout included a jetty set aside for passenger traffic, with a pleasant railway station and facilities for transfer from train to steamer. The 'amazing' Great Central seem to have thought of everything at Immingham, and it cost them nearly £3 million, even in those days. At the opening ceremony His Majesty the King knighted the General Manager, Sir Sam Fay. One further enterprising proposal in connection with Immingham did not, however, materialize, at any rate in the form originally intended by the Great Central, namely to include a naval repairing dock.

To locomotive lovers the Great Central was a sheer delight. John G. Robinson, formerly with the Waterford, Limerick and Western Railway, was appointed chief mechanical engineer in 1900, and he will go down in history as the man who never built an ugly locomotive. From his gracious express passenger classes down to humdrum goods and shunters they were a beautifully proportioned lot. That some of the express passenger classes were larger than the traffic warranted is perhaps apart from the point; but Robinson's goods engines had to work hard enough. It was fully in the spirit of the Great Central of 1900 to 1914, that special classes had to be built for special duties. There were, for example, no fewer than four varieties of outside cylinder 4-6-0s, all of closely similar appearance introduced between 1902 and 1907. They could be broadly distinguished as shown in the table on the facing page.

They were all most beautifully proportioned engines and did their work well. The two 6 ft. 9 in. engines were built simultaneously with a couple of 'Atlantics' of generally identical proportions, to test the relative suitability of the 4-4-2 and the 4-6-0 type for fast main line work. With the light loads generally prevailing the 'Atlantics' were of course quite adequate. How their use developed after World War I I shall tell later.

For the slower and heavier freight traffic, including the coal train hauls over the Pennines,

Coupled wheel diameter		Designation	Number of engines in class	Running Numbers
ft.	in.			
6	9	Express passenger	2	195–6
6	6	'Immingham'	10	1095–1104
6	0	'Fish'	14	{ 1067–1072 180–187
5	3	'Fast Goods'	10	1105–1114

Robinson designed a very powerful 0-8-0, with outside cylinders. It is indicative of the need for locomotives in such a power class that they preceded, by two years, the main line express passenger 'Atlantics'. Furthermore, while the big passenger engines came to be built in twos and half-dozens, a total of no less than eighty-nine of the 0-8-0s was built. They were, without any question, the most elegant looking coal engines ever produced. The last batch of them appeared in 1910. But good though these were something still more powerful was needed for the heavy traffic expected to arise from the completion of Immingham Dock, and in designing a superheated version, with a larger boiler and consequently increased weight at the front-end, the 2-8-0 type was adopted. These proved extremely successful, and by the end of 1913 there were 127 of them in service on the Great Central. How they came to be a War Office standard in later years is yet to be told. But in addition to these very heavy mineral hauls there was a great deal of ordinary goods work to be done, all over the line, and Mr. Robinson had not long been in office before he introduced a smart 0-6-0—another remarkably good-looker—with 5 ft. 1 in. wheels, and a large boiler. They proved most useful general service engines, being able to take a passenger train, if not at top class express speed, then certainly at what was needed for seaside excursions and other specials. They were nicknamed the 'Pom-Poms', and a more graceful 0-6-0 has never run the rails. I suppose ex-Great Central men could draw some satisfaction from the fact these engines were selected by Edward Thompson to be an L.N.E.R. standard in the scheme of post-war reconstruction drawn up in 1945; but many of them would have been horrified—as I was—by the way in which their appearance was transformed into that of an ugly nondescript workhorse, by the simple process of putting on a Great Northern type 'flowerpot' chimney and a button-size dome cover.

One of the most important Great Central locomotive designs of the early 1900s was that of the giant 0-8-4 hump-shunting tank engine introduced for purely yard work in the extensive marshalling yard at Wath. This could be quite superficially described as a tank engine version of the 0-8-0 main line mineral engines. The coupled wheel diameter, and the fixed wheelbase was the same; but instead of the two 19-in. diameter cylinders on the 0-8-0s the humping engines had *three* 18-in. cylinders—an increase of 35 per cent in cylinder volume. They had a large tank capacity, and large coal bunkers to enable them to

keep continuously at work in the yard for long periods. It was, however, the three-cylinder drive that was of greatest interest to locomotive men. The cranks were arranged at 120 degrees to each other, and there were six exhausts for each revolution of the driving wheels. This gave very smooth starting under a heavy load, and the idea was followed in some 4-8-0 tank engines built by the North Eastern Railway in 1909 for similar duty in the Erimus hump marshalling yard near Middlesbrough. Robinson's use of three-cylinder drive on his Wath humping engines had indeed 'started something'. On the North Eastern, Vincent Raven was so impressed with the Erimus shunters that he began to use three cylinders on most of his important main line engines, and I have told in chapter eleven how H. N. Gresley adopted the principle on his Great Northern engines. The curious thing is that Robinson himself did not follow it up on his Great Central engines, except for one experimental 'Atlantic'. When his express passenger and heavy mixed traffic engines reached proportions that could not conveniently be provided for by two cylinders he followed Great Western and London and North Western practice, by using four.

Having briefly mentioned the 'Atlantics', it is now time to describe in some detail these most beautiful and successful engines. There were two varieties apart from the one experimental three-cylinder engine. There were the standard two-cylinder simples, originally built as non-superheaters, with balanced slide valves, some having 180 lb. per sq. in. pressure, and others 200. There were in addition four that were built as 3-cylinder compounds, on W. M. Smith's system, as used on the Midland compounds. They became known collectively as the 'Jersey Lilies', but this nickname was actually not the compliment to their beauty that is commonly supposed. I have told the true story before,* but it is worth repeating. One of the greatest stage beauties of the day was Lily Langtry—the 'Jersey Lily' as she was affectionately known; but at the time the Great Central 'Atlantics' were first introduced an extremely fat woman of 32 stone had been on exhibition at one of the 'Pubs' near the works. She was advertized, sarcastically, as 'The Jersey Lily'. When the first of the new 'Atlantics' arrived from the neighbouring works of Beyer, Peacock & Co. the girth of its boiler created something of a sensation, and some wag thinking of the fat woman in the 'Pub' dubbed it 'The Jersey Lily'; and so the Great Central 'Atlantics' were thereafter known as the 'Jersey Lilies'.

The majority of the tasks allotted to these engines in the years before World War I were very easy, involving the haulage of no more than four- and five-coach trains, at average speeds of around 60 m.p.h. between Marylebone and Leicester. The show train of the whole line, the 3.15 p.m. 'Sheffield Special', normally conveyed five coaches, one of which

36. GREAT CENTRAL PASSENGER TRAINS

(a) Down semi-fast train on the Metropolitan joint line near Pinner, hauled by 'Director' class 4-4-0 No. 430 *Purdon Viccars*.
(b) One of the earliest Manchester expresses on the London Extension, near Harrow, hauled by 4-4-2 No. 1084.
(c) Liverpool–Manchester express on the Cheshire Lines, hauled by one of Robinson's first 4-4-0s, No. 1016.

* In *British Steam Railways*.

was slipped at Leicester. The train itself was non-stop to Sheffield, covering the $164\frac{3}{4}$ miles in 177 minutes, at an average of 55.9 m.p.h. The Leicester slip coach was due to arrive in 109 minutes from London, 103 miles. One of the most interesting trains run by the Great Central Railway, and run moreover at very high speed for that era, was the special newspaper express originally put on shortly after the completion of the London Extension, which event roughly coincided with the birth of the *Daily Mail* newspaper. This train, which at first left Marylebone at 2.45 a.m. was exclusive to the *Daily Mail* for several years, but was later made available to other newspapers, and also included accommodation for ordinary passengers. At the period of which I am now writing it left at 2.40 a.m., and on a typical run the load consisted of two bogie vans, two small four-wheeled vans and two coaches for passengers. Although heavily charged with newspapers the total tonnage for the engine to haul was only 140 tons—a featherweight for a 'Jersey Lily', when one considers the kind of loads that were being taken out of Euston by 4-4-0 engines at the same period. It is startling, too, to find small four-wheeled vans included in the formation of a train which, within the compass of fifty-five miles had to attain maximum speeds of 79, 82, 82, $83\frac{1}{2}$ and $83\frac{1}{2}$ m.p.h. to keep time. Actually, on the run of which I have details before me, one of the little vans did suffer what the report calls 'a slight mishap', and had to be detached at Brackley. I am not surprised, and just wonder in what state the other one was on arrival at Nottingham after such a ride!

In the year that Immingham Dock was opened in such ceremony and splendour one saw a notable change in the locomotive practice of Mr. Robinson. Six very large and imposing 4-6-0 express locomotives were built at Gorton Works, but with *inside cylinders*. The boiler was enormous for that period, but the shapeliness of Great Central engines was fully maintained. They represented a change in another respect, in that all engines of the class were named. The first of them was *Sir Sam Fay*, and the other five were named after cities served by the railway. It seemed that three at any rate of this new class were intended for fast goods work, possibly in anticipation of increased traffic from Immingham, because they were painted in the 'goods' livery—black, with red and white lining. The other three, including the *Sir Sam Fay*, were finished in the splendidly ornate passenger style. In those early days they worked from Manchester over the heavily graded route across the Pennines to Sheffield. This class was followed, in 1913, by what was Robinson's greatest express passenger design, the ten 4-4-0 engines of the 'Director' class. The reversion to the 4-4-0 type, after so long a usage of 'Atlantics' was interesting; but the application of superheating to a splendidly designed and massively constructed engine was most successful. The 'Directors' took over the principal express workings that were operated from the London depot of Neasden, and the 'Atlantics' were mostly quartered at Leicester and Sheffield from that time onwards. The significance of this allocation became apparent to me in post-war years when I began to use the line, and take lengthy lineside observation. The third new engine class of the Robinson 'inside-cylinder' period was a very powerful mixed traffic 4-6-0, of which eleven were built at Gorton in 1913. They were virtually a smaller-wheeled version of the *Sir Sam Fay* class with 5 ft. 7 in. instead of 6 ft. 9 in. coupled wheels.

The First World War, which played such havoc with many British institutions profoundly affected the Great Central Railway; and if the affairs of the company had not brought any joy to the ordinary shareholders, from a time even before the London extension was completed, they could take some proprietorial pleasure that the resources and staff were called upon to render notable service in the national emergency. But first of all, however, there came the inevitable cessation of all normal shipping across the North Sea; and this virtually sounded the death-knell of all the high hopes that had been cherished for the great development of trade through Immingham Dock. The situation was greatly changed by the time the war was ended, and the prolonged period of industrial unrest and strikes in the British coal industry made our former customers across the North Sea look to alternative supplies of fuel. At an early stage in the war Sir Sam Fay was called to Government service, and in January 1917 was appointed Director of Movements on military railways; and in March 1918 he succeeded Sir Guy Granet of the Midland Railway as Director General, incorporating all three branches of the transportation services, namely 'Movements', 'Railways and Roads' and 'Inland Waterways and Docks'. From his pre-war experience on the Great Central it will be appreciated how well he was fitted for this onerous task.

While it was probably through his influence that the Robinson 2-8-0 freight engine of the Great Central was chosen as a standard for general service overseas with the Railway Operating Division, and no fewer than 521 were built by various firms, it was an admirable design for such a purpose in its massive construction, generous bearing surfaces, a fine steaming boiler, and extremely simply machinery. Possibly the only feature that would not be appreciated by a later generation of locomotive engineers was the inside Stephenson link motion; but as that feature of the design contributed to the strength of the engines in lifting a heavy train away from rest little more need be said. Among locomotive officers of the R.O.D. in France they were highly appreciated engines. Towards the end of the war another batch of 2-8-0s, for service on the Great Central itself, was built at Gorton. So far as the 'engine' and machinery was concerned these were the same as the original version of 1911, and as the R.O.D. engines, but had a very much larger boiler. There were 20 of these engines, but their usefulness was not proportional to their weight and cost, and they were, unhappily, only the beginning of the last and least successful phase of J. G. Robinson's career as an engine designer. His large 4-6-0 engines, built from 1918 onwards, had four cylinders, and although very large and imposing machines were, by comparison with his 'Atlantics' and even more so with the 'Director' class 4-4-0s, little short of failures.

The end of the war brings me to the time of my own personal observations on the line. It was a time when most railways in Great Britain were looking rather 'shop-soiled', after the four lean years; the previous impeccable standards of cleanliness of rolling-stock had been allowed to slide, and so long as engines did the job, and coaches could carry lots of people all was well. Not so on the Great Central! I used to walk over to Marylebone station in the early evening to see the 6.20 p.m. Bradford express go out. It was followed by a 6.25 p.m. semi-fast, and this had hardly gone before the porters were gathering to receive the 6.38 p.m.—the crack 'up Manchester', which had come up non-stop from Leicester. Normally one saw three different classes of locomotive, and it was their condition that fairly took the breath away. Immaculate was not the word for it—they positively glittered. The 6.20 p.m. out, which always had a 'Jersey Lily' was an interesting train. It carried two separate slip coaches—huge, elliptical-roofed affairs, which of course had to include their own luggage compartments. and which each weighed 37 tons tare. One was slipped at Finmere, and worked forward from there to serve roadside stations; the second was slipped at Woodford. The main train ran non-stop to Leicester, and because of the intense service over the Metropolitan Line to Aylesbury at that time in the evening it was routed via High Wycombe. Over the Great Western and Great Central Joint Line, from Northolt Junction it followed closely in the wake of the heaviest and most popular of all the Great Western's two-hour Birmingham expresses, the 6.10 p.m. from Paddington. At holiday times, when the latter had to be run in two portions the congestion sometimes extended back to the Great Central train. and I remember being very disgusted once when delays on the Joint Line made the 6.20 p.m. from Marylebone 10 minutes late by the time we got clear of 'joint' ownership at Ashendon Junction. The 6.20 was a flyer in its own right, and had to cover the $107\frac{1}{2}$ miles to Leicester, via this route, in 114 minutes.

The Great Central was a fascinating line to watch. I spent many hours walking the track out in the Chiltern Hills, pedalling down the by-roads that led to overbridges between Harrow, Northwood and Rickmansworth as well as my evening walks to Marylebone. There were not many trains to see, but it was a beautiful countryside in which to spend leisured summer Saturdays with a camera. Despite the relatively few trains there was plenty of variety in motive power. The crack 3.15 p.m. down was one of those trains on which the engine worked through to Manchester; on Saturdays it was a Gorton turn and one could expect, equally, a 'Director', a 'Sir Sam Fay' or one of the 4-cylinder 4-6-0s of the 'Lord Faringdon' class. The midday, and early afternoon up expresses were always 'Atlantic' hauled, and the 2.15 up from Manchester was one of the through workings, and on Saturdays it was always a 'Director' from Neasden shed. The use of the 4-4-0s on the through workings between Manchester and London, and 'Atlantics' on trains that changed engines at Leicester puzzled some observers, because the 'Atlantics' had the higher tractive-effort— 21,658 lb. against 19,644 lb. Both classes had the same tube heating surface, but the boiler barrel was much shorter on the 'Director', 12 ft. 3 in. against 15 ft. This would not only make the 4-4-0s freer in steaming, but on a long run trouble from the partial sooting up of the tubes would be less pronounced. The big 4-6-0s of the 'Sir Sam Fay' and 'Lord Faringdon' classes were, through some mistaken policy of standardization, given the same size of grate as the 'Directors'; and since the power of a locomotive is to a large extent its capacity to burn coal, the big engines in the ultimate extent did little better, if at all, than the 'Directors', and they were used indiscriminately with them on the Manchester–London turns.

While the London area was a good place for seeing the Great Central in rapid action, to see its amazing variety of engine power one had to spend a few hours on the platforms of

Sheffield Victoria station, as I did one day not long before the grouping. But before leaving the London area I must not forget to mention those splendid 4-6-2 tank engines that did all the suburban workings on both the Wycombe and Aylesbury routes. Up in the Chilterns, where the line was jointly owned with the Metropolitan, there seemed a healthy rivalry between the local trains of the Great Central, and those of the Metropolitan which were then steam-hauled from Harrow. The Metropolitan had recently added a class of very handsome 4-4-4 tank engines to their stud, and on Saturdays the outer residential trains came in fairly quick succession from about 12.30 p.m. onwards; and from Rickmansworth in particular the Great Central 4-6-2s and the Metropolitan 4-4-4s always seemed to be trying to see which could get their trains more rapidly into speed, on the heavy climb towards Amersham. The Great Central 4-6-2 tanks were not seen outside the London suburban area in pre-grouping days. They were about the only Great Central standard class not seen going through Sheffield Victoria; for there one saw the freight, *in excelsis*. I still have a copy of the notes I made on a day in September 1922, and the 'bag' included five varieties of 4-6-0; both large boilered and standard boilered 2-8-0s; the smaller 4-4-0s of the 'Sir Alexander' class; both simple and compound 'Atlantics', and finally the 'Director' class 4-4-0 that hauled my train to Marylebone. A further item of variety was the Lancashire and Yorkshire 4-6-0 which took over the haulage of the 10 a.m. express from Marylebone to Bradford. By that time, however, the Lancashire and Yorkshire had amalgamated with the London and North Western, and the former L. & Y. system was known as 'B' division of the L.N.W.R.

CHAPTER SIXTEEN

Shap

THE FASCINATION OF the steam locomotive always seemed to reach its greatest heights when fighting a severe gradient. It was certainly impressive to stand by the lineside in level, open country and see an express train sweep by at 70 m.p.h. or so, with hardly a sound from the engine except the rush of movement. But see the same train up in the hills: the exhaust loud and fierce; volumes of smoke shooting skywards from the chimney, and the rhythmic beat measured, and symbolical of intense effort. Shap was such a gradient. But it was much more; it provided the challenge, the yardstick of requirement against which the skill of the Crewe drawing office and the capacity of the great works was constantly matched. Shap was something else in addition. It was not a case of mere statistics—gradients, vertical rise, and so on; there are far longer and steeper gradients elsewhere in Great Britain. What made steam train working over Shap such a fascinating study from a technical angle was the way it was included—taken in the stride—of an otherwise fast-running main line. The fact that the climbing of Shap took place in glorious northern fell country added immense zest and purely emotional appeal to a major task of locomotive and train operation.

In London and North Western days the run was from Crewe to Carlisle, 141 miles, made non-stop by nine trains a day; and while the average speed scheduled over the comparatively level Southern Division of the line, between Euston and Crewe, was 54 to 55 m.p.h., the only concession to the inclusion of Shap in the Northern Division run was a reduction to 52 or 53 m.p.h. The physical disposition of the heavy gradients was itself a handicap. For the first 78 miles of the run northwards from Crewe to the passage through Carnforth, one had a relatively easy road. Much of it was level, and while there were some sharp gradients, as in the two miles just after passing Wigan, they were what the Americans call 'momentum grades'. They could be rushed, and in consequence did not rule the load. If the going was good one could cover that first 78 miles, to Carnforth, in about 83 or 84 minutes; but then, just when a fireman might be digging down to some less-good coal on the tender, or the fire itself might be getting 'dirty', there lay immediately ahead a gruelling 31 miles, in which the

192   *(g) Brighton and South Coast Railway. Brighton Elegance—the 'Southern*
Belle' in the early twenties.

line rose from little more than sea level to an altitude of 915 ft. at Shap Summit. Quite apart from steam raising, and the techniques of managing the fire, there was the question of engine design; and in this the physical make-up of this part of the line had no small influence. It was not a continuous uniform upward slope from Carnforth to Shap Summit, though of course the aggregate effect could be considered the same. The average gradient, for 31 miles, is 1 in 186, but the really hard climbing comes in two marked stages: the Grayrigg Bank, beginning near the eighty-fifth milepost from Crewe, and continuing unbroken for 13 miles, at an average inclination of 1 in 143; and the Shap Incline proper, which is $5\frac{3}{4}$ miles long, with the last four continuously at 1 in 75.

What came to influence the design of locomotives allocated to the Crewe–Carlisle section was not only the fast running needed to as far north as Carnforth, but that interspersed in the mountain section were two stretches where it was necessary to run at least up to 65 m.p.h. to keep time. The first piece of climbing, that began less than a mile beyond Carnforth could certainly be regarded as a momentum grade—$2\frac{1}{2}$ miles at 1 in 134 followed by $3\frac{1}{2}$ miles of downhill and level before one struck the foot of the Grayrigg Bank. There could be no dawdling there. Then when one had topped Grayrigg and might be a little breathless with the effort, there are $5\frac{1}{2}$ miles of downhill, and level track through the Lune Gorge before reaching the foot of the Shap Incline itself. Those easy gradients were again no place for snatching a respite. Speed had to be piled on to take a full-blooded 'charge' at Shap. While those last four miles, at 1 in 75, could not in any circumstances be regarded as a 'momentum grade' when there was a chance of taking a flying run at them—as the easy gradients through the Lune Gorge did permit—there was every advantage in doing so. And as if to give some encouragement there was a set of water troughs near Dillicar signal-box, at the very foot of the incline. So quite apart from the section northwards from Crewe to Carnforth, the mountain section itself called for an engine that could run fast, as well as climb reliably; and this was the design parameter that faced the Crewe drawing office for more than sixty years.

In the nineteenth century that great individualist among engine-designers, F. W. Webb, had built locomotives that were virtually identical to his standard express passenger classes—both simple and compound—but which had considerably smaller driving wheels. The idea was undoubtedly that a 'lower geared' engine would climb the gradients more readily. But climbing the gradients at higher speed meant the development of greater power; and as the boilers of both large-wheeled and small-wheeled engines were the same it is difficult to imagine where the additional power was expected to come from. The difference in wheel diameter on the single-expansion 2-4-0s was between 6 ft. 9 in. and 5 ft. 6 in. Whatever may have been expected from them, the 5 ft. 6 in. 2-4-0s were a failure as far as main line engines were concerned, and some of them were converted into branch line tank engines. But the rebuilding of an earlier class of Ramsbottom 2-4-0s, with 6 ft. 3 in. coupled wheels produced an excellent engine for the Crewe–Carlisle line; and at a time when the loads of express trains on this route had outstripped locomotive capacity and, for a time, nearly every train required double-heading, it was common practice to run a

6 ft. 3 in. 'Whitworth' 2-4-0, and a 6 ft. 9 in. 'Precedent' together on many trains, thus seemingly getting the best of both worlds.

When, at the beginning of the period covered by this book, George Whale was engaged on the modernization of the L.N.W.R. motive power stud he built the 6 ft. 9 in. 4-4-0s of the 'Precursor' class for general express service, and the 6 ft. 3 in. 4-6-0s of the 'Experiment' class—in the first place for work on the Northern Division. But while the men found some difficulty in firing the 'Experiments' at the start, and their performance consequently fell somewhat short of expectations, in one respect they produced a surprise, in that despite their smaller wheels they proved freer runners than their 6 ft. 9 in. 4-4-0 counterparts. One of them, indeed, attained a maximum speed of $93\frac{1}{2}$ mp.h. descending from Shap, towards Carlisle. When C. J. Bowen-Cooke began building his remarkable superheater engines at Crewe, the 6 ft. 9 in. 'George the Fifth' class 4-4-0s were put on the Carlisle run and, as briefly mentioned in chapter twelve, brought unheard of loads unpiloted over Shap. In maximum performance the superheated version of the 'Experiments', the 'Prince of Wales' class did not seem to do any better; but both these superheated classes brought a very high degree of reliability to the working of heavy express trains over Shap.

It is fascinating to recall what was actually involved, in the years 1911 to 1914. The 10 a.m. Scottish express from Euston was divided at Crewe, and the Glasgow portion was booked to run the 141 miles onwards to Carlisle in 159 minutes—53·3 m.p.h. The 'working' timetable allowed 88 minutes to pass Carnforth, 39 minutes for the $31\frac{1}{2}$ miles up to Shap Summit, and then 32 minutes for the downhill run to Carlisle. The successive average speeds required were 53·3, 48·5 and 59 m.p.h. In consideration of the differing nature of the road the uphill allowance was very severe. In practice, the drivers of heavy trains used to try to get a little time in hand when they passed Carnforth, so as to offset the severe sectional time laid down for the mountain section. The timing was originally planned for a six-coach train, and with this totalling up to about 205 tons, the non-superheated 'Experiment' class engines could keep good time; but once the 'George the Fifth' class engines were on the job, the traffic department piled on the tons, and no one dreamed of doubleheading. A run with the engine *Deerhound*, while not exactly typical, was an example of the optimum performance, for the load was no less than 370 tons.

Carnforth was passed at 65 m.p.h., and on the first sharp rise speed fell away to 52, with the first sight of the fells crowding into the picture ahead of the train. With the respite that

37. THE ATTACK ON SHAP

(a) Edinburgh and Aberdeen portion of 10 a.m. express from Euston, climbing Grayrigg Bank: engine No. 2268, 'Claughton' class, later named *Frobisher*.

(b) Down goods train restarting from Tebay after attaching rear-end bank engine: the train engine is a '19-inch goods' 4-6-0, No. 2600.

(c) Liverpool–Glasgow and Edinburgh express on Tebay troughs: 'Prince of Wales' class 4-6-0 locomotive No. 1400 *Felicia Hemans*.

follows speed quickly rallied, and the foot of the Grayrigg Bank was struck in good style with speed back to 64 m.p.h. Then the driver and the fireman really began to step up the effort, and with the speed still only a little below 50 m.p.h. the beat of the engine gradually sharpened into a real 'bark'. It was on a short length of 1 in 111 gradient that observers could usually guess if a stop was going to be made at Oxenholme for a pilot. In the days of the non-superheater engines a small stud of well tuned-up 2-4-0s were kept at Oxenholme for assisting heavy trains over Shap. Because of the fast running made in the Lune Gorge the 2-4-0 was coupled on ahead of the train engine, and went through to Carlisle, to be available there for assisting southbound trains. On a train wanting assistance that stretch of 1 in 111 would find the engine flagging, and approaching Oxenholme would come the 'two crows' on the whistle—the recognized code for calling out a pilot engine. On this particular run *Deerhound* was going in positively thunderous style, and as she passed through the dark, smoke-blackened station at 43 m.p.h. the exhaust was a veritable cannonade. So up the steep hillside, overlooking the picturesque town of Kendal. The gradients steepened noticeably above this point: 1 in 104, 1 in 124, and the track is winding along the contours. The lineside structures are in white limestone hereabouts, and gradually a magnificent panorama is opening out to the west. While the engine is hammering away up the bank the distant profiles of famous Lakeland mountains can be recognized, with the very distinctive outlines of the Langdale Pikes in the centre of this particular vista.

At many different times I have seen the varied aspects of L.N.W.R. working in this robust fell country. Many times I cycled from Barrow to spend an afternoon by the lineside at Hay Fell, where seven crack expresses passed within a space of about two hours. The southbound trains were skating effortlessly down the gradient, on the wings of the wind. One after another they came: Edinburgh to Euston; Glasgow to Euston—with a Great Western coach for Plymouth; Glasgow to Liverpool and Manchester, and finally Aberdeen to Euston. Then, not long after the last of this procession had gone, the signals were pulled up for the first of the northbound trains. Hay Fell was a tiny little cabin—never, it seemed, had the term 'signal-*box*' been more appropriate. But there was nothing tiny about those signals. Some of them were 70 ft. high, to be seen for miles over the shoulder of some hillside; and in case there was thick mist shrouding the fells, a second arm on the post, at driver's eye level. I used to stand on a convenient ridge where the length of a high embankment was entirely in view, and beyond which on the western side was that great panorama of the Lakeland mountains. Long before an ascending train emerged from the rock cutting and came round the curve past the little signal-box you could hear her beat, pounding up the grade. It is a place of cherished memories for me, because photographs can no longer be conveniently taken there. Saplings that one barely noticed have grown into tall trees, and obscured the most favoured view of the line, and much of the wide prospect beyond.

Deerhound was doing 35 m.p.h. with her heavy train at this point, and while passengers not having an afternoon nap might be admiring the view, the prospect ahead for the driver and fireman was of lofty fells crowding into the picture, and making it appear as though the line was heading into some mountain *cul de sac*. On that high embankment the gradient is

1 in 131, and for the last two miles of the Grayrigg Bank it steepens to 1 in 106. Tough going, in a tough mountain country; but the speed was magnificently held, and the summit was topped at 32 m.p.h. I must not dilate on the sublime scenery of the Lune Gorge, for there are only two thoughts on the footplate at this stage—working up as much speed as possible to 'charge' the Shap Incline, and getting a good refill of water at Dillicar troughs. Despite the all-out effort from Carnforth *Deerhound* had passed Grayrigg summit 'strong in wind and limb', as it were, and her 6 ft. 9 in. wheels enabled the most to be made of the respite in the grading. Speed rose to a full 70 m.p.h. at the troughs, and a long, wild scream on the whistle told the engine shed at Tebay that they were going through at full speed, and not stopping for a bank engine. I should explain that there were two regular ways of taking assistance on the mountain section: either to stop at Oxenholme and couple on a pilot ahead of the train engine, in which case both engines usually went through to Carlisle; or, if Grayrigg had been taken unaided to stop at Tebay for rear-end 'pushing' assistance just up the Shap Incline itself. *Deerhound* took no assistance at all, and climbed the $5\frac{1}{2}$ miles from Tebay up to Shap Summit in $8\frac{3}{4}$ minutes, with a very lowest speed of 27 m.p.h. That schedule of 39 minutes, for the $31\frac{1}{2}$ miles up from Carnforth, was planned when the load of the train was little more than 200 tons; *Deerhound* took $39\frac{3}{4}$ minutes—an average speed of $47\frac{1}{2}$ m.p.h. with a load of 370 tons!

If I had enjoyed those afternoons of long ago by the lineside at Hay Fell, as much as journeys over the line in the train, it was even more so on that most beautiful stretch of line through the Lune Gorge. The vistas around Hay Fell have been obscured by trees; the whole stretch between Low Gill and Tebay has been changed by the construction of the 'M 6' motorway through the valley—quite apart from the complete superseding of steam by the diesels, and the impending further change from diesel to electric traction. It was the quietest of North Country mountain valleys when I did my earliest train watching and photography there—quiet that is, between the passage of the trains; and when I first went there were five, and not seven trains in the early afternoon. The morning Anglo-Scottish expresses in each direction had the Glasgow and Edinburgh sections combined, and were daily made up to huge loads. The superheater 4-4-0s were not often seen on the mountain section after World War I. Many additional 'Prince of Wales' class 4-6-0s had been built, and in the four-cylinder 'Claughton' class 4-6-0s the L.N.W.R. had an engine that could take a 440-ton train over Shap without assistance. Two days in 1921 remain particularly in my memory. The first was at Easter during the school holidays. There was a coal strike, and the train service was much restricted. I had been up at Hay Fell, and 'bagged' a couple of down freights; but time was pressing on, and I cycled back to Oxenholme to photograph the down Scotsman from Euston. I was richly rewarded, for the engine was none other than the very celebrated war-memorial 4-6-0 No. 1914 *Patriot*—the pride of the line, and going magnificently with an enormous train of about 450 tons. From my photograph Jack Hill has painted the splendid picture facing page 177.

The second occasion was in the late summer, just before I went to London to commence my engineering training. This time I cycled from Barrow to Oxenholme, and then took a

38. SPEEDING IN THE LUNE GORGE

(a) Liverpool and Manchester—Scotch Express on Tebay troughs: engine No. 2222 *Sir Gilbert Claughton.*

(b) Aberdeen–Euston express in 1922 hauled by two 'Jumbos': No. 1521 *Gladstone* and 1678 *Airey.*

(c) Preston–Carlisle semi-fast train near Tebay, hauled by an unnamed
'Prince of Wales' class 4-6-0 No. 490.

local train, to Tebay. Motorways through the Lune Gorge indeed! The mountain track from my stance at Hay Fell over the fells to Tebay was more than a venturesome rider of sixteen years was prepared to tackle in the middle of a long day's outing, and that local train had its merits. We were standing in Low Gill station, where the heavily canted track, designed for the smooth passage round the curve of expresses at 60 m.p.h., made a passenger in a standing train feel his carriage was going to topple over on to the platform. But in the few moments we stood the first up 'Scotsman' approached; the first 'Euston' with the Glasgow and Edinburgh sections combined. The sight of that train approaching, weaving round a succession of curves, of seemingly endless length and hauled by a 'Claughton' was thrilling indeed. But the impression was to be pushed into the background by what met me at Tebay. I hopped out of the train and made off smartly down the road towards the water troughs. While I was on my way, and about 100 yards from the overbridge the up line signals were pulled off. I ran for that bridge, and got my camera set just in time for the Glasgow–Liverpool express. Remember that Tebay is just at the foot of the Shap Incline, and the track down that incline is little removed from the straight. Well, that train had come down like a thunderbolt with another 'Claughton', doing about 85 m.p.h. I did not secure much of a picture, but from that bridge I saw her hit the water-troughs, and the spray from the pick-up scoop shot to twice the height of the carriages!

Tebay at that time was a fascinating little railway colony. It had one of those dark rather grim stations that characterized the smaller junctions and outposts of the L.N.W.R. Oxenholme was another, and Carnforth even more so. The purely country stations were delightful little period pieces, and why the junctions should have been so forbidding I cannot imagine. Tebay was a junction with the North Eastern cross-country line to Darlington, an offshoot of that patriarch of all railways, the Stockton and Darlington, and the gay little North Eastern engines that brought three-coach trains across that wildest of North Country railways over Stainmore summit, made an interesting contrast to the black North Westerns. The L.N.W.R. had a fair sized engine shed at Tebay, and the stud there was employed exclusively on giving rear-end banking assistance up Shap. This was necessary on practically all the freights, but not often with passenger trains. Occasionally a train would be double-headed throughout from Preston, or Crewe; others would have taken the pilot at Oxenholme; but the 'Claughtons' used to bring trains of up to 420 tons unassisted up Grayrigg Bank, and they usually stopped for a bank engine at Tebay. When the exigencies of wartime working led to the combination of the Glasgow and Edinburgh sections of the 10 a.m. from Euston, with no additional time allowed, it was left to the driver's discretion whether he took the banker from Tebay. I have records of two instances, one with a load of 420 tons, and one with no less than 440 when no bank engine was taken. On the former run the *E. Tootal Broadhurst* passed Tebay at 60 m.p.h. and climbed Shap without falling below 24 m.p.h.; on the second the pioneer engine, the *Sir Gilbert Claughton* began the climb at 62½ m.p.h. and finished at 22 m.p.h.—both engines keeping exact point-to-point time from Tebay up to the summit, 10 minutes for the 5½ very difficult miles.

The most powerful L.N.W.R. engines attached to Tebay shed were the 4-6-2 superheater tanks. They were not only used as 'pushers' on Shap itself. I have seen them couple on as pilots to heavy down expresses taking assistance from Oxenholme, and also as pilots from Carlisle up to Shap Summit. For many years however, the rear-end banking from Tebay was performed by standard 0-6-0 goods engines of the class nicknamed 'Cauliflowers'. There were nevertheless times when the locomotive yard at Tebay presented a most animated and colourful spectacle. In chapter six I mentioned the cross-country mineral train service between Barrow and Bishop Auckland worked by the North Eastern and the Furness Railways. One could have an N.E.R. 0-8-0 black mineral engine, and a red Furness 0-6-0, with a North Eastern '901' class 2-4-0, or a 'Tennant' in pale green to add to the variety. But while freight workings, and the attaching of rear-end bankers was always full of interest, to me the greatest thrill was to see one of the through expresses double-headed with one of the little 'Jumbo' 2-4-0s. To see such a train come from Shap, down the bank and dash through Tebay at about 80 m.p.h. was a railway spectacle that I have never seen surpassed in the fifty years that have elapsed since I did my first train watching at Tebay.

I always found Shap Summit itself rather a dreary place. After the magnificent scenery farther south the line climbs over storm-swept open moorland to the very 'roof of the world', and the shallow cutting at the summit itself cuts off the distant outlines of the Haweswater mountains. With the activities of the Shap Granite Company, and the laying in of many sidings it has, in more recent times, become a busier place; but when I first knew it, rather more than fifty years ago, its main concern was that of detaching pilot engines that had assisted heavy trains up from Carlisle, and the getting of 'pushers' back to Tebay as quickly as possible. As in ascending from the south side the arrangements for piloting varied. If a Carlisle engine was used—4-6-2 tanks, a 19-inch small-wheeled 4-6-0 goods, or occasionally a second express engine, as in the case mentioned in chapter twelve, when the morning Glasgow to Euston express had two 'Claughtons'—then a stop was made at the summit, to detach. But if it happened to be an Oxenholme 'Jumbo', working home, then the train continued double-headed through to Oxenholme itself. It was in circumstances like these that Cecil J. Allen once clocked a '90' between Shap Summit and Tebay, with a 'Jumbo' piloting an 'Experiment'. Having arrived at the 'Summit' as it were, the rather different conditions existing on the north side must be discussed.

Physically, the aggregate ascent is almost exactly the same. The summit box is precisely half way between Carnforth and Carlisle and the two stations stand roughly the same height above sea level. But in London and North Western days the engines of up expresses were always starting 'cold' from Carlisle; and with all the power and all the steam in the world a locomotive is not at its most *puissant* in the first twenty miles particularly if that initial stretch is heavily graded. It is not a peculiarity of steam locomotives. In recent years I have found that the mightiest of British diesels are noticeably weaker on the first twelve miles of ascent out of King's Cross than later in the same journey on gradients of the same inclination; and as a motorist who for many years began his daily journey to work by driving up a steep hill I was constantly aware of the weakness of a 'cold' engine. This disability was well recognized in the working timetables of the London and North Western Railway. I have already referred to the sharp timings of the crack trains between Carnforth and Shap Summit. The Glasgow portion of the 10 a.m. from Euston had only 39 minutes for that 31·4 miles, and the very heavy 2 p.m. 'Corridor' was allowed 42 minutes. In the reverse direction, however, the fastest trains were allowed 50 minutes for the same distance up from Carlisle, as an obvious concession to that 'cold' start. The differences was not expected to be recovered later, and the fastest non-stop expresses were allowed 125 minutes to cover the remaining $109\frac{1}{2}$ miles to Crewe, compared with 127 minutes in the reverse direction.

On the other hand, while the aggregate vertical rise between Carlisle and Shap Summit was the same as that uphill from Carnforth there was no gradient steeper than 1 in 125, and less in the way of intermediate respite. There was normally no means of getting temporary help on the way up, as with rear-end banking from Tebay on the north-bound run. If an engine should have been in really dire straights the driver could have stopped at Penrith, in the hopes of getting one of the 2-4-0 'Jumbos' that worked on the Keswick line to couple on ahead; but there was no regular arrangement for doing this such as existed at Oxenholme. At this latter station the 'Jumbos' were there for no other purpose. The heavily graded line to Keswick was a rather surprising last haunt of some of the 'Jumbos', and a number of them were to be seen there until well after the grouping—some painted in Midland red! And delightfully incongruous names some of them had: *Cuckoo*, *The Queen*, *Bee* and *Tartarus* were amongst them, and rather more appropriately, *Skiddaw* and *Merrie Carlisle*.

Some of them lingered on for many years after grouping. I found *Tartarus* at the back of the little yard at Penrith looking quite forlorn and indescribably shabby in the spring of 1931. She was scrapped later that year.

One of the most extraordinary aspects of train running on the Crewe–Carlisle section, in years just after World War I, was the occasional use of 'Jumbos' in pairs, on quite important expresses. Although the North Western had 90 4-6-0s of the 'Prince of Wales' class, and 60 'Claughtons' in service by the end of the war, there were times evidently, when pressure of traffic in other directions resulted in there not being a 4-6-0 available. On a summer day in 1921 the midday 'non-stop' from Carlisle to Crewe was worked with tremendous gusto by *Airey* and *Avon*, and in the following summer when I was at Hest Bank one day the 'up Aberdeen' came along headed by *Gladstone* and *Airey*. I was not the only lineside observer to see this latter train, for the veteran photographer, H. Gordon Tidey was at Tebay, and duly 'bagged' the combination. But perhaps the most remarkable instance, in the late autumn of that same year, was the use of a similar pair on no less a train than the Glasgow portion of the 10 a.m. from Euston. The load was down to its minimum of seven coaches, weighing only 205 tons behind the tender; and instead of the usual 'Claughton' or 'Prince of Wales' there was provided the little 'Jumbo' No. 857 *Prince Leopold*. To assist, there was a second 'Jumbo', one of the regular main line pilots at Crewe, No. 883 *Phantom*. This latter engine was putting in quite a substantial mileage in piloting express trains at that time, and shortly before this run she did some good work coupled ahead of a 'Claughton' with an exceptional load of 460 tons.

The fascination of the Northern Division, especially north of Carnforth, was boundless in the variety of the passing trains, and in the engines working them. It was always so. One delights in turning through old copies of *The Railway Magazine*, and seeing pictures of 'double-headers' of 70 years ago labouring up Shap: a 'Jumbo' and an 'Alfred the Great' 4-4-0 compound; a 'Jumbo', and one of the rather fantastic 'John Hick' 2-2-2-2s. It seemed plainly evident from these old pictures that it was the little 'Jumbo' that was doing the lion's share of the work, with a tremendous volume of exhaust steam positively erupting from the chimney, while a dignified plume of white exhaust came from the compound. That greatest of contemporary railway photographers, F. E. Mackay, was often at Shap, but he never managed to catch a double-header on the bank itself. One would dearly have liked to see recorded the occasion when *Phantom* was assisting the 'Claughton' No. 250 *J. A. Bright* with that 460-ton train. One would have needed a modern tape recorder to have completed the documentation. *J. A. Bright* was quite a regular engine on the 10 a.m. from Euston, before it was divided regularly into separate Edinburgh and Glasgow sections north of Crewe. I was at Oxenholme one afternoon when she gave the 'two crows' and stopped opposite the sheds for a pilot. And no wonder; that day she had 'sixteen' on, a load which with passengers and luggage must have been nearly 500 tons. Oxenholme had a 4-6-2 tank waiting to couple on, and the *noise*, as those two restarted that great train, and got away up the Grayrigg Bank was terrific.

Heavy trains are invariably coupled with memories of the London and North Western

Railway, though in the earlier half of the period covered by this book there was always some uncertainty about the tonnage actually carried. Until October 1913 train loads were reckoned in 'coaches'. A six-wheeler counted as 'one'; an eight-wheeler bogie coach as '$1\frac{1}{2}$' and a 12-wheeler as 'two', and because of the variation in weight of individual vehicles there could be considerable disparity. When the 'Claughton' class engines were first introduced a regular turn was the 5.19 p.m. from Crewe to Carlisle. This was the 2 p.m. 'Corridor' from Euston, and the load from Crewe to Preston was '$20\frac{1}{2}$', made up by eight 12-wheelers, and three 8-wheelers—about 430 tons. On the return working, on the 1 a.m. from Carlisle to Crewe the load was also '$20\frac{1}{2}$', but the latter train, although a heavy and well-patronized sleeping car express, did not carry so many 12-wheelers. But the 'Claughtons' were required to take 'equal to $20\frac{1}{2}$' from Carlisle to Shap without assistance. It would be interesting to know the heaviest load ever taken over the mountains in L.N.W.R. days. There is a record of a train of 585 tons, being worked by a 'Jumbo' and a 'Claughton' from Crewe to Lancaster; but the load was reduced to a little under 500 tons from Lancaster. Those were great days on the West Coast Route, and it is good to recall personal memories of what one saw of it from the lineside.

CHAPTER SEVENTEEN

The track of the 'Southern Belle'

AT THE LATTER end of the nineteenth century the London Brighton and South Coast was at the same time the most glamorous and one of the least efficient of all the old railways of Britain. But by 1902 a great transformation was in progress. Those who loved the Brighton, despite its many shortcomings as a transportation concern, were not sure that all the changes that were becoming evident were for the good. Stroudley the master engine-designer had been dead some years. His successor, R. J. Billinton, had not got away to a very good start. Not only had he departed from the cherished precepts of Stroudley regarding the wheel arrangement of express locomotives, but in doing so he produced engines that were quite definitely not so good as their predecessors. Stroudley, in flat contrast to all his contemporaries in Great Britain, had adopted the 0-4-2 type for his principal express locomotives, arguing that the 'front-coupled' 'Gladstone' class were smoother riders than engines of the 2-4-0 or 4-4-0 types. There is no doubt that the 'Gladstones' were very good engines, if not quite the marvels that the more ultra-ardent of Brighton supporters would have us believe. It is equally true that Billinton's first 4-4-0s, built in 1895 and nick-named the 'Grasshoppers', were not so generally useful, or reliable. There were acid comments about the folly of changing Stroudley's practice, and forsaking the individualism in locomotive design for which the 'Brighton' was famous, for the apparent sake of going into conformity with what other British railways were doing.

But having stumbled a little over his first express locomotive design R. J. Billinton made no mistake with his second—the very excellent 'B4' class 4-4-0, introduced at the end of 1899. Outside the ranks of Brighton men, and Brighton railway enthusiasts, these engines are not known so well as perhaps they ought to be. The mere fact that the unorthodox 0-4-2 had been abandoned for the commonplace 4-4-0 took some of the glamour away, even though the engines were at first painted in the famous 'yellow' livery; but in the earliest years of the twentieth century the heat of publicity had been turned in other directions, and the fact that the 'B4' class had a greater tractive effort than such contemporary stars as the Great Eastern 'Claud Hamiltons' and the London and North Western 'Precursors' passed more or less unnoticed. Furthermore, the Brighton engines did not have to work so hard and, on the face of it, there was nothing very spectacular in running the 51 miles from London to Brighton in 65 minutes. One of the fastest and hardest runs made by one of these engines in their very early days, at a time when only three of them existed, was with Queen Victoria's funeral train, of all occasions, after delays had occurred in the early stages of the journey from Gosport. To avoid keeping King Edward VII waiting at Victoria a very fast run was made, reaching 80 m.p.h. at times, though the details of this extraordinary journey were not made public until nearly forty years later. The first three engines of the 'B4' class were built at Brighton works; but after they had been well proved in service an order for a batch of 25 was placed with Sharp, Stewart & Co. of the Atlas works, Glasgow, and for this reason the 'B4' class as a whole were always known on the Brighton railway as the 'Scotchmen'.

They had one glorious flash of publicity in 1903. It may seem odd that the intense rivalry of the north-going railways—'Aberdeen Awa' '—in 1895 should have sparked off a record run from London to Brighton; yet so it was! The daily newspapers of 1895 were full of exciting stories of the racing trains leaving Euston and King's Cross each night at 8 p.m., and some journalists fairly let themselves go in describing the ever-quickening tempo of travel to the north. Season ticket holders, and others who travelled regularly *south* of London read all this at first with rather cynical eyes. Then someone wrote to *The Times* under the heading 'The Crawl to the South' and this just opened the floodgates. Letters poured in, retailing experiences of slow and delayed running; one correspondent interpreted the initials L.B. & S.C.R. as the 'Long Blighted and Slow Coach Railway', and altogether it was quite a time before the editor declared the correspondence closed. As always however, there were clever people with an instant remedy, and a 'group' announced with much publicity their intention to construct an entirely new, all-electric, railway which would do the journey between London and Brighton in 50 minutes. All this was nevertheless taking place when the management and traffic operators of the Brighton railway had turned over to a very new leaf, and reforms were rapidly taking effect. They took this threat of a competitive all-electric railway very seriously, and on 26 July, 1903, set out to demonstrate to the world that there was no need to change to electric traction in order to get to Brighton in 50 minutes; it could be done with steam, and existing standard locomotives.

For a few years previously the L.B. & S.C.R. had been running an all-Pullman 'Limited' train to Brighton on Sundays, making the 51-mile journey from Victoria in the level hour. The 'Scotchmen' were used on this train, and some fine runs had been made already. One of the fastest recorded up to that time had also been made on an unexpected occasion— festive rather than lugubrious this time—on Christmas Day 1901. The engine *Marlborough* ran the Pullman Limited to Brighton in exactly 51 minutes on that day. On 26 July, 1903, however, a deliberate attempt was made to break all records—with official blessing, and carrying a speed recording apparatus designed and operated by Mr. Billinton himself. They succeeded so well that the record time made 70 years ago has only once been surpassed to this day, though nowadays it is density of traffic on the line rather than inadequacy of

39. TRACK OF THE 'SOUTHERN BELLE'

(a) Newhaven Continental Boat Express near Coulsdon, hauled by superheated 'Atlantic' engine No. 421.

(b) The down afternoon 'Southern Belle' (four cars only) at Tooting Common: 4-6-2 tank engine No. 326 *Bessborough*.

motive power that has prevented it being regularly beaten with modern equipment. The engine concerned was the *Holyrood*, and her time from start to the dead stop was 48 minutes 41 seconds. In the course of this run she ran several miles in the neighbourhood of Haywards Heath at 90 m.p.h. This killed any suggestions of alternative routes to Brighton, and in many ways set the seal on the general smartening up of the service, and upon the vastly improved punctuality that henceforth became a characteristic of the railway. But the luxury service to Brighton did not become a daily run until 1908. Before then also, as if to close the door finally on the bad old days of the nineteenth century, Mr. Billinton's successor as locomotive engineer, Douglas Earle-Marsh, changed the engine livery from the gay yellow of Stroudley's day to a more practical chocolate brown, albeit very smartly picked out with yellow and black lining.

Many new engine classes were introduced. Marsh came from Doncaster, and he had

(c) The 'Sunny South Special', through express Liverpool to Brighton and Eastbourne and composed of L.N.W.R. stock, at Tooting Common: Billinton 4-4-0 No. 213, *Bessemer*. This engine, although of the 'B2' class (Grasshoppers) had a much larger boiler than the rest of the class.

built by Kitsons, of Leeds, five 'Atlantic' express engines very similar in appearance to the famous Ivatt 'Atlantics' of the Great Northern. There does not seem to have been any urgent need for these engines, as the 'Scotchmen' were master of all tasks then set to Brighton engines; but Marsh followed these main line engines with a series of 4-4-2 tank engines for the outer suburban services in London. With these, however, history was very much repeated, in that their performance was disappointing in comparison with the stalwart efforts of the Stroudley 'D2' class 0-4-2 tanks. Performance apart, the scene at Victoria at the height of the evening suburban rush was as animated as it was intensely varied. Many of the engines would still be in yellow, for the craftsmanship of the paintwork was superb; 0-4-2 tank engines took many of the trains; there would be an occasional 'Terrier' 0-6-0 tank, used on the South London line shuttle service between Victoria and London Bridge, and among the new 4-4-2 tanks on the outer 'residentials' many of the Billinton 'radial' 0-6-0 tanks would be seen. The onlooker might be lucky to see one of the new 'prestige' 'Atlantics'; but the majority of the express trains would be taken by 'Scotchmen', or 'Gladstones', with the 'B2' 'Grasshoppers' on the Portsmouth trains. It always seemed rather strange to me that this line, which included some heavy gradients where it crossed the North Downs between Dorking and Horsham, should have been worked by engines that were something less than the best. In Stroudley's time, when his 'Gladstones' were running the Brighton express, the Portsmouth line had to put up with the 2-2-2 'singles' of the 'G' class; and Billinton followed this by bequeathing his somewhat ineffectual 'Grasshoppers' to the route. All the same I cannot imagine that the lineside enthusiasts, or photographers of those days would mind very much; for both the 'Grasshoppers' and the 'G' singles were very pretty little engines.

It was in 1908 that the L.B. & S.C.R. put on 'The Southern Belle'—an all-Pullman, all-first class train running four times a day between Victoria and Brighton in the level hour. The load varied. The down morning service leaving London at 11 a.m. carried 7 cars; but at first, on the up midday train and the down afternoon trip there were only 4, leaving 7 again for the final run up in the evening. Luxury travel or not it was a very cheap train, for the return fare to Brighton by it was a modest twelve shillings. It became the veritable 'flagship' of the Brighton passenger service. It ran 'between times', as it were, and so was assured of a clear road; but with this reservation, it kept immaculate time, and Brighton enthusiasts delight in the legend of the country people setting their clocks and watches by its passage—that being very long before the days of the B.B.C. 'pips'. Whether Marsh altered the colour of the engines in anticipation of this duty one cannot say; but his chocolate brown was a precise 'match' with the body colour of the Pullman cars, and the cream upper panels of those cars blended perfectly. Whatever the Brighton railway may have lost in publicity by the suppression of the yellow engine livery it gained ten-fold by the mere name of the 'Southern Belle'. It became a legend on the railways of Britain, as much as the Irish Mail, or 'Flying Scotsman' or—tell it not in Gath!—the Cornish Riviera Express.

To the photographers also, the 'Southern Belle' could be a plunge in the lucky bag so far as locomotive power was concerned. The down morning service from London was an absolutely 'crack' working. From quite early days a majority of the express engines were stationed at Brighton, and a 'star' engine was always set aside for the 8.45 a.m. up to London Bridge—for obvious reasons nicknamed 'The Stockbrokers Express'. Arrived at 9.45 a.m., the engine then ran tender first round the South London line to be at Victoria, pointing in the right direction, ready for the 11 a.m. down Southern Belle. In the early days of the Pullman train the engine was almost invariably an 'Atlantic'—and very splendid those engines looked at the head of the seven-car, chocolate and cream train. The up Midday train, leaving Brighton at 1.20 p.m. was often worked by a 'Scotchman', and after the exploit of 26 July, 1903 it can well be imagined that no difficulty was experienced in running a four-car train up to Victoria in the hour. When Marsh produced his celebrated tank-engine version of the 'Scotchman'—the 'I3' class of 4-4-2—these were sometimes used on the morning turn, instead of an 'Atlantic', and the variety in the lucky bag was increased in 1910 when March produced the first of the large 4-6-2 tanks with outside cylinders, the *Abergavenny*; she, and her companion engine of 1912, the *Bessborough* were frequently on the 'Southern Belle'.

On my first photographic expeditions on the Brighton line the passage of the 'Southern Belle' on one or more of her regular runs was a centre-piece on which one planned the day's itinerary and timetable; but coming to what one could see and photograph along the track of the 'Southern Belle' I must tell of an offshoot of the main line, for it was there I first did my systematic train watching on the L.B. & S.C.R. That offshoot was the Eastbourne line, and in 1919 it was a very good place for seeing Brighton motive power. On the mid-morning London express the type of locomotive could be anyone's guess. The first time I saw it there was a superheated 'Atlantic' on, and I was caught without my camera. I went again next day and found a 'B2X' on the job—one of the 'Grasshoppers' rebuilt with a larger boiler. Having dealt appropriately with the London express, within the next half hour I bagged a 'Gladstone', a 4-4-2 tank, and a type not often seen on the Brighton lines in London, a 0-4-4 tank. In travelling to Eastbourne and back from London we were hauled by a 'Scotchman' in each direction; but as a schoolboy my most lasting recollection of those journeys is the rather primitive—or so I thought—carriages, on a main line express train. They were all flat-roofed non-corridors, looking most unpretentious compared to the main line stock of the North Western and the Midland, with which I was then more familiar. 'Not even as good as the Furness', was my unspoken comment, I remember only too well. But the thing that struck me so forcibly was the most forthright advertising in them. Instead of pictures of the Peak District, coloured photographs of Cathedrals, or mountain resorts one read:

> When knights were bold they all wore armour
> Nights hot or cold wear Swan's pyjama

with a gaily coloured picture of a natty gent reclining in a bedroom armchair! There were other advertisements, that one might now classify as 'period brash'!

But I must return to the track of the 'Southern Belle'. In the London area the Brighton

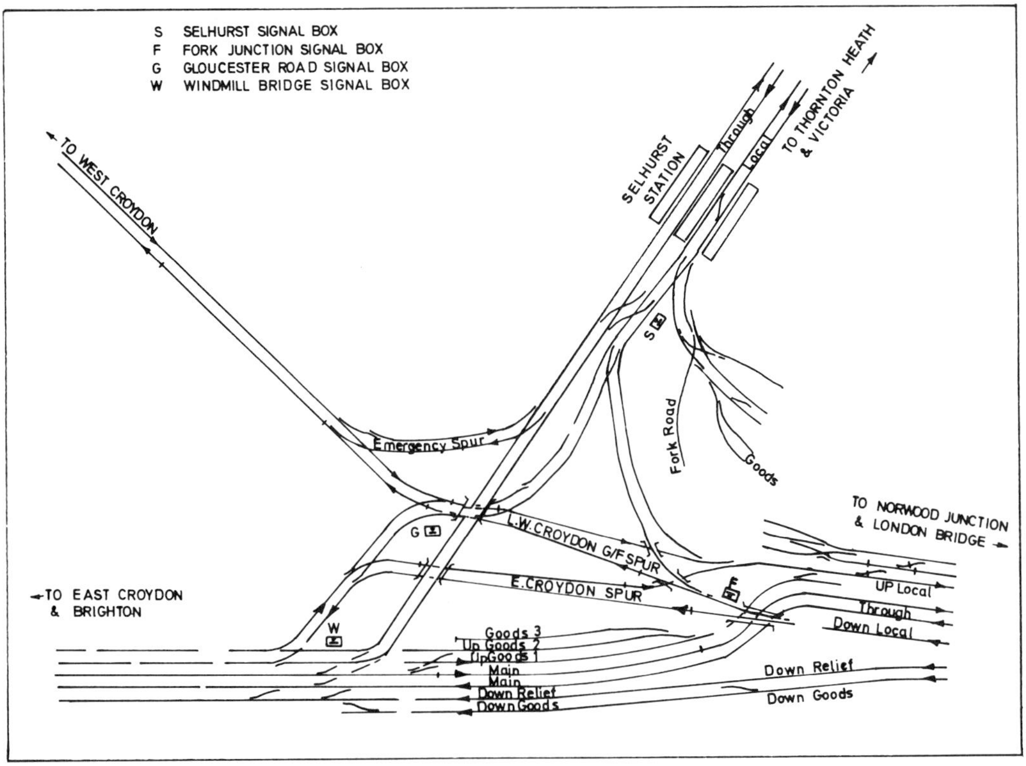
S SELHURST SIGNAL BOX
F FORK JUNCTION SIGNAL BOX
G GLOUCESTER ROAD SIGNAL BOX
W WINDMILL BRIDGE SIGNAL BOX
TO WEST CROYDON
SELHURST STATION
Through
Local
TO THORNTON HEATH & VICTORIA
S
Fork Road
Goods
Emergency Spur
G
L.W. CROYDON G/F SPUR
E. CROYDON SPUR
F
TO NORWOOD JUNCTION & LONDON BRIDGE
UP Local
Through
Down Local
TO EAST CROYDON & BRIGHTON
W
Goods 3
Up Goods 2
Up Goods 1
Main
Main
Down Relief
Down Goods
Down Relief
Down Goods

MAP 5: L.B. & S.C.R. THE CROYDON TRIANGLE

main lines were very thoroughly encompassed. Recalling earlier photographs in *The Railway Magazine* I went by bus out to Tooting Common, and what with massive railings and overhead electric wires the previous haunts of F. E. Mackay were of no further use. But to the amateur photographer the Brighton was the most friendly of railways, and providing one kept away from the electrified areas lineside walking passes were readily forthcoming. Before exploring south of Purley, however, I had seen, from station platforms and other vantage points that amazing complex of tracks lying between the three nodal points of Selhurst, Norwood Junction and East Croydon. The London and North Western was one of the earliest users of the principle of the 'flying' junction; but the Brighton used it 'in excelsis' in the area just north of Croydon, as will be appreciated from the accompanying sketch map. The company could also claim some of the most picturesque station and signal-box names. The places where the main lines from Victoria and London Bridge converged, just short of East Croydon was, and is still in fact, known as 'Windmill Bridge Junction'. Norwood Junction was originally 'Jolly Sailor' and outside Brighton there was a signal-box named 'Lovers Walk'. Once through the busy Croydon area the main line drives on into what, in my earliest explorations, was approaching open country. Certainly I can recall with pleasure the journeys I made thence by push-bicycle from South Kensington.

The really fascinating part of the Brighton main line in those days began at Coulsdon—'Stoats Nest Junction' as it was originally known. John Rennie's original line to Brighton had no gradient steeper than 1 in 264. It involved him in a tremendously deep cutting through the chalk of the North Downs, which because of the stability of the ground had exceedingly steep sides, and was excitingly impressive in consequence. It ended in the long Merstham Tunnel. But as a legacy from early railway politics the Brighton had to share that line with the South Eastern, and that 'sharing' was not very congenial to the owners, whatever the South Eastern might have paid for their running powers. And so, around the turn of the century the Brighton committed themselves to the expense of building a new line of their own from Stoats Nest Junction. With the greatly improved locomotive power of the day gradients were not so vital, and so the Brighton were not involved in such immensely deep excavations as on the original line. The new line diverged to the west of the old one, and on slightly steeper gradients at first climbed parallel to, and overlooking the old line. Then at Star Lane the difference in levels was such that the new line could cross the old one to the eastern side before entering Quarry Tunnel.

It was a fascinating stretch of line to walk. The gleaming white cuttings made a splendid background for photographs, and in addition to the Brighton expresses on the new, or Quarry line, one had various 'slows', and the South Eastern locals trundling up and down on the old line. By that time also the large L. B. Billinton 4-6-4 tank class was being multiplied. One could be fairly certain of getting one of them on the 'Southern Belle', while by that time the afternoon 'Belle' had become a very popular train, and loaded as heavily as the morning one. Mention of the 'Southern Belle' reminds me of the interim stage through which that train passed when it was restored to service after World War I. To avoid additional mileage at first a number of ordinary third-class carriages were attached to the Pullman set, and as these were run next to the engine they completely ruined the photogenic aspect of the down train; but after a relatively short time third-class Pullmans were included, and the all-Pullman feature of the train was restored—except in one respect. Passengers seemed to be travelling with more luggage than previously and to avoid congestion of baggage in the cars themselves a bogie luggage van of ordinary stock was run on many occasions. But the inclusion of third-class Pullmans, at lower fares of course, so increased the popularity of the train that it was loading to 10, 11 and sometimes 12 cars. This of course greatly increased the task of haulage, since the schedule remained the same, and the locomotive people were glad to have the big 4-6-4 tanks available for the job.

Another new locomotive class that added a further spice of variety to the Brighton main line scene, was L. B. Billinton's rebuild of his uncle's celebrated 'B4' Scotchmen. In the last year before grouping there were only two of these engines rebuilt, Nos. 55 and 60, and they were much sought after by photographers. I used to visit F. E. Mackay in his home in Battersea at that time, and he had a source of 'inside information' at Brighton works, as to the trains these engines would work. They were highly regarded, and were taking turns with the bigger engines on all the principal expresses, except the 'Southern Belle'. On

Friday evenings Mackay would phone to the hostel where I lived in South Kensington giving the latest expectations; but they never seemed to work out. Those two engines always seemed to turn up when least expected! But the increase in the number of 4-6-4 tanks to seven and the availability of the two splendid 4-6-2 tanks, *Abergavenny* and *Bessborough*, made it possible to spare one or two 'Atlantics' for the Newhaven boat trains. From that time onwards the morning Continental boat expresses became as much a certainty for an 'Atlantic' as the 'Southern Belle' was for a 4-6-4 tank. The last of these latter engines, No. 333, was made the L.B. & S.C.R. 'War Memorial', following the precedent set by the London and North Western in naming an engine *Patriot*. The Brighton engine was named *Remembrance*, and in keeping with the solemnity of the gesture was painted grey, instead of the usual chocolate brown.

Apart from the brief excursion to Eastbourne, skipping over the intervening country, all my comments on the Brighton railway have so far concerned that busy and intricate part of it north of the Merstham and Quarry tunnels. Once through the latter tunnel drivers of the Brighton expresses really began to pile on the speed. Today the convergence of the old line with the new, at Earlswood, is subject to a 60 m.p.h. speed restriction; but no such limit—if it ever existed—was observed in the old days of the L.B. & S.C.R. and it was a thrilling sight to stand on the platforms of that station and see the 'Southern Belle', or one of the evening 60-minute Brighton trains come sweeping down from the tunnel abreast of Redhill, and roar through at a full 70 m.p.h. But this was only the beginning. Acceleration continued till the train was doing little short of 80 m.p.h. at Horley. They were then fully launched on the sweeping ups and downs of Rennie's original line, all at 1 in 264, and impetus from the dash through Horley carried them up through Three Bridges to the crest of the ridge covered by the old Balcombe Forest—about midway between the North and South Downs. Three Bridges became an important junction, for its westward cross-country cut to Horsham. It was favoured as a route for expresses heading for resorts on the western reaches of the Sussex seaboard as affording an alternative and less steeply graded way out of London to the normal route of the Portsmouth expresses via Sutton and Dorking. A few years after the grouping I used occasionally to travel by the 6.20 p.m. express from Victoria to Bognor, which ran non-stop over the 37·9 miles to Horsham, via Three Bridges. In certain areas the Brighton seemed to vie with the London and North Western in the height of its semaphore signals, and at one time there was a group of three, on a gantry across Three Bridges station that could well have claimed to be the highest in England.

The Brighton main line was quadruple tracked from Earlswood to the southern approach

40. BRIGHTON EXPRESS ENGINES

(a) One of Earle-Marsh's celebrated '13' class 4-4-2 superheated tanks No. 29.
(b) L. B. Billinton's rebuild of the 'B4' class, known as 'B4X': a very successful modernization.
(c) The first of L. B. Billinton's 4-6-4 express tanks of 1914, named after the Deputy Chairman of the L.B. &. S.C.R.

to Balcombe Tunnel, and there the four lines converged into two. With heavy trains the rising 1 in 264 gradient had usually pulled the speed down to little more than 50 m.p.h. at Balcombe Tunnel; but this was only the prelude to what was normally the fastest piece of running on the journey from London to Brighton. It was a stretch of great engineering interest, for in maintaining the perfectly uniform gradient of 1 in 264, downhill again after the tunnel, the line was carried high across the wide valley of the Sussex Ouse, on a magnificent stone viaduct of 37 arches. It is one of the disadvantages of travelling by train, or indeed of nearly all forms of travel, that the passenger cannot see the engineering works by which his route strides across the countryside. There are, of course, stretches in difficult mountain regions where sharp curves in the line give glimpses of viaducts, approaching tunnel entrances and so on; but such is certainly not the case with the Ouse Viaduct, because the line for many miles on either side is little removed from dead straight. I would hazard a guess that not one in ten thousand passengers is conscious there is a viaduct at all! With the speed back at about 70 m.p.h. it is crossed in less than a quarter of a minute!

It was here, on the record run of July 1903, that the 'Scotchman' 4-4-0 *Holyrood* was putting on such a tremendous spurt. By Haywards Heath the speed was getting near the 'ninety mark', though such fast running was not normally needed in running the 'Southern Belle', and the other 60-minute trains of L.B. & S.C.R. days. After all there is a world of difference between 60 and 48¾ minutes on a 51-mile run. Drivers on the 'Southern Belle' prided themselves on their precise time-keeping, and if one had covered the 29·5 miles to Three Bridges in the scheduled 37 minutes from the Victoria start the engine could usually be taken down through Haywards Heath under easy steam, at little more than 70 m.p.h. By the time Keymer Junction was neared, where the Eastbourne line takes such a sharp turn to the left, the long ridge of the South Downs is stretched athwart the track, and from the maximum speed on the Ouse Valley descent, attained somewhere near Keymer Junction, the pace begins to fall off again, on the last stretch of climbing, at 1 in 264, to a summit point under the North Downs, in Clayton Tunnel. This tunnel has a very fine castellated entrance, and looking most incongruous on this splendid façade, a little cottage set right in the middle, between the bastions, with its little windows just peeping over the parapet wall. Once through Clayton Tunnel drivers of down expresses could ease their engines completely, for the downhill run thence into Brighton had naturally to be taken easily. The country hereabouts is some of the prettiest on the whole line.

The railway layout at Brighton is complicated. The Central station not only provides a terminus for the main line from London but also constitutes a staging point on the west to east line along the south coast from Portsmouth to Hastings. Trains arriving from the west, after berthing at one or another of the most westerly platforms in the terminus, had to reverse direction before proceeding eastwards towards Lewes, Eastbourne and Hastings, and in so doing, crossing all the main London lines. It is, however, possible to reach the West lines direct from the London direction without going into Brighton terminus at all, by a spur leaving the main line near Preston Park. At one time through carriages for Hove and Worthing used to be slipped from the direct London–Brighton trains at Preston Park.

The track layout outside the Central station included a multitude of crossovers and spur connections, and at the time of which I am now writing, entirely mechanical signalling. It was controlled by no fewer than nine signal-boxes with a total of 662 levers. The largest boxes were the West station (120 levers), South station (240 levers), Lovers Walk (60 levers) and Montpelier (98 levers). By the early part of the present century, the picturesque Bannister type of semaphores, working in a slot in the post, and mostly mounted on the roofs of the signal-boxes had been replaced with the later standard Brighton type of semaphore—not so picturesque, but a better mechanical job.

One of the most curious signalling features coming at the very end of the track of the 'Southern Belle', was to be seen at the entrance to the main arrival platforms. It was to be seen also at the entrance to certain platforms at Victoria, and at London Bridge. The signals were 'two-arm' and looked exactly like the combination of 'home' and 'distant' semaphores at locations where the working between two closely adjacent boxes was interlinked—or 'slotted', to use the usual signalling term. The normal understanding of such a combination is that with the upper or home arm clear, and the 'distant' at danger the signal may be passed but the driver must expect the next signal ahead to be at danger. If both arms are clear, it is an authority to pass the signal at full speed, and an indication that all the signals at the next signal box are also at clear. The visitor to Brighton, or to those platforms where it applied at Victoria and London Bridge might wonder how such a combination came to be used at the entrance to a terminal station, where there was obviously no 'next signal-box' ahead. Now all three terminal stations concerned have all-over roofs; they are very busy, there was frequently the smoke of other locomotives drifting inside, and in all cases there was not a clear sight along the platforms. At Brighton Central, for example, the main line platforms are curved throughout. Those signals have therefore a special and entirely local meaning. If the upper arm only was clear a driver was authorized to enter the platform cautiously, at such a speed that he could stop short of any obstruction he saw was in the way, such as a standing carriage, van, or even a light engine. If both arms were in the clear position the line was clear right up to the buffer stops.

On the way down from London I referred particularly to the Ouse Viaduct. Although Rennie was the engineer for the Brighton railway most of the detail work was done by John Urpeth Rastrick, and it was he who designed the Ouse Viaduct. It is a magnificent piece of work, and it has its counterpart in the London Road Viaduct at Brighton immediately to the east of the Central station on the line to Lewes. This is another of Rastrick's master-pieces, and although it is taking the story nearly twenty years ahead from the grouping, an incident during World War II may be recalled, as showing the quality of the construction work put into these viaducts, at that time nearly 100 years old. The London Road Viaduct at Brighton has 27 arches, and carried the line at a height that reaches a maximum of 70 ft. above street level. During the war a heavy bomb from a tip-and-run raider scored a direct hit on one of the piers. Only work of first class quality would have withstood such a blow without collapsing altogether. But here only the pier against which the bomb exploded was demolished. The other piers stood solid as a rock, while the rails, and even one parapet hung in mid-air across the gap. The engineers were, indeed, able to complete a temporary bridging structure and get the line open again only five weeks after the incident, and the viaduct was completely restored in four months.

And so, in concluding this chapter, I come back once more to the 'Southern Belle'. Up to the outbreak of World War I it had no imitators, though of course Pullman cars in ones and twos were run on certain boat expresses of the South Eastern and Chatham Railway. But after the war there came many new all-Pullman trains, though not at first including the qualification 'Belle'. There was the Thanet Pullman Limited, and after grouping the Eastern Belle and the Northern Belle, run by the London and North Eastern Railway. The last mentioned was not a Pullman train at all, but a luxury 'land cruise' train including sumptuous sleeping cars. But it was when the Southern Railway, as inheritor of the L.B. & S.C.R. and its traditions, began to extend the regular running of all-Pullman trains to other parts of the system that the famous title 'Southern Belle' began to lose its significance; and with the inception of the 'Bournemouth Belle', the progenitor of them all became the 'Brighton Belle'. But other administrations in the grouping era may well have been glad of the pioneer work done on the Brighton, by the launching of the 'Southern Belle' in 1908. One thinks particularly of the 'Queen of Scots' and 'West Riding Pullmans' on the L.N.E.R., though the Great Western venture into a 'Torquay Pullman' was a complete failure. The unique character of the 'Southern Belle' itself began to disappear with the grouping, when the chocolate brown engines gave place to Southern Green. It was certainly one of the 'great' trains of Britain.

CHAPTER EIGHTEEN

Eve of the Grouping

IT WOULD PERHAPS be an over-simplification of a situation hedged round with manifold difficulties to say that the grouping timetabled to come into effect on New Year's Day 1923 involved a series of mergers that no one wanted—no one, that is, within the railway service itself. At this distance in time there may well be very many who would ask why the grouping took place at all. The old railway companies were well run, and with a few exceptions they paid steady, if not spectacular dividends. Why indulge in a general scramble that pleased very few people, least of all the unfortunate shareholders of some pre-grouping companies, to whom grouping was a financial disaster! To appreciate the problems that beset the Government, the newly-formed Ministry of Transport, and the higher managements of the major companies, one must go back in history for about a dozen years. Then, in the early years of the twentieth century, although the railways of Britain had reached an age of pre-eminence when competition from other forms of transport had not begun to be seriously felt, there was much to cause deep concern around the board tables. One factor was the rising cost of practically every item of raw material and supplies in regular use, while relations between management and labour were entering into a distinctly restless stage. The only way to maintain dividends at an acceptable level was to economize in operating costs, because rates and fares were regulated by law.

Under the stress of competition, and particularly arising from the opening of the London Extension Line of the Great Central many fast and attractive passenger services were run that could scarcely hope to pay their way; and although the Midland Railway in particular carried out extensive rearrangements of service in order to save engine mileage the heat of competition admitted of no relaxation. Fully appreciating that such practises would lead eventually to ruin some important moves towards rationalization of hitherto competitive services were initiated between the large north-going companies. It was not surprising that the Great Central was concerned in one of the earliest of such movements, and proposals got to the state, in 1907, of complete amalgamation between the Great Eastern, the Great Northern and the Great Central. This scheme held out prospects of major economies in

41. HIGHLAND ENGINES

One of the celebrated 'Jones Goods' engines—the first 4-6-os in Great Britain—alongside the *Ben Wyvis*, Peter Drummond's 'Small Ben' class.

operating, and in the co-ordination of engineering and administrative staffs. At that time however, public opinion, as represented by Parliament, was strongly adverse to any business arrangements that savoured of monopolies; and although the three companies concerned in this particular project were not directly competitive on many major routes, the first public intimation of the proposed merger received such a generally hostile reception that it was eventually dropped. The friendly relations that had developed did, however, lead to certain working arrangements between the three companies, though such operating econo-mies as were effected did not help the Great Central to pay any dividend. Another working agreement that was of greater benefit to the parties concerned was organized between the London and North Western, Midland, and Lancashire and Yorkshire Railways. But again it was purely a matter of operating, in its broadest sense; the management remained entirely separate. Then, with the outbreak of war in 1914, the working of all railways in Britain was co-ordinated under the management of the Railway Executive Committee, and existing inter-company working agreements were extended on a national scale. The financial implications of this vitally necessary procedure were at first of no immediate account, because the arrangement under which the Government took control of the railways in 1914 guaranteed each of the companies the same net revenue as they had earned in 1913, for the duration of Government control irrespective of the traffic they were required to carry.

As the war progressed matters became very complicated, through the inter-working made

218

Highland Railway: One of Peter Drummond's 0-6-4 tanks, built 1909,
for banking on the Druimuachdar Incline.

necessary, changes in wage agreements and such like, and it became clear that to hand the companies back to the owners on the basis of pre-war achievement would border on the chaotic. In the meantime a very important change in national responsibility for the working of the railways was made by the creation of the Ministry of Transport. Hitherto the responsible authority had been the Board of Trade. The first Minister of Transport was Sir Eric Geddes, who had won high distinction in Lloyd-George's war-winning coalition Government; previously he had been a professional railwayman, and before he joined the Government, Assistant General Manager of the North Eastern Railway. So Geddes, unlike the great majority of his successors at the Ministry of Transport, was fully conversant with the intricacies of railway management and operation; and under his guidance Parliament turned a complete somersault in its attitude towards railway amalgamation. From being instinctively opposed to any movement that gave the slightest hint of setting up a monopoly, the Parliament elected immediately after the Armistice in 1918, and which gave the Coalition Government such a huge majority, quietly accepted the principle of a major 'grouping' of the British railways. I think the great majority of senior railway officers were convinced that some form of permanent co-ordination was not only inevitable, but urgently necessary. It was the scheme finally authorized by Parliament that pleased nobody.

It is interesting to recall the different proposals that were made and subsequently rejected. The Government White Paper, published in the summer of 1920, represented the ideas of Sir Eric Geddes himself, and proposed the setting up of seven groups, namely:

1. The *Southern*, combining the South Eastern and Chatham, the Brighton, and the South Western.
2. The *Western*, embodying an amalgamation of all the local Welsh lines with the Great Western.
3. The *North Western*, combining the North Western, the Midland, the Lancashire and Yorkshire, the North Stafford, and the Furness.
4. The *Eastern*, combining the Great Eastern, Great Northern and Great Central.
5. The *North Eastern*, taking in the existing North Eastern with the Hull and Barnsley.
6. The *London Group*, consisting only of local lines.
7. The *Scottish*, combining all railways north of the border.

It will be seen at once that groups 3 and 4 set up complete amalgamations of companies already working in close unison, while 1 and 2 were obvious geographical combinations. It is interesting to see that Sir Eric Geddes proposed to keep his old company separate, save for its absorption of the Hull and Barnsley. This was an arrangement that was actually adopted 25 years later when the railways were nationalized, and a separate 'North Eastern Region' was set up. The idea of a 'London' group envisaged a unification of local services; and although it was dropped later the proposal eventually materialized 10 years later when the London Passenger Transport Board was set up. Lastly, the proposal to merge all Scottish railways into a single group showed a striking lack of understanding of local conditions. It might look admirable on paper, but to anyone who knew Scottish railways and railwaymen it spelled disaster.

It was not surprising that the detailed proposals for amalgamation came under severe criticism. *The Railway Gazette*, under the guidance of that great editor John Aiton Kay, had its finger very surely on the pulse of railway opinion in England, both of senior and middle management, and stockholders, and in the late autumn of 1920 it published its own ideas of how the railways might be grouped. It was a remarkable document, because in most respects it took account very definitely of factors in amalgamation that led subsequently to much unrest when they were ignored in the final set-up. One of the most drastic proposals of *The Railway Gazette* was a complete 'carve-up' of the Great Central Railway. This, while horrifying to the traditionalists, was logical enough from the financial point of view, because as a whole, with its enormous capital involvement, it would be an incubus to any group in which it was included. *The Railway Gazette* proposed no appreciable amalgamation south of the Thames, leaving the S.E. & C.R., the Brighton and the South Western independent, except that the last mentioned absorbed the Somerset and Dorset. The Great Western was even larger than the Geddes White Paper, taking in also the L.N.W.R. line west of Craven

42. VINTAGE HIGHLAND 4-4-0S, EARLY 1920S
(a) A 'Skye Bogie' No. 88A, shunting at Inverness.
(b) 'Strath' class 4-4-0 No. 89 *Sir George* on the roundhouse turntable, Inverness.
(c) Jones 4-4-0 No. 133 *Loch Laoghal* at Aviemore.

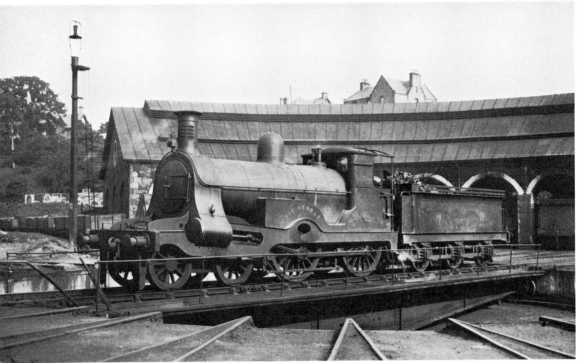

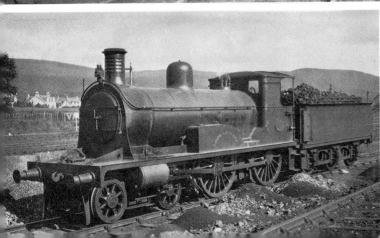

Arms, the Midland West of Hereford, and all Great Central lines south of Woodford, including Marylebone station. But it was in connection with the main north lines that *The Railway Gazette* showed an imagination lacking in the White Paper.

It is true that the North Western, the Midland, and the Lancashire and Yorkshire were working closely together; but full amalgamation is a very different thing, when the individuality of three great industrial empires was concerned. And *The Railway Gazette* proposed the formation of three separate companies, incorporating local lines on the way. The new North Western, for example, would take in the North Staffordshire, the Furness, and the smaller local lines in Cumberland, while the Midland—horror of horrors at Marylebone—would take the Great Central main line from Woodford to Manchester. But the empires of the North Western and Midland were not confined to England in *The Railway Gazette* scheme. Each company would absorb the line of its Scottish partners as far as Edinburgh and Glasgow was concerned, so that the Midland would take the whole of the Glasgow and South Western, and the Waverley Route of the North British, while the North Western would take the former Caledonian main line from Carlisle to Glasgow, and Carstairs to Edinburgh. It was similarly proposed that the entire East Coast Route from King's Cross to Edinburgh would be under one company—the 'London and North Eastern'—which would include the whole of the Great Northern and North Eastern, and the North British from Berwick to Edinburgh. Oddly enough, *The Railway Gazette* proposed to give the Hull and Barnsley to the Midland! The Lancashire and Yorkshire remained much the same.

It was in Scotland, however, that the proposals of *The Railway Gazette* seemed most unrealistic. The enlarged Highland Railway was to take in the Great North of Scotland, but also the Callander and Oban, and the West Highland north of Helensburgh. Both these lines were completely isolated from the main Highland line, though perhaps it was envisaged, though not definitely specified, that the Highland might take over the Caledonian line between Perth and Stirling. But just imagine the situation arising over the 'remains' of the original Caledonian and the North British! Two proud, efficient and highly individualistic railways and one of them had lost its main south line to the North Western, and its scenic Oban line; the North British was even more mutilated, having lost the East Coast main line south of Edinburgh to the new 'L.N.E.R.'; the Waverley Route, to the Midland and the West Highland to the new 'Highland'. And two central 'rumps' of these two onetime great companies were supposed to come together amicably and form 'The Edinburgh and Glasgow Railway'. What a hope! It is extraordinary how the pundits of Westminster and the new Ministry of Transport seemed abysmally ignorant of the sentiments that lay so deep in Scottish railroading. One might have expected *The Railway Gazette* to be better informed, but on the grounds of geography alone its proposals were a good deal clumsier even than those of the White Paper. By way of a footnote to *The Railway Gazette* scheme, the mileages of the proposed eleven railways are appended:

43. WARTIME AUSTERITY LIVERIES

(a) G.W.R. Falmouth and Newquay express leaving Paddington, hauled by 4-cylinder 4-6-0 No. 4060 *Princess Eugenie*, in plain all-over green.

(b) S.E. & C.R. Through morning express leaving Bexhill for Cannon Street, hauled by 'L' class 4-4-0 No. 776 in plain dark grey.

44. FIRST SIGNS OF GROUPING LIVERIES

(a) A G.N.R. 'Atlantic' No. 1419 fitted with booster, enlarged cab, and painted in the new style.

MILEAGES IN *Railway Gazette* SCHEME

New Railway	Route Mileage
Great Western	3,600
London & South Western	1,200
London Brighton & South Coast	500
South Eastern & Chatham	700
Great Eastern	1,400
London & North Eastern	3,400
London & North Western	2,800
Midland	3,200
Lancashire and Yorkshire	800
Edinburgh and Glasgow (or Caledonian)	1,500
Highland	1,000

By the end of 1920 it was still not clear whether the Government proposed actual amalgamation, or grouping for collective operation, and the Railway Companies Association, strongly critical of the White Paper, put forward its own proposals for grouping. This was precisely the series of alignments that was eventually adopted, leading to the setting up of the 'Big Four' in January 1923. But these proposals did not represent a unanimous recom-

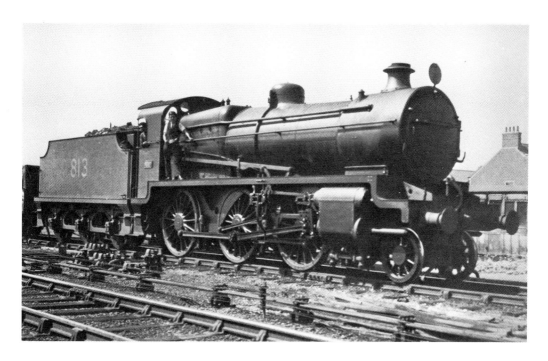

(b) S.E. & C.R.; one of the Maunsell 'Moguls' No. 813, following the wartime prototype, No. 810.

(c) A G.N.R. large-boilered 2-cylinder Mogul No. 1671, hauling a down stopping train near New Southgate.

mendation. The North Eastern, for example, stood out strongly against it, preferring to constitute a group of its own, as proposed in the White Paper. But when Sir Eric Geddes introduced 'The Railway Bill, 1921' in the House of Commons the proposals provided for six groups; there were to be two separate groups in Scotland, and the North Eastern and the Hull and Barnsley were to be included in the Eastern group, with the Great Eastern, Great Northern and Great Central. The actual line-up of the companies underwent some considerable modifications during the Committee stages of the Bill. A strong move to omit the Midland from the London and North Western—Lancashire and Yorkshire alignment was defeated, and instead this already large combine had included in it the three western Scottish companies, Caledonian, Glasgow and South Western, and the Highland. Similarly, the Eastern group had attached to it the North British and the Great North of Scotland. It was in this form that the Bill went forward to its third reading. The overriding argument for not having a separate Scottish group, or pair of groups was that the establishment of a new wage structure on a national basis would have so increased Scottish operating costs— which hitherto had been much lower than in England—as to make the economy of the once-independent Scottish companies impossible to sustain.

Thus the grouping scheme, authorized by 'The Railways Act, 1921' was ultimately effected purely on the basis of the old companies, without any attempt at the rationalization of routes, elimination of duplicate facilities, or even a geographical tidying up of the railway map. There were many glaring anomalies, arising from the activities of the old companies. In Scotland, for example, the West Highland line from Helensburgh to Fort William and Mallaig became part of the London and North Eastern Railway; this latter penetrated into West Cumberland as far as Silloth, while in the London area, the London Midland and Scottish ran to Southend and Shoeburyness. The London and North Eastern Railway was saddled with the entire financial burden of the Great Central, as well as having to bolster up two Scottish companies. No wonder the old North Eastern had struggled for independence! It was the only one of the Eastern group that could be classed among the really 'rich' railways, and before long that wealth was dissipated. So far as the Great Central was concerned the Grouping did not make the slightest difference to its competitive position in the Midlands. Its through train networks remained as before. But perhaps the most extraordinary outcome of the grouping, seen in retrospect, was the retention of many joint lines. They had been jointly owned by two or more of the old companies, and because those companies passed into different groups they still remained joint. A few instances are shown on the facing page, giving in each case the original companies concerned and the new owners from 1 January, 1923.

Many other examples could be quoted. The point was that the majority of these lines lay almost entirely in the territory of one or other of the new groups. There is no doubt that Sir Eric Geddes was deeply anxious to get the measure through Parliament, and he several times warned that any delay would mean 'chaos'—to quote his own word. As a result of the shipwreck hurry imposed upon the consideration of the Bill, the line of least resistance was taken in far too many instances, and the careful co-ordination, which in the first case was

Railway	Original Joint Owners	Owners after January 1923
Somerset and Dorset	London & South Western Railway, and Midland Railway	Southern and L.M.S.R.
Midland and Great Northern Joint	Midland Railway Great Northern Railway	L.M.S.R. and L.N.E.R.
Shrewsbury and Hereford	London & North Western Great Western	L.M.S.R. and Great Western

claimed as the prime object of grouping was lacking. The grouping purely by existing companies was the easiest and quickest way out. One feels that Sir Eric Geddes was fairly carried away with the rosy prospects of grouping when he stated that within four or five years an aggregate economy in operating expenses of £25 million should be effected. Lord Knaresborough, Chairman of the North Eastern Railway countered this optimistic forecast by saying that in his opinion £3 or £4 million was about the best that could be hoped for, and Sir Frederick Banbury of the Great Northern—always a strong opponent of grouping— said that what was really needed was a revision of the statutory charges for various classes of traffic, which had remained unchanged from an era of totally different economic circumstances.

While all this discussion was in progress in railway board rooms and in the committee rooms of the House of Commons the future prospects were viewed with varying degrees of apprehension by the men who had to continue to run the railways, and with openly expressed concern by all others interested in railways, whether as passengers, shareholders, or merely as friendly onlookers. Of course there were neophytes who looked forward to the changes, because there would be new things to see, but to many onlookers there were lugubrious speculations as to what the mergers would bring; as to what colours engines and carriages would be painted, and who among senior officers would get the top jobs. The attentions of not a few were turned towards the Great Western, as being the only one of the old companies to remain in a recognizable form. At that time, curiously enough, the Great Western was one of the least attractive of British railways. Its locomotives of all types were still painted in the plain unlined green of wartime, with all the bright parts suppressed. They were not being kept very clean either, and with the carriages in crimson lake the line was not one of the most attractive to the spectator. I remember travelling to Llandudno in the summer of 1921 by the London and North Western, and at Chester we were joined by a Leeds friend with whom I had enjoyed many hours of train-watching on his home ground. As we were leaving Chester, I told him to look out for the Great Western engine sheds; but what a dull, if not shabby spectacle the massed engine power displayed there presented.

It was the first time my friend had seen any Great Western engines; and he was not impressed. And having seen them in all their pre-war glory, neither was I!

In the years 1919–22 the companies to be merged into the new Southern Railway were not a very colourful group either. Only the Brighton had retained its pre-war style. The locomotives of the South Eastern and Chatham were painted a dark 'battleship grey', without any lining, and with their numbers rendered in large white *sans-serif* characters on the tenders. Admittedly they were being kept smart and clean but again one missed the 'glorious technicolour' of pre-war years. The London and South Western was in the course of transition. The old salmon-coloured carriages were giving place to plain green of the same shade as that of the locomotives. The Chief Mechanical Engineer, R. W. Urie, had abandoned some of the more colourful touches on the Drummond locomotives, such as the rich brown surrounds to the tender panels; but they were still fully lined out in black and white, even though the shade of green was rather dull. To an outsider it seemed that the South Western would inevitably take the predominant place in the new combine. Handsome and powerful though the Brighton 4-6-4 tanks were, they did not appear likely to be used on the longer-distance runs to the West of England, and the big Urie 4-6-0s of the 'N 15' class seemed the most likely standard for the new group. At that time we, who were on the touch-line as it were, did not know how far those imposing engines were falling short of expectations. They were much sought after by the photographers.

The year 1922, the last of the old companies, saw an exciting competition between the Great Northern and the North Eastern in 'Pacific' engine building. Until then the Great Western had been the only English railway company to own a 'Pacific'; and while the Great Northern design, by H. N. Gresley, had long been expected it was evident that the North Eastern—the reluctant partner in the East Coast alliance—did not intend to leave the Great Northern alone in the field. A successful Doncaster engine of such size would, if unchallenged, have presented a strong claim to becoming the standard heavy main line locomotive of the new London and North Eastern Railway. So Sir Vincent Raven, the N.E.R. Chief Mechanical Engineer, put Darlington Works on to the design of a huge new engine—a 4-6-2 version of the very successful Class 'Z' three-cylinder 'Atlantics'. It was a larger and heavier engine than the Gresley 'Pacific' and was completed just in time to have the words NORTH EASTERN and the old company coat of arms on the tender. The new management was thus clearly faced with making a choice between the Gresley and Raven designs of 'Pacific', for future standardization. But by the oddest twists of fortune the first chief mechanical engineer of the L.N.E.R. was very nearly a man from the Great Central, of all railways. Whatever the financial position of that company may have been its technical achievements were first class, and with Sir Vincent Raven of the North Eastern due for retirement, the post was actually offered to the next most senior mechanical engineer, John G. Robinson. He himself, however, felt that he was too senior in years to undertake the job, and that it needed a younger man who could look forward to many years in office, and secure the continuity in practice that he felt was essential in co-ordinating the mechanical engineering work of the large new company. On Robinson's recommendation the post went

45. ON THE L.N.W.R. IN 1922

(a) The Royal Train near Euxton Junction, Lancashire, hauled by two 'Claughton' engines, Nos. 179 *Private W. Wood V.C.* and 207 *Sir Charles Cust*. The leading engine was named after one of the three L.N.W.R. men who won the V.C. in the First World War.

(b) Down goods train leaving Oxenholme, hauled by a Class 'G2' 0-8-0 No. 253.

to H. N. Gresley. It was a pity for the sake of the development of locomotive practice elsewhere, that other engineers of senior years did not have the same kind of attitude as J. G. Robinson, when the time came for appointments to high office in the grouping era.

A significant, and not very welcome, development took place at the end of 1920, while proposals for grouping were still under discussion, and before Sir Eric Geddes had launched 'The Railways Bill, 1921' into Parliament. On 31 December, 1920, Sir Thomas Williams, the able and popular General Manager of the London and North Western Railway retired, and was accorded the honour of a seat on the Board. It had generally been assumed that whatever form the grouping of the railways eventually took the London and North Western and the Lancashire and Yorkshire would be brought into the same fold. Their interests were deeply interlinked in the teeming industrial districts of South Lancashire; but what was not expected, at any rate by the great majority of L.N.W.R. men, and interested members of the public, was that the reigning General Manager of the Lancashire and Yorkshire, Arthur Watson, would be appointed General Manager of the L.N.W.R. while retaining his existing appointment. It was a move much resented by North Western men, all the more so because Watson's methods were somewhat alien to those that had prevailed at Euston for more than fifty years. Unfortunately it was only the first step in the chain of events that led to the apparent derating of what had hitherto been Britain's greatest railway. It is certainly true that the early 1920s caught the North Western in a weak moment. By death and retirement the company had lost three of its greatest men in quick succession. The terrible post-war influenza epidemic claimed Sir Guy Calthrop as a victim; Bowen-Cooke died at the early age of 62 years, and the outstanding chairman, Sir Gilbert Claughton, had retired. The door was wide open for the senior men of the Lancashire and Yorkshire to wade in, and when full amalgamation of the two companies took place in 1921 in several key appointments, quite apart from that of the General Manager, one found men of the North Western taking second place.

From the viewpoint of railway enthusiasts the most important development was that the post of Chief Mechanical Engineer went to George Hughes of the L.Y.R. It would at once be acknowledged that in years and tenure of major office he was far senior to H. P. M. Beames, who had succeeded to the post of C.M.E. on the L.N.W.R. only on the death of Bowen-Cooke, in 1920. But Hughes's record on the L.Y.R. had not been a very successful one, as engine designer at any rate, and his final contribution to the motive power position on the L.Y.R. had been the reconstruction of a class of four-cylinder 4-6-0 passenger engines which, in their original form, could well be stigmatized as one of the worst-ever to run the rails in Great Britain. The reconstruction certainly transformed a very bad engine into a reasonably good one; but the rebuilt engines were not the marvels some of their admirers would have had us believe. The Lancashire and Yorkshire locomotive department at Horwich had, to quote another commentator, 'gone all scientific . . .', and comparative trials were run between the rebuilt Hughes 4-6-0s and the L.N.W.R. 'Claughton' class 4-6-0s. No details of these trials were published, but information 'leaked' out to railway journalists of the day, suggested that the honours were definitely with the L.Y.R. engines.

It was not until more than forty years later, when I was privileged to examine the actual results that I discovered that the outcome was precisely the opposite of what we had all been led to believe in the 1920s.

The results of those engine trials, on the enlarged London and North Western Railway were unhappily typical of much of the atmosphere that pervaded the months before and after the actual grouping of the British railways. What happened on the L.N.W.R., and which was continued in a much more intensified form when full grouping took place, was paralleled, if not in locomotive matters then in other forms, in other facets of the various mergers, and it was many years before sober fact began to take the place of much of the propaganda and—to be frank, 'ballyhoo'—that had surrounded the amalgamations. Loughnan Pendred, the great editor of *The Engineer*, aptly summed up the situation when he concluded a leading article, commenting upon another series of locomotive trials with the words: 'publicity has gained more than science'!

In whatever way one regards it, whatever one's partisan feelings towards one or other of the old companies may lie, there is no doubt that the lights of the golden age of steam railways in Great Britain were beginning to go out in those last months of 1922. We can let our imaginations range over the prospect of how different the immediate outcome might have been had, for example, Sir Guy Calthrop still been at the helm at Euston; had Sir Henry Thornton not been tempted to recross the Atlantic, and take over the chairmanship of the newly-formed Canadian National Railways, or had it been made worthwhile for Sir Cecil Paget to return to railway service after his brilliant wartime career. Giant personalities apart, the railways of Great Britain were on the threshold of a new age—an age that lies beyond the period and the spirit of this book. It is always fascinating to speculate how men who loomed so great in their own age would have fared in meeting the challenges of the inter-war years, of the Grouping Era on the railways of Great Britain. In locomotive circles, the Drummonds were both dead before the end of the 'golden age'; so was Bowen-Cooke. Lawson Billinton, Raven, Robinson and Urie retired, and Churchward, seeing which way the wind was blowing, told the shop-stewards of Swindon: 'It's time the "Old Man" got out!' Collett, Gresley and Maunsell were left to gather in the sour-apple harvest of the early grouping years, and to display in the searching context of mechanical engineering that priceless British attribute of an ability to switch tactics rapidly to meet changing conditions. But I am straying beyond that epoch-marking New Year's Day of 1923, and it is time that I also closed down on this particular theme.

Index